CAPTIVATE

CAPTIVATE

The Science of
Succeeding with People

Vanessa Van Edwards

PORTFOLIO / PENGUIN

An imprint of Penguin Random House LLC
375 Hudson Street
New York, New York 10014

Dedicated to anyone who has ever felt awkward in a social situation.

You are so not alone.

CONTENTS

CAPTIVATE

INTRODUCTION

Hi, my name is Vanessa, and I'm a recovering awkward person.

At school dances, I'd volunteer to watch the punch bowl. Growing up, if a cool kid accidentally bumped into me, I would start hiccupping uncontrollably. When my family got AOL, my first IM buddy was the school nurse. In second grade I tried to get a permanent dismissal from PE by saying I had menopause pains. If only Google had been around in those days.

To prove it, as painful as it is, I present Exhibit A, a photo of me circa 1993:

Me, circa 1993

As you can see, I went for "helmet hair" without actually playing a sport requiring a helmet—or any sport, frankly—while clinging to the belief that nothing complements a baggy T-shirt quite like a sharp vest. A plaid one, though truthfully I wasn't too picky in the vest department.

On particularly socially anxious days, I would break out in hives right before walking into school and wear long sleeves and pants to cover my swollen, red, itchy limbs. As you might have guessed, the rashes covering my face and scalp didn't help my popularity rankings.

It wasn't all bad, though. On Valentine's Day, my teachers gave me cards.

HUMAN BEHAVIOR HACKING

It's an understatement to say that people skills did not come naturally to me. I had to learn them the hard way, so I could teach them to you the easy way. Here's how it happened: Early on, I figured out that I could learn human behavior just like I studied for math or foreign language tests. I made facial expression flash cards, looked for small-talk patterns, and tried to spot the hidden emotions of my teachers—although that last one sometimes got me into trouble!

I read everything I could get my hands on about people—psychology textbooks, sociological studies, and every human behavior book ever written. Eventually, I began to create my own tests and experiments. For one mini-experiment, I created flash cards of conversation starters based on studies of dopamine, carried them in my purse, tried them on strangers, and then catalogued their reactions. For another, I tried to adopt the alpha body language moves of chimps to see if people would mirror me (that one did NOT work). In yet another, I used persuasion techniques in a business pitch competition to see if I could game the system.

On a whim, I decided to document all of my misadventures and take-aways as a human guinea pig on a blog, ScienceofPeople.com. To my surprise and delight, I found I wasn't the only person struggling to get along with people. As our articles started to pop up all over the web and our videos began going viral, we caught the attention of media outlets like NPR, *Inc.*, and *Forbes*, which covered our unique approach. This is when I decided to do larger research experiments and turn Science of People into a human behavior lab.

In our lab, we start every endeavor by finding the latest scientific studies and then turn them into real-life experiments and tactics. We then share these strategies with our readers and students to test them. In this way, each skill in this book has already been refined by thousands of students who have used them in real-life situations and reported their results back to us to perfect.

This method is our secret sauce:

Step One: Find fascinating research.
Step Two: Create actionable real-life strategies.

Step Three: Test, tweak, and perfect.
Repeat.

I call our approach behavior hacking. Over the last eight years, I have developed shortcuts, formulas, and blueprints for getting along with anyone. Our unique approach has reached millions of students through our online courses and in-person workshops. I've helped corporate teams at Fortune 500 companies increase their interpersonal intelligence, singles make connections at speed-dating workshops, and entrepreneurs win pitch competitions using science-based behavior hacks. My columns and appearances in the *Huffington Post,* in *Forbes,* and on CNN are seen all over the world by people who want to improve their relationships.

We have streamlined all of our best findings into a universal framework that makes up this book. Each chapter of *Captivate* will teach you one of the fourteen behavior hacks. These are simple, powerful tools that you can use to level up your career, improve your relationships, and increase your income.

WHAT YOU WILL LEARN

This book will teach you how people work. If you know exactly what makes people tick, you can optimize your behavior, interactions, and relationships. Trying to get along with people without a framework is a bit like solving complex math problems without any equations. It's both difficult and involves a heck of a lot of unnecessary suffering along the way. This book will give you the people skills you never learned in school.

As diverse as we all seem on the outside, our inner workings are quite similar—if not eerily predictable. **There are hidden rules to human behavior.** We just have to find where to look.

Part I is all about helping you master the **first five minutes** of any interaction—starting a conversation and creating instant likability. First impressions are fundamental to everything else I can teach you.

In Part II, I will teach you skills that will help you get to know someone better in the **first five hours** of any interaction. My system for speed-reading people and decoding behavior will help you whether you are on the first five dates or in the first five meetings. I call this system the matrix—it doesn't involve Keanu Reeves, but it's just as cool. This is what happens when you want to level up a casual connection to something deeper.

Part III is about the **first five days**. In order to get to know someone on a deeper level, you have to learn how to influence people, lead teams, and increase your impact with everyone you meet. This is the ultimate level of connection and the final and most advanced step for interacting with people.

You can also keep your eyes peeled for Fast Facts, where we pulled in data from our Twitter polls and online surveys that are relevant to the content. They look like this:

FAST FACT BOX

Our Twitter poll indicated that 96 percent of users believe people skills are a bigger contributor to career success than technical skills.

> **Vanessa Van Edwards**
> @vvanedwards   ± Follow
>
> I believe the most important factor in career success is:
>
> 4% Technical skills
> 96% People skills
>
> 71 votes · Final results

You will also see that we reference our "Digital Bonuses." These are sections of the book that have corresponding videos, photos, and exercises to help you learn as you go. Get all of the resources at www.ScienceofPeople .com/toolbox.

Here's my promise: Learning people skills will change your life. Developing your PQ—or interpersonal intelligence—is like adding a catalyst to your success. By the end of the book you will be able to engage anyone you meet in memorable conversation. You will know how to leave a lasting first impression with clients, colleagues, and friends. And you will have more confidence, control, and charisma in all of your interactions.

- **People with high PQ make on average $29,000 more per year than people with average PQ.**
- 90 percent of top business performers have high PQ.

- Individuals with strong interpersonal communication report being 42 percent happier and more fulfilled with their lives.

I joke that people skills are the social lubricant of life. When you understand the laws of human behavior, everything goes more smoothly:

Professionally, you will know how to negotiate a raise, connect with colleagues, build rapport at networking events, and nail your elevator pitch.

Socially, you will make unforgettable first impressions, reduce relationship drama, enjoy stronger and more supportive friendships, and get along with everyone you meet.

Romantically, you will impress your dates, deepen your relationships, flirt authentically, and prevent partner miscommunications.

Bottom line: There is a science to winning friends and influencing people, and learning it will completely change the way you interact.

Let the adventure begin!

YOUR PQ SCORE

In every job that must be done, there is an element of fun. You find the fun and—SNAP—the job's a game.

—Mary Poppins

I have developed the following quiz to test your people skills, or your PQ. This quiz will help you assess your current level of interpersonal intelligence. The good news is our PQ can be improved, stretched, and hacked. No matter where you are now, each hack you learn in this book will help get your PQ up.

We will take this test again at the end of the book, and my goal is to help you level up your score by at least fifty points.

Ready? Play.

The PQ Test

1. Which smile is real?

A   B   C   D

2. Where is the best place to stand at a networking event?
   A. Near the entrance to the event
   B. At the food table so you can sit with people
   C. Where people exit the bar
   D. Next to someone you know

3. What does this face mean?

   A. Amused
   B. Sad
   C. Bored
   D. Contemptuous

4. Which saying about people is most true?
   A. "Opposites attract."
   B. "Birds of a feather flock together."
   C. "One bad apple spoils the bunch."
   D. "Never bite the hand that feeds you."

5. How much of our personality comes from our genes?
   A. Very little. Our personality is mostly formed by how we are raised.
   B. 35 percent to 50 percent
   C. 55 percent to 75 percent
   D. A lot. Our personality is mostly formed by our genetics and DNA.

6. The best way to show someone you care about them is to:
   A. Tell them all the reasons they are awesome
   B. Get them a gift
   C. Do their to-do list for them
   D. All of the above
   E. It's different for each person

7. Which phrase corresponds best with this facial expression?

   A. It smells weird in here.
   B. This makes me angry.
   C. I'm confused.
   D. I'm afraid.

8. Which emoticon would best represent this face?

    A   B   C   D

9. If this man walked into your office, what would you guess about him? (Hint: Only one of these personality assessments is correct.)

A. He is an introvert.
B. He is an extrovert.
C. He is laid-back.
D. He is quiet.

10. Our brains are most active when we are chatting about:
    A. Our crush
    B. The latest juicy gossip
    C. Ourselves
    D. The latest thriller

11. What does this face mean?

    A. Excitement
    B. Giddiness
    C. Interest
    D. Surprise

12. In the average conversation, people typically hold eye contact what percent of the time in a conversation?
    A. 31 percent
    B. 51 percent
    C. 61 percent
    D. 91 percent

13. The best way to get someone on the same page as you is to:
    A. Tell them a story
    B. Pay them a compliment
    C. Make them laugh
    D. Say something surprising

14. What does this face mean?

    A. Surprise
    B. Hatred
    C. Fear
    D. Confusion

15. Which of these habits tends to annoy people the most?
    A. People who are too talkative
    B. People who are too quiet
    C. People who are fake
    D. People who show off

16. People will pay more for something that:
    A. Their friends have also bought
    B. A doctor recommends
    C. Matches their personality
    D. They customized

17. When you first meet someone, you are LEAST likely to be able to accurately guess:

A. How extroverted they are
B. How much they worry
C. If they are open to new ideas
D. Their IQ
E. How organized they are

18. The easiest way to know if your new colleague is neurotic is if they:
    A. Put up inspirational posters
    B. Show up early to every meeting on the first day
    C. Introduce themselves to you immediately
    D. Wait for you to introduce yourself

19. What does this face mean?

A. Embarrassment
B. Confusion
C. Irritation
D. Disgust

20. Making someone feel _____ is the best way to improve their mood.
    A. Flattered
    B. Attractive
    C. Valued
    D. Powerful

Answer Key:

Whew! Now it's time to check your answers. Go through and give yourself 0 points for every wrong answer and 10 points for every right answer:

1. C _____ Points (Chapter 6)
2. C _____ Points (Chapter 1)
3. D _____ Points (Chapter 6)
4. B _____ Points (Chapter 5)
5. B _____ Points (Chapter 7)
6. E _____ Points (Chapter 8)
7. B _____ Points (Chapter 6)
8. D _____ Points (Chapter 6)
9. B _____ Points (Chapter 7)
10. C _____ Points (Chapter 4)
11. D _____ Points (Chapter 6)
12. C _____ Points (Chapter 2)
13. A _____ Points (Chapter 10)
14. C _____ Points (Chapter 6)
15. C _____ Points (Chapter 1)
16. D _____ Points (Chapter 11)
17. B _____ Points (Chapter 7)
18. A _____ Points (Chapter 7)
19. D _____ Points (Chapter 6)
20. C _____ Points (Chapter 9)

Add up the total to get:

Your PQ Score = _____

Take note of this score. By the end of the book, we will blow it out of the water.

0 to 50 points

I'm so excited you're here! Let me tell you, this is exactly where I was when I first started, and I couldn't be more thrilled to start you on this adventure. Get ready, big change is a comin'.

51 to 100 points

You got this. In fact, this is the range for most people. But you and I both know you are not average. You're exceptional; it's time to show it.

101 to 150 points

You're well on your way. You already have good interpersonal intelligence, but good is never enough. Let's make it great!

151 to 200 points

Well, well, well smarty-pants. You're a natural! Hey, if you're already this good with people, imagine where this book can take you. Say it with me: "total world domination."

Did some of these answers surprise you? They should!

We have not learned many of the fundamental forces that drive human behavior. But don't worry, I will explain the fascinating research behind each and every one in the chapters to come.

PART I

THE FIRST FIVE MINUTES

Whether you're going to a housewarming party, networking event, or first date, you face the same initial challenges:

- How do I make a good first impression?
- Who should I talk to?
- What should I say?

Part I is all about the first five minutes of an interaction. How can you use your first impression, conversation starters, and introduction to get to know someone? The first five hacks are all about tapping into what intrigues people so you can be the most memorable person in the room.

CHAPTER 1

CONTROL

How to win the social game

Once upon a time, a boy named Harry was teased for wearing thick glasses and having a bookish streak. When the time came to apply to college, he took jobs as a timekeeper in a railroad construction company and as a shelf duster in a pharmacy to support his family. No one would have guessed that this shy boy would one day become the thirty-third president of the United States.

The story of Harry S. Truman is surprising because he doesn't fit the stereotypical booming presidential personality. On July 19, 1944, this posed a problem. Truman was facing the biggest opportunity of his career. He was vying for the vice presidential nomination at the Democratic National Convention. The odds were not in his favor. Then-president Franklin D. Roosevelt had already publicly supported his contender, Henry Wallace, a gifted public speaker *and* the current vice president.

Truman was not a gifted public speaker—and he knew it. His team had to draw the battle off the main stage to make the convention work to Truman's strength: one-on-one rapport building. All day, they pulled delegates into a private, air-conditioned room underneath the platform, called Room H. The convention hall was stiflingly hot, so delegates literally breathed a breath of fresh air as they listened to Truman's pitch and began to cool off. Then he spent hours standing at the end of the hallway, shaking hands with passing members. Instead of waiting for the results in his hotel room (which is what Henry Wallace and most of the candidates tended to do), Truman ordered a hot dog and sat with his wife in the audience.

In the first ballot, Wallace had 429.5 votes and Truman received 319.5

votes. A second ballot was called immediately. Truman had to win friends and he had to win them fast. Instead of making a grand speech, Truman and his team kicked into full gear, working party leaders, delegates, and influential members of the crowd one by one. He worked a solid connection with the right person and then let them convince their people *for* him.

At 8:14 p.m. the results were announced. Truman led with 1,031 votes to Wallace's 105. He gained 712 votes in a matter of hours. A few minutes later, Truman gave one of the shortest acceptance speeches in history. He stood patiently at the bank of microphones, and when the audience had finally quieted down he said, "Now, give me a chance."[1]*

Truman understood his strengths and played to them. He optimized his interactions for success, and so can you.

THE SCIENCE OF FAKE

Imagine it's your dream to play professional basketball. You're fast and have great ball-handling skills. You also happen to be six feet two inches tall. You have two choices: You could play center, but the average height of an NBA center is six feet eleven inches.[2] If you went for center, you would have to fake your height by wearing lifts during games and spending a ton of extra hours after practice working on your vertical jump. Or you could play point guard, where the average height is six feet two inches.[3] You wouldn't have to make up for extra inches with your jump— you could just focus on playing.

Feigning extroversion is like trying to play center with lifts on. Trying to socially fake it until you make it burns a whole lot of extra energy and doesn't really work. It also comes across as inauthentic.

In a Science of People survey, we asked 1,036 of our readers the following question:[4]

Which of these people habits annoy you the most?
A. People who are too talkative
B. People who are too quiet
C. People who are fake
D. People who show off

---

* Want to watch Truman's acceptance speech at the 1944 convention? See all of our extra Digital Bonus material for this book at ScienceofPeople.com/toolbox.

Can you guess which won? "C. People who are fake" led the board by far with 63 percent. "D. People who show off" was a distant second (22 percent).

Fake doesn't just happen when you're trying to be something you're not. If you don't like someone, they will feel it. If you are unhappy at an event, people will sense it. **Pushing through, faking it, trying to make it work—simply *doesn't* work.**

Dr. Barbara Wild and her associates found that our emotions are infectious. First, her team showed people pictures of happy or sad faces. Then they gave them a series of mood tests. They found they could "infect" participants with the emotions in each image. Very simply, after viewing a happy face, participants felt more positive. After viewing a sad face, participants felt more negative.[5] Here's what's crazy: They only flashed each image for 500 milliseconds! Only 500 milliseconds is barely enough time for participants to even register they had seen a face, and they still caught the emotion.

Dr. Wild even found that our smile muscles unconsciously tend to mimic the smiles around us. We are happier around happy individuals, and we thrive with thriving people.[6] When you force yourself to go to events you are dreading, you are not only miserable, **but your misery is contagious.**

Think you can just fake it until you make it? Think again! We can spot a fake smile a mile away. Over 4,361 people have taken our virtual Body Language Quiz to test their nonverbal intelligence. In one question we show participants a genuine smile hidden among three fake smiles. Over 86.9 percent of participants are correctly able to pick out the genuine smile.

Researchers at the University of Finland showed one group images of fake smiles and another group images of real smiles.[7] Like this:

A   B

Can you guess which smile is real and which is the fake? Image A shows a fake smile, and Image B shows a genuine smile.

When participants looked at the real smiles, they felt a positive mood change. But when participants looked at the fake smiles, their mood remained the same. (For more on how you can tell the difference, turn to Chapter 6.)

Faking it until you make it is not worth the effort. Happy people make us happy,[8] but fake happy people—they are forgettable. The first step in winning the social game is to control the situations you play in. Only interact in places where you don't have to fake it. **No matter how many behavior hacks you learn, if you go to events that make you unhappy, it will be incredibly difficult to increase your memorability.**

When you feel great, other people pick up on it and want in on it. When you drag yourself to an event because you feel like you "should make an appearance," you are the party pooper. And you smell up the event.

This is why you need to have a Social Game Plan.

> *Confidence is contagious and so is lack of confidence, and a customer will recognize both.*
>
> —Vince Lombardi

YOUR SOCIAL GAME PLAN

Here's the worst piece of advice I was ever given: Say yes to everything. Say yes to networking events, coffees with strangers, and random conferences, because you never know what opportunity might come your way. As the science shows, this is a big smelly sack of baloney.

Unfortunately, it took me years to figure this out. When I first started my blog, I was trying to find any paid writing gig I possibly could. So almost every weeknight, I trudged out to the professional circuit. I prepared for these networking events like I was going into battle, loading up on fat stacks of business cards, fistfuls of no-nonsense pens, and multiple personalized name tags. My uniform consisted of sensible shoes, casual professional attire, perfume, and a news anchor smile.

I fought. For attention, for business, for a break from the interminable boredom of having the same conversation over and over again. After three years of this nonsense (and at least ten pounds from eating so many platters of pigs in a blanket), I threw in the towel. I wasn't making any real connections, I wasn't drumming up business, and I certainly wasn't having a good time.

Why? I wasn't working to my strengths. Like Truman, I do much better in one-on-one situations. I get overwhelmed by loud rooms with lots of people. Trying to cover up my anxiety with fake smiles just made me come across as inauthentic—and that's the problem.

What I needed was a game plan.

HACK #1: The Social Game Plan
Take control of your interactions and play by your social rules.

Who says you have to play by other people's rules? Not me! I want you to create your own.

Your Social Game Plan will help you find the position that's perfect for you: where you play your best, feel the most comfortable, and are set up for the greatest success.

Skill #1: Play Your Position

Most people skills books try to force you into one approach—the bubbly extrovert. They want you to fake it until you make it. They expect you to be "on" all the time with everyone you meet. This is impossible.

You *can* get along with anyone, but you don't have to get along with everyone. The Social Game Plan isn't just about mapping out your strategy, it's also about leveraging your social strengths. Athletes aren't expected to play every position on a team, so you shouldn't try to engage in every social role. Play to your position. This will also make it easier to try all of the hacks you've learned.

At our human behavior lab, "The Thrive Test" asks participants about their favorite places to socialize. Before seeing the results, fill out your answers below.

Check off all the places where you greatly ENJOY spending time with other people—and feel free to fill in your own at the bottom. We'll call these your thrive locations:

_____ Bars	_____ Nature
_____ Nightclubs	_____ Pool Parties
_____ Restaurants	_____ Dinner Parties
_____ House Parties	_____ Movie Nights
_____ Cafés	_____ Casinos
_____ Boardrooms	_____ Concerts
_____ The Gym	_____ Black-Tie Events
_____ Office Meetings	_____ Cocktail Parties
_____ Conferences	_____ Backyard Barbecues
_____ Coffee Shops	_____ Theme Parks
_____ Phone Calls	_____ Festivals
_____ E-mail Check-ins	_____ Networking Events
_____ Video Chats	_____ Sporting Events
_____ IMs	

Check off all the places where you greatly DISLIKE spending time with other people—feel free to fill in your own at the bottom. We'll call these your survive locations:

_____ Bars	_____ The Gym
_____ Nightclubs	_____ Office Meetings
_____ Restaurants	_____ Conferences
_____ House Parties	_____ Coffee Shops
_____ Cafés	_____ Phone Calls
_____ Boardrooms	_____ E-mail Check-ins

_____ Video Chats

_____ IMs

_____ Nature

_____ Pool Parties

_____ Dinner Parties

_____ Movie Nights

_____ Casinos

_____ Concerts

_____ Black-Tie Events

_____ Cocktail Parties

_____ Backyard Barbecues

_____ Theme Parks

_____ Festivals

_____ Networking Events

_____ Sporting Events

Can you guess which answer was the most popular?

Trick question! There weren't any clear winners. We couldn't find a statistically significant pattern because the answers were evenly split. Everyone thrives in different scenarios. This is why it's hard trying to learn how to "work a party" if you don't actually like parties. It's silly trying to learn how to "charm people at a conference" if conferences make your skin crawl. That's like saying a quarterback should also be able to play as a kicker and linebacker. Maybe he could, but it wouldn't make for a very successful game.

Let's identify the positions where you thrive and the ones where you merely survive:

- **Thrive:** Look at the first set of places you checked off in the exercise above. Put the top three to five under "My THRIVE Locations" below. These are the places you look forward to going to and where you are your best self.
- **Neutral:** Certain social situations could go either way depending on your mood or who's there. They aren't your favorite, but you don't dread them. Look at the places that you didn't check off in either exercise and add the ones that you encounter the most under "My NEUTRAL Locations" below.
- **Survive:** Other places or scenarios always make you feel uncomfortable, bored, or unhappy. Take three to five of the places you checked off in the second set and write them under "My SURVIVE Locations" below.

My THRIVE Locations: _____

My NEUTRAL Locations: _____

My SURVIVE Locations: _____

Now you know which invites to say yes to and which ones to skip. Put yourself in a position to be successful before you even arrive.

You are much more likely to triumph with each of the behavior hacks if you try them at your thrive locations. And if you have to go to a neutral or survive event, no worries—the next two skills have you covered.

Skill #2: Work a Room

Before you go to an event, imagine drawing your social interactions on a map, from the door you enter through to the location of your first conversation to the location of your last. Many of us follow the same paths over and over again without even realizing it.

At the Science of People, we partner with event organizers who let us film and track people's movement through the venues. At each event, we assign every attendee a number and then observe his or her interaction patterns. At the end of the night, we count how many connections they made, ask them how many business cards they received, and look at their connections on LinkedIn. We have found that the most successful connectors use specific patterns. **In other words, this social map can be hacked.**

Here is a map of a typical social event:

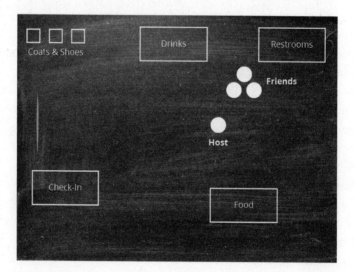

Whether you're at a networking event, holiday party, wedding, dinner at a friend's house, or in a conference ballroom, most events have this basic setup. There is a check-in area or a table to drop off gifts. You can easily spot the bathroom and the bar or food area. There are usually a few people you recognize—maybe colleagues, friends, or acquaintances gathered and already catching up. And of course, the host or boss is milling around the room.

Let's reimagine Truman's social map at the 1944 convention:

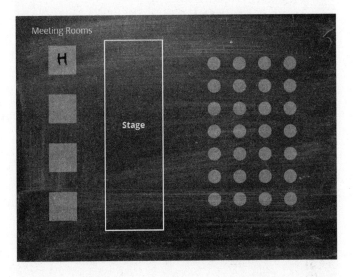

An audience sat before a big stage. Private meeting rooms were in the back.

Most of the candidates devoted their energies to getting onstage before roaming through the audience to do obligatory schmoozing. Their map looked like this:

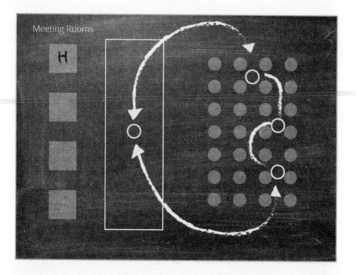

To be effective and win votes, the shy Truman had to avoid both the typically traversed path and his own personal traps. The *X*s mark potential traps:

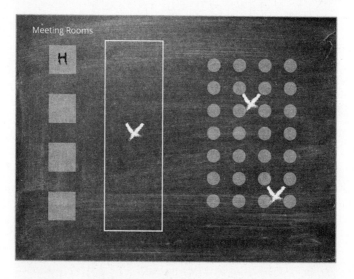

Truman did his networking at the end of a long hallway on the side of the stage and in the privacy of Room H. I call locations that work to our strengths social sweet spots. On the next map, a star marks the sweet spot.

All Truman had to do was follow his sweet spots to work the room in his favor.

I want you to do the same thing. Let's revisit the typical social map. I split every event up into three basic zones: the Start Zone, the Social Zone, and the Side Zone.

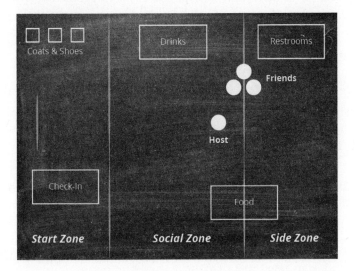

The Start Zone is the starting point at all events. Emotionally, it's the place where nerves are running highest. When people have just arrived, they're usually juggling lots of thoughts. They are running late, checking in, taking off their coats, surveying the room, seeing if they know anyone, worrying about first impressions, silencing their phones, running to the bathroom, or praying for a good time.

The biggest mistake I see at events is when people hover at the boundary of the Start Zone. It's a social trap. You're catching people at a confidence low. We noticed that the people who collected the least amount of business cards tried to pounce on people right in the Start Zone. What they didn't realize was that they were trying to connect with people who weren't open to connection yet.

When you approach someone before they get oriented to an event, they are not only more distracted during your conversation, but they will also be looking over your head to scope out the room and find people they know—you'll have a much harder time engaging in eye contact. They are also more likely to excuse themselves to get their drink, grab some food, say hi to the host, or go to the bathroom—and less likely to be receptive to anything you have to say.

The Side Zone is also filled with secret traps that people often fall into. I call it the Side Zone because we noticed that when people fall into these traps, they become sidelined and don't get to meet many new people. The first trap in the Side Zone is an easy one to remember: the bathroom. Sure, go to the bathroom, but don't hover outside it. It's creepy.

The second Side Zone trap is making a beeline for the food and then floating around it all night. This isn't a terrible trap, but it isn't a great place to plant yourself. Not only will you eat too much and contend with a food baby all night, but you will also make it hard for other people to get their food and eat. It's difficult to strike up conversations when people are trying to load up their plates, almost impossible to shake hands, and makes for awkward chatting-while-chewing moments.

The third Side Zone trap is immediately going to people you know. Once you join up with your colleagues, friends, or acquaintances, it is incredibly challenging to get out and meet new people. The best thing to do is wave or give your friends a quick hug when you arrive, and then say you will circle back to them. You can hang out with them as the crowd thins out, but capitalize on your fresh energy at the beginning of an event to hit the Social Zone.

Here are the traps to avoid:

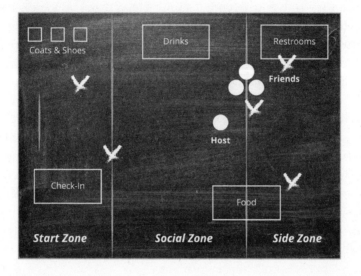

The Social Zone is where the magic happens. First, the best place to start working a room is right where people exit the bar. By the time they're here, the emotional, high-anxiety feeling of the Start Zone will have died down. Drinks in hand, people are ready to mingle, if not desperate to have someone to talk to. **You become their savior if you rescue them from drinking alone.**

There are two sweet spots on either end of the bar. At our networking events, we noticed the people who collected the most business cards and had the most connections on LinkedIn dominated these sweet spots (and never ran out of people to talk to). Your opening line can be contextual: "How do you like the wine tonight?" Or just, "Hey, cheers! I'm Vanessa..."

The other great sweet spot in the Social Zone is right near the host. Once you have your drink, you can continue to work the room by saying a brief hello and thank-you to the host. You can also ask them to introduce you around before they carry on greeting people. You can say, "Thank you so much for having me! This looks like a great group. Anyone I should meet?"

After they have introduced you, let them do their hosting duties, but if possible, stay in their line of sight. I do this when I don't know many

people, because the host is more likely to see me while talking to someone and say, "Hey, you should meet my friend Vanessa. Vanessa, come
over here!" Score!

While I don't recommend standing around the food, hidden sweet
spots are at the couches or bar tables where people are already eating. They are often hoping for someone like you to set their plate
down beside theirs. Something like, "Hey, can I join you while you eat?"
works well.

Bonus: If you are an introvert and don't like big groups, I highly recommend being what I call a Grazer. Instead of hitting the buffet once for
a heaping plate, go up first for appetizers, again for the main course, and
then again for seconds or dessert. Why? This is an easy way to take a
break from a conversation or move to a new one-on-one.

I'm a Grazer myself. If I need a longer break, I'll go to the bathroom
and refill my drink, too. Conserving my social energy helps me have multiple quality conversations in one night.

In summary, work a room by hitting your social sweet spots and
avoiding common traps. This map will help you optimize meeting people
at events:

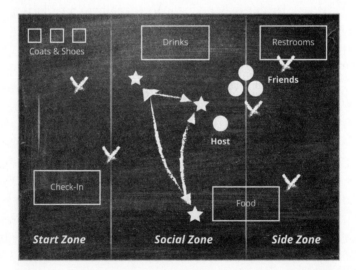

Don't take my word for it. Next time you are at an event, pretend you
are on our Science of People observation team. You'll notice people moving in and out of traps and sweet spots:

Approach Me!	Avoid Me!
I've just gotten my food.	I'm only talking to people I know.
I'm close to the host.	I just got here.
I have a fresh drink in my hand.	Where's the bathroom?

Maybe you'll find even deadlier traps or even smarter sweet spots. And you can always redraw your social map based on your skills and goals. I strongly recommend it.

Skill #3: Know Your Team

About two weeks after an online body language course I taught went viral, I got a random e-mail from a guy who wanted to give me some unsolicited advice. He told me—in not very nice words—that he thought I should wear a business suit in my videos (in most of my videos I wear a button-down or a dress). He said I didn't look "professional enough" and "business wear would appeal to more students." He also advised against using jokes, as they "distract from the message."

I panicked. I immediately began to think about reshooting my videos to look more formal. Should I start from scratch? Try to edit out clips piece by piece? Devastated, I asked some mentors for advice.

Right after I told them the story, one of my mentors asked me, "Vanessa, why are you listening to this guy? Is he one of your people?"

I had no idea what he meant by "my people." He explained, "Your goal is not to reach every person—it's to reach the right people. If this guy gets distracted by what you are wearing, he is not one of the right people."

This was a turning point for me and my business. I began to define my ideal student very specifically. Surveys and interviews told me that the people who bought my courses are above average in all areas. They are high performers with above-average intelligence and a super-busy schedule. My goal is simply to help as many of them as possible. Instead of going after every type of student, I started to target my type of student.

With this ideal customer in mind, I began to create short, digestible videos power-packed with actionable tips. If a video wasn't supercharged with valuable intel or was too wordy, I didn't post it. Within a few months, our business started snowballing. Our YouTube channel views ballooned to over nine million. Our Twitter following grew by a factor of twelve. As of this writing, we have over 132,000 students in our online courses and over 104,000 in our online community. This only worked because I knew exactly who I was looking for. I found my people.

Whether you are trying to find ideal clients, a great partner, or friends who bring out your best self, you have to make sure you are with the *right* people. You can take the Superman approach, stealthily preventing awkwardness and optimizing your interactions on your own. Or you can partner up. Batman has Robin, Iron Man has Jarvis, and Bert has Ernie. Better yet, you could join the Avengers and have a team to support you.

There is an African proverb that says:

> **If you want to go fast, go alone.**
> **If you want to go far, go together.**

My question for you is: Who are your people? You can accelerate your learning pace by drawing from the strength of others. We all need supporters in our lives. So let's take stock of who's on your team. Read the following prompts and write down the person who pops into your head for each:

Who do you love spending time with? _____

Who makes you laugh? _____

Who makes you feel valued? _____

Who do you go to when you need to strategize? _____

Who do you most look forward to seeing? _____

Who do you call in a crisis? _____

Who makes you feel like your best self? _____

Who do you wish you could get to know better? _____

Take a moment to look at your answers. Identify the following people:

Your Winger: Did anyone come up more than once? Is there someone who could join you on a social adventure, who could help you be more comfortable as you try out social hacks, and who shares your desire for growth? I call this person your Winger—a gender-neutral form of wingman or wingwoman. Write their name below. *Your Winger:* _____

Your Riser: Is there someone you wish was on this list? We all have people in our lives with whom we want to improve our connections. Maybe an office colleague, a new friend, or a potential business contact who could be a career game changer. Use the fourteen behavior hacks with your Riser to level up the relationship.
Your Riser: _____

Knowing what scenarios you thrive in, what positions you're most comfortable in, and what teammates you trust in will save you both energy and time. Use your thrive list to help you only make social decisions that serve you. Reach out to and rely on the people who truly support you and make you feel valued.

Bottom Line: You do not have to like everyone. It takes far more work to get along with people or try new behavior hacks in a location that makes you nervous or uncomfortable. **By controlling where, how, and with whom your interactions take place, you can set yourself up for more success.**

> *I started to say no. I'm not doing that. I don't want to do that. I'm not taking that picture. I'm not going to that event. I'm not standing by that because that's not what I stand for. And slowly but surely, I remembered who I am, and then you go home, and you look in the mirror, and you're like, "Yes, I can go to bed with you every night." Because that person, I know that person. That person has balls, that person has integrity, that person has an opinion.*
>
> —Lady Gaga[9]

TAKING CONTROL

Whether you are a quiet, contemplative conversationalist or a wild, silly party animal, you can succeed by playing to your strengths.

When Truman was an unknown senator, for instance, he came up with an ingenious plan for climbing the ladder. The obvious strategy was to speak out on the Senate floor, but Truman preferred research to rhetorical flourishes, so he played the cards he had. He wrote in his memoirs: "Sitting as a 'hearing committee' is a dull, boresome procedure and it requires patience and persistence, so I soon became the 'patient and persistent' member of the subcommittee."[10]

His Social Game Plan was two-pronged. First, he threw himself into researching a topic he knew well from his experience on the railroad: transportation. Then he spent hours in the Library of Congress learning every arcane detail. Second, he built a relationship with a person with similar interests and goals. His Riser was Senator Burton K. Wheeler, the chairman of the Interstate Commerce Committee at the time. As Truman showed off his transportation knowledge in committees, he began to level up his relationship with Senator Wheeler. Finally, after Truman dutifully attended many meetings, Wheeler made Truman a formal subcommittee member. Not long after, Wheeler promoted him to vice chairman of the committee. Other senators noticed his work ethic and unique approach for dealing with people—and it carried him all the way to the White House. Even though Truman might not have been the most traditionally charismatic of individuals, he optimized his skills, mapped out his goals, and worked the right people.

Succeeding with people is about engineering what works for you.

CHALLENGES

1. Say no to an event that you are dreading.
2. At your next event, use the Social Game Plan to find at least two sweet spots.
3. Identify the person who you want to "level up"—your Riser. Keep them in mind while you apply the next 13 hacks.
4. **Bonus:** Reach out to a potential Winger about joining your social adventure. Get them this book and invite them to be on your superhero team.

CHAPTER REVIEW

There is no one definition of charisma. There are many flavors of social influence—and that's a good thing. The world would be incredibly boring (and loud) if everyone were an extrovert. We need you. Use your Social Game Plan, show up on your terms, and interact with people who matter to you. Your confidence is contagious.

- Stop forcing yourself to socialize in ways that drain you.
- Go where you thrive, avoid where you survive.
- Say no so you have the energy to say yes.

My biggest takeaway in this chapter is: _____

CHAPTER 2

CAPTURE

How to make a killer first impression

The audience sits in hushed anticipation. The Pittsburgh Symphony Orchestra is already assembled onstage, tuning their instruments expectantly. The sold-out Heinz Hall is filled with 2,676 people. Everyone is waiting for conductor Arild Remmereit to take the stage.

The problem is that Remmereit is not supposed to be here. The audience knows it, the orchestra knows it, and Remmereit certainly knows it. When the famed German conductor Christoph von Dohnányi became ill a few days before the show, the Pittsburgh Symphony Orchestra had to find an immediate replacement. They turned to Remmereit.[1]

In a matter of days, Remmereit, a tall, energetic Norwegian, had to find a way to learn and conduct Dohnáyi's entire program with an orchestra he had never worked with before. Of the three scheduled pieces in the program, Remmereit had only ever conducted one before in concert.

When I interviewed Remmereit, he confessed, "Before walking out I was incredibly nervous and was going on almost no sleep to get ready for the performance."[2] To add even more pressure, *New York Times* reviewer James R. Oestreich was in the audience.

As Remmereit finally takes the stage, the audience holds its breath. He has only a few seconds to make a strong first impression. For Remmereit it's all about "finding a way to create trust." He has to convince the audience that he can lead them through a new set and show the orchestra they should follow him.

"He approached the podium like a diffident schoolboy. But once there he showed utter self-assurance, using clear and wide-ranging gestures," observed Oestreich.[3]

Remmereit leads the orchestra through a sensational performance of Wagner's *Siegfried Idyll* and then a dynamic reading of Schumann's Fourth Symphony. He finishes with Brahms's Second Piano Concerto and finally a Chopin waltz as the encore. The audience is thrilled.

"The only thing listeners seemed to want to talk about afterward was Mr. Remmereit," reported Oestreich. "Mr. Remmereit radiated a joy in music-making, several listeners said. Inevitably, his boyish good looks, expressive podium manner and understated charisma were noted, but so was what some perceived as an unusual rapport between conductor and players."

The news of Remmereit's magnetic performance spread. He was quickly re-hired in Pittsburgh and made additional debuts with the Baltimore Symphony, Milan's Filarmonica della Scala, Munich Philharmonic, and the Vienna Symphony.

"The musicians know within five minutes whether a new conductor is any good or not," he said later.[4] What did he do right in those first five minutes?

THE SCIENCE OF FIRST IMPRESSIONS

Have you ever met someone who you just clicked with—within the first few seconds you somehow knew that you would get along? Have you ever met someone who rankled you right from the start—you don't know exactly what it was, but something about them just bothered you?

Whether we like to admit it or not, we decide if we like someone, if we trust someone, and if we want a relationship with someone within the first few seconds of meeting them.[5] However, we rarely think about our first impressions. And if we do, we aren't quite sure how to make them better. So we practice what we want to say, we plan witty jokes, and hope for the best when it comes to those early moments.

Researchers Nalini Ambady and Robert Rosenthal at Harvard University wanted to test the power of our snap judgments. They decided to look at students' perceptions of their professors.[6] Our judgments of teachers *should* only be made based on their actual teaching content—not on their looks, behavior, or presence. However, this is not how we operate.

For the experiment, Ambady and Rosenthal showed muted ten-second video clips of professors teaching to outside participants, who rated the teachers on fifteen dimensions of effectiveness, including warmth, optimism, and professionalism. The evaluators had to make judgments based entirely on nonverbal cues.

Ambady and Rosenthal looked at the results and wondered if they could change the ratings by shortening the clips. So they cut the clips from ten seconds to five seconds. The ratings did not change. Then they cut the clips from five seconds to two seconds. **The ratings still did not change.** They concluded that we make a snap judgment in the first two seconds of meeting someone and we rarely adjust it—even when we get more information. **We decide if we believe someone, if we like someone, and if we trust someone before we have even heard him or her speak.**

What character judgments could you confidently make after watching someone move in a room for two seconds? Could you guess how honest they are? How nice? How supportive? Even though you would have very little content to judge, you already mentally ask and answer these questions within seconds of meeting someone. And the crazy part is you're pretty accurate!

Here's the most interesting part of the study. Ambady and Rosenthal took the ratings from each of these clips and compared them to the student evaluations of these same teachers after an entire semester of classes. Again, they were surprisingly similar. **Teachers who got poor rankings from the two-second clips also got low rankings from students who took a semester's worth of classes.**

You can bet that those teachers spent many hours agonizing over their curriculum, practicing their teaching method, and spending time bonding with students before and after classes. According to Ambady and Rosenthal, this is not what really mattered. Students decide how effective teachers are within the first few seconds of walking into the room. The same thing happens to Remmereit when he takes the stage. And the same thing happens to you when you enter a room.

Intimidated by the speed of the first impression? Don't be! This is good news. If it takes only a few seconds to convince someone you are worth talking to, let's supercharge these first few seconds. **You can use the first impression to hack an entire interaction.**

LEVELING UP

First impressions are a survival mechanism. When you meet a new person, you have to quickly decide if you want them in your life. Ever heard of the fight-or-flight response? It is a way your body instinctively reacts to external stimuli and decides if you should stay or flee. This is why first impressions are so swift and decisive.

We are trying to answer three basic questions about a new person during the first few moments of an interaction.

Level One: Are you friend or foe? This is our subconscious personal safety check. We're thinking, "Darlin' you got to let me know. Should I stay or should I go?"

Level Two: Are you a winner or loser? When we first meet someone, we want to quickly assess their confidence—do they look like a leader or a follower?

Level Three: Are you an ally or an enemy? It's one thing to see someone as nonthreatening, but the last level is when you decide whether someone should be on your team. Your brain wants to know if this person likes you enough to back you up.

When someone successfully answers all three questions, we "level up" and trust them more. Strangers become acquaintances. Acquaintances become friends. Prospects become clients. (These are, of course, the three questions people are also trying to quickly answer about *you*.) How does this phenomenon play out when a speaker is in front of a big audience? In a TED Talk, for example?

I'm a TED Talk junkie. Most days, I find a juicy talk at lunch to accompany my sandwich. One day, I typed "leadership" into the search bar and two videos popped up. One was "How Great Leaders Inspire Action" by Simon Sinek, and the other was "Learning from Leadership's Missing Manual" by Fields Wicker-Miurin.

Both talks were about eighteen minutes long. Both talks came out in September 2009. Both talks were given by respected thought leaders in their field. But there was one difference—and it was a big one. Sinek's talk had 24,905,052 views, while Wicker-Miurin's had only 725,663. Why such a big discrepancy? By virtue of being selected for TED Talks, both speakers were vetted prior to their presentation. TED goes to great lengths to keep their presentation style consistent and pick the best speakers from around the world. All of these speakers have amazing ideas. What gives?* I designed a research experiment in our lab to find out.

---

* Watch Simon Sinek and Fields Wicker-Miurin's TED Talk in our Digital Bonuses at www .ScienceofPeople.com/toolbox.

We wanted to see if Ambady and Rosenthal's findings could be applied to TED. First, we had a group of participants watch full-length TED Talks and give each speaker a score on credibility, charisma, intelligence, and overall performance. Participants were not able to see the view counts (to avoid skewing their perceptions) and we verified they had not seen the talks before.

Next, we gave scoring sheets to a second group, who saw seven-second clips of the same TED Talks. Guess what? No significant difference in opinion.

Is it possible that we decide if we are going to like a TED Talk within the first seven seconds? How do the top TED Talkers pass through all three levels of trust so quickly?

We had our coders analyze hundreds of hours of TED Talks looking for differences between the least and most viewed videos. We counted hand gestures and measured vocal variety, smiling, and body movement. We found that there were patterns. **The power of our first impression lies not in *what* we say, but *how* we say it.**

The most popular TED Talkers leveled up their audiences before even getting to their big idea. They did this by using what I call:

HACK #2: The Triple Threat
Make a powerful first impression by nonverbally hacking all three levels of trust.

In showbiz, performers are a Triple Threat when they can act, sing, and dance. With a first impression, you are a Triple Threat when you use your hands, your posture, and your eye contact. These are the three nonverbal weapons you can use to pass through all three levels of trust. These are what Arild Remmereit uses when he enters the stage. They are what the top TED Talkers use on that little red carpet. And they are what you should use anytime you are interacting with someone.

Skill #1: Use Your Hands

The top TED Talkers use a very specific mechanism to instantly build trust with their audience: hand gestures.

- The least popular TED Talkers used an average of **272** hand gestures—yes, our coders painstakingly counted every single one.

- The most popular TED Talkers used an average of **465** hand gestures—that's almost double!
- Temple Grandin, Simon Sinek, and Jane McGonigal topped the hand gesture charts with over **600** gestures in just eighteen minutes.

This effect isn't specific to TED Talks. Robert Gifford, Cheuk Fan Ng, and Margaret Wilkinson found that job candidates who use more hand gestures in their interviews are more likely to get hired.[7] Why do hand gestures have such an impact? Hands show intention.

Think back to caveman days for a moment. When a stranger approached our caveman ancestors, the best way to tell if the stranger had good or bad intentions was to look at their hands. Were they carrying a rock or a spear? As the stranger introduced themselves, our ancestors watched their gestures to make sure they weren't going to reach out and attack or steal precious belongings. Even though in modern times we aren't often subjected to physical harm, this survival mechanism remains. This is why in most cultures we shake hands as a way of greeting. And why the first thing police officers yell at criminals is "Get your hands up!"

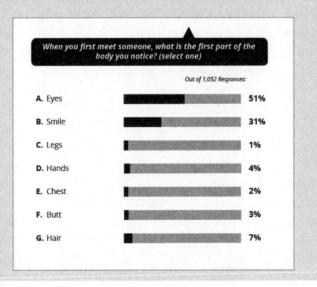

FAST FACT BOX

Most people think that we look at the eyes or the smile when we first meet someone. We don't realize how important hands are.

When you first meet someone, what is the first part of the body you notice? (select one)

Out of 1,052 Responses:

A. Eyes	51%
B. Smile	31%
C. Legs	1%
D. Hands	4%
E. Chest	2%
F. Butt	3%
G. Hair	7%

When someone can see your hands, they feel more at ease and are more likely to befriend you. This is an easy one to implement. When you walk into a room or are waiting to meet someone, keep your hands out of your pockets.

I know, I know, putting your hands in your pockets is so comfortable! It's so casual! It's so cowboy! I don't mean to get drastic, but pockets are *murderers* of rapport. Yeah, I said murderers. That's because the absolute easiest thing you can do to improve your first impression is to keep your hands visible. Every time you put your hand in your pocket, just scream "MURDERER!" in your head. That will help you remember.

Pockets aren't the only problem. Don't let desks, purses, or laptops block your friend-makers. Whenever possible, keep your hands above the desk in a boardroom, on the table during a coffee meeting, and out of your purse during an event.

Getting handsy is a one-two punch for trust. First, you have your hands visible, and then you go in for the perfect handshake.

How to Give a Perfect Handshake

Are you friend or foe? A handshake shows a stranger you are safe enough to go palm to palm. But not all handshakes are created equal. Here are the top things you need to know about a great handshake:

- **Dry:** Nothing is worse than a slimy handshake. If you get nervous and your palms sweat, use my favorite "napkin wrap" trick. When you get to an event, order a drink from the bar and wrap a napkin around the glass. Hold this with your handshaking hand so the napkin catches your sweat before you shake.

- **Vertical:** Always keep your hand vertical with your thumb toward the sky. Offering your palm up is a nonverbal submissive or weak gesture. And forcing someone into the palm-up position by putting your hand out palm down can be seen as domineering and controlling.

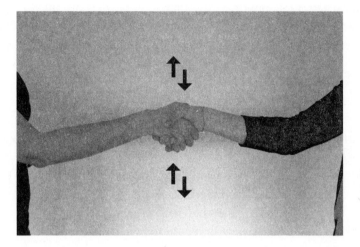

- **Firm:** Have you ever squeezed a peach to see if it was ripe? This is kind of the effect you want when shaking a hand, because everyone has slightly different ideas of firmness. With a peach, you squeeze until you feel a tiny bit of resistance. If it's really ripe, this comes fast and you stop squeezing. If it's not ready to be eaten, you can squeeze pretty hard without bruising the fruit. Same goes for people. Squeeze until you feel their muscles tighten, and then stop. And for goodness' sake, never give someone a limp hand a.k.a. the "dead fish"—it's deadly for rapport.*

Never, ever skip a handshake. Don't replace it with a wave or a high five or—heaven forbid—a fist bump. Why? The moment we have skin-to-skin touch with someone, our body produces something called oxytocin.

Oxytocin is the connection hormone. Researcher Paul Zak discovered the power of this little hormone, which he calls "the moral molecule,"

---

* Want more handshake tips? Find out what to do if someone's handshake is too strong or if you don't like touch, or how to handle the double handshake. Watch our digital bonus video at www.ScienceofPeople.com/toolbox.

to facilitate trust—this is why it is an essential part of answering the question "friend or foe?" Two million people have viewed his TED Talk. In it, he describes conducting experiments with oxytocin in which he manipulated the trust of participants simply by giving them a dose of the hormone.

When you shake hands with someone, your body produces the exact hormone you both need to build trust—and then a deeper connection.

Bottom Line: Keep your hands visible. Never skip a handshake.

Skill #2: Be a Winner

Answer the following question:

> **What is the most influential factor for professionals who want to earn the trust of potential clients?**
> A. Being an established, proven expert
> B. Having a high degree of confidence
> C. Demonstrating advanced expertise in their area
> D. Having a well-respected reputation

What did you guess? If you guessed "B. Having a high degree of confidence," you are correct! According to a major study done by Carnegie Mellon University,[8] a professional's confidence is more important than that professional's reputation, skill set, or history!

Why is confidence so important? As humans, we are constantly looking for winners.

> **Winner:** *n.* Victor; a person likely to be successful.

We like to have winners on our team. We like to be associated with winners. We like to be led by winners. Whether we like it or not, in the first few seconds of an interaction, we are trying to decide if the person we are speaking with looks more like a winner or more like a loser. The question is: What does a winner look like?

Researchers Jessica Tracy and David Matsumoto wanted to know if there are universal winner and loser behaviors. Specifically, they examined how humans respond to success and failure. To do this, they compared how Olympic athletes behave after they win or lose a race. Do sighted, blind, and congenitally blind (blind since birth) athletes display the same forms of pride and shame after a match? The answer is yes—**across cultures, the behavior of winning and losing athletes was the same.**

Even congenitally blind athletes, who have never seen an athlete finish a race or suffer a crushing defeat, somehow mimic the gestures of other athletes.[9]

Winners typically take up as much space as physically possible. Frequently called "Power Posing" this is when we raise our arms over our head, expand our chest, and tilt our head up:

Losing athletes take up as little physical space as possible. Also known as "Low Power Posing," defeated athletes usually bow their head, slump their shoulders, and pin their arms tightly to their sides.

The fact that athletes instinctively use the same body language shows us how innately programmed we are to broadcast victory and defeat nonverbally. But why? Tracy and Matsumoto propose that pride and shame factor significantly in social signaling, providing rich information we use to make judgments of ourselves and others.

Like athletes, when we are proud, we want people to notice us, so we take up space. When we feel defeated, we try to deflect attention by taking up as little space as possible.

Now, as much as I want you to look like a winner, the traditional winner's pose is a bit much for everyday interactions. It would be odd if you ran into your meetings or dates like you just crossed a finish line—highly powerful, but a bit socially aggressive.

Instead, I use something I call the Launch Stance. This is a slightly toned-down version of the winner's posture. **Whenever you are talking to people, use your Launch Stance:**

- Keep your shoulders down and back.
- Aim your chin, chest, and forehead straight in front of you or slightly up.
- Keep space between your arms and torso.
- Make sure your hands are visible.

Body language is the fastest way you can showcase confidence to others and hack your winning first impression.

Special Note: Sometimes we accidentally go into loser body language when we check our phones. Think about it: You bow your head, cross your arms in front of your chest, pin your arms tightly to your sides, and slump your shoulders in. What do most of us do while waiting for a client or before going into a meeting? We check our phones! This terrible cycle has to stop now!

If possible, chat with colleagues, look calmly around the waiting room, or read a newspaper before an important engagement. If you want to check your phone, just do it like a winner. Pivot the phone out and up to align with the Launch Stance:

Bottom Line: Stand like a winner. Look like a winner. Interact like a winner.

Skill #3: Engage with Eye Contact

Once we have decided someone is both trustworthy and a winner, we want to know if they should be on our team or not. This is the differentiator between a good first impression and a great one. Specifically, we are looking for indicators of alliance. Does this person like me? Would this person respect my opinion? Will this person include me? Sure, we like people who are trustworthy and confident, but if we don't think they will respect us, we never level them up.

Most TED Talkers pass only the first two levels. They may indicate their trustworthiness with hand gestures and capture confidence with a broad stance. However, most don't know how to make the individuals in their audience feel cared for. They speak to the cameras, they speak to the slides, but they don't speak to YOU.

How do you communicate your desire for an alliance? Imagine you're sipping on coffee during an afternoon break in a park. You see a mother reading a book on a blanket beside her toddler. The toddler spots a duck, so he looks up at his mom and says, "Look, a duck!" The mother doesn't hear him, so her son pulls on her hand and says louder, "Mom! Look, I see a duck!" This time, Mom registers it and murmurs, "Uh-huh, nice, sweetie." But the toddler isn't fooled. His mom wasn't *really* paying attention. So he starts jumping and tugging on his mother's arm, chanting "Mom, Mom, Mom, MOM, MOM! MOM!!" Finally, right as the toddler begins to cry, the mother puts her book down, looks at her son and says, "What is it?" The toddler smiles and points at the duck. "Oh!" she exclaims, and looks over at the duck with him. "How great! You love ducks," she says, turning to him and smiling. He sighs happily, and they both resume relaxing.

What happened? The toddler just wanted someone to share an experience with. Like all of us, he wanted an alliance. The best TED Talkers act much like a doting mother with their audience. They make eye contact with specific faces in the crowd and speak directly to them—making everyone watching feel like they truly matter. The sense of togetherness you get during a stellar TED Talk comes when you feel you are experiencing the slides and presentation along with the speaker. Viral TED Talkers speak *to* you, not *at* you.

One of the most powerful examples of eye contact is in a video done by activist Jae West and her team at Liberators International. Their organization's stated mission on their website: "We aim to coordinate, record and distribute monthly global acts of freedom."

Their YouTube channel is filled with many daring acts of kindness and unique public service announcements. In one video, the Liberators lead Australian subway passengers to sing an impromptu rendition of "Over the Rainbow." In another video, a woman stands in her underwear on a public street blindfolded. She asks people to draw hearts on her body with a permanent marker to raise awareness for eating disorders.[10]*

One of their most popular videos is called "The World's Biggest Eye Contact Experiment." In this video, Liberators ask strangers to participate in one minute of sustained eye contact with another stranger. "We were definitely nervous going into it . . . it's quite confronting to stare a stranger in the eye and allow yourself to be vulnerable," said West.

The results were overwhelming. Over 100,000 people participated in the experiment in 156 cities around the world. After just one minute of eye contact, stranger after stranger ended their moment in tears, hugs, and astonishment. As West concluded, "Holding eye contact with another person can evoke many feelings . . . it calls on true courage to trust another being."[11]

Why is eye contact so powerful? It produces oxytocin, the chemical foundation for trust. We're programmed to interpret it as a nonverbal signal of goodwill. When you like someone, you look at them more. Author Allan Pease describes it this way:

---

* Watch some of our favorite Liberators International Videos at www.ScienceofPeople
.com/toolbox.

When person A likes person B, he will look at him a lot. This causes B to think that A likes him, so B will like A in return. In other words, in most cultures, to build a good rapport with another person, your gaze should meet theirs about 60 to 70 percent of the time. This will also cause them to begin to like you. It is not surprising, therefore, that the nervous, timid person who meets our gaze less than one third of the time is rarely trusted.[12]

In those first few seconds, it's especially important that you override the impulse to look away shyly.

You may be worrying that you'll use *too* much eye contact. How much is ideal? You may remember this question from the PQ quiz:

In the average conversation, people typically hold eye contact what percent of the time?

1. 31 percent
2. 51 percent
3. 61 percent
4. 91 percent

I have asked this question to hundreds of audiences. The answers are usually evenly split. People have completely different ideas about how much eye contact is normal.

British social psychologist Dr. Michael Argyle found that when Westerners and Europeans are in conversation, they tend to hold eye contact for an average of **61 percent of the time** (answer C). He found that 41 percent occurs while talking and 75 percent while listening.[13] Next time you're talking to someone, try to objectively evaluate where you tend to fall on the spectrum. Some other things to keep in mind:

- Notice their eye color.
- Don't look over their head to scope out the scene.
- Hold eye contact for 60 to 70 percent of the time.

Bottom Line: Use eye contact to build trust. Gaze to produce connection.

THE ULTIMATE SOCIAL WEAPON

Making a killer first impression is not about banishing social anxiety once and for all. Before Arild Remmereit takes the stage, he still feels incredibly nervous. Famed TED Talker Dr. Brené Brown says giving her TED Talk was terrifying—and her talk is one of the most viewed TED videos of all time.

"One of the most anxiety-provoking experiences of my career was speaking at the TED Conference in Long Beach. In addition to all the normal fears associated with giving a filmed, eighteen-minute talk in front of an intensely successful and high-expectation audience, I was the closing speaker for the entire event," recalled Brown.

However, Brown took the stage like a champion, her shoulders back and her hands out. Then she made sure she could see her audience. "When I finally walked onto the stage the first thing I did was make eye contact with several people in the audience. I asked the stage managers to bring up the houselights so I could see people. I needed to feel connected," said Brown.[14]

The Triple Threat is a tool you can turn to when your nerves are high. It will both simplify the process of making good first impressions— once you understand the science, it's not so big and scary—and allow you to relax by living more in the moment. Along with the most popular TED Talkers and Remmereits, you can make your first few seconds count by nonverbally showing your audience: You can trust me, I have a winning idea, and I'm here to help you. That's how we become memorable.

CHALLENGES

1. Don't guess on your handshake. Do a handshake audit with a trusted friend or colleague—ask for honest feedback to make sure your grip is just right.
2. Use your Launch Stance during your next interaction—feel the difference?
3. Practice engaging in 60 to 70 percent eye contact during your interactions.

CHAPTER REVIEW

You have only a few seconds to make a killer first impression.

- Confirm trust by showing your hands.
- Be a winner with your Launch Stance.
- Use the right amount of eye contact.

My biggest takeaway in this chapter is: _____

CHAPTER 3

SPARK

How to have dazzling conversations

In the heart of Bogotá, there are treasures. And Jeffer Carrillo Toscano is our treasure hunter. A small group of us diligently follow him as he weaves through the small cobblestone alleys that make up La Candelaria—one of the oldest neighborhoods in Colombia.

"Keep your eyes peeled," he says, pointing to the tops of Spanish colonial houses and crumbling baroque balconies, "they could be anywhere." We climb up a set of narrow stairs, barely disturbing a family of napping kittens and stumble upon our first find. What are we looking for? Graffiti.

Nestled between two boarded windows is one of the most beautiful pieces of art I have ever seen. An indigenous woman looks up at the sky as if in prayer or search of rain. It takes my breath away.

Street after street, Jeffer points out drawings I never would have noticed before—a portrait on the side of a drainpipe, a mushroom on the corner of an art deco door, a tiny hummingbird next to a patio. As he walks and talks he is constantly surveying the group for interest. He notes when and where people take pictures, who says "Ooohh!" and who looks bored.

In between streets he plays a memory game and tags each person's name to where they are from—by the end he has all twenty-six names memorized. Then he asks each of us for our story. He wants to know what brings each person to his graffiti tour—not exactly the typical choice for a tourist.

One by one he finds something relevant for each person on the tour. One woman works at an international nonprofit to preserve the rain forests of South America. To her delight, he brings her to a large mural depicting the Colombian rain forest.

Jeffer then learns one of our group members is an American journalist. He weaves around the streets to show him a political graphic on the base of a cement slab. It shows a black-and-white image of Edward Snowden with the words "Hero or Traitor?" emblazoned in large block letters. The journalist is blown away and begins scribbling away in his notebook for his next story to send home.

Without realizing it, Jeffer is tapping into a fundamental law of human behavior. He creates sparks. His ability to captivate attention has made his Bogotá Graffiti Tour the second-highest-rated activity on Trip-Advisor and has been featured in the *New York Times* as a must-see if you have only thirty-six hours to spend in Bogotá.*

THE DEATH OF SMALL TALK

One of the greatest days of my childhood existence could be summed up in two words: Space Mountain. Every summer while I was growing up, my family went to Disneyland. This was the highlight of my year, and my siblings and I counted down the days until we could run through the perfectly manicured, cotton-candy-scented park with abandon.

There was only one problem. In the beginning, I was not tall enough to go on the best rides—specifically, Space Mountain. I watched as the top of my older brother's curly hair grazed the ominous height

---

* See more Colombian street art pictures in our Digital Bonuses at www.ScienceofPeople
.com/toolbox.

requirement line. Then my parents left me to babysit my little sisters as the three of them went down the dark tunnel of excitement without us. I was stuck in the Tiki Room. The thrill of my day came when my youngest sister almost flew out of a spinning teacup because I dared her to not hold on (never, EVER tell Mom).

One glorious summer, the top of my pigtail reached that forbidding line. I strapped into my rocket car and gripped the sweaty safety bar. The next two minutes were life defining. Space Mountain blew my mind. All my life I had an inkling I had been missing out, but really I had no idea. The slow, monotonous humps of Dumbo the Flying Elephant did not even come close to comparing to the exhilarating dips and whirls of Space Mountain. The "speed" we reached on the Disneyland Railroad was laughable compared to the daredevil pace of a rocket! That day, my brother and I rode Space Mountain over and over again, and I swore I would never go back to the kiddie rides.

This is exactly how it works with conversations. For most of our lives, we chitchat on the kiddie ride. Our conversations aren't memorable because we aren't very stimulated or excited. Our energy level during most small talk looks something like this:

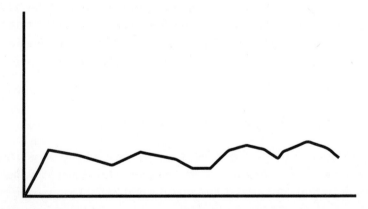

This is small talk. With no high peaks and no interesting hooks, our conversations come and go—we are lucky to remember our partner's name, let alone what we talked about. I want to introduce the concept of Big Talk.

Big Talk is like Space Mountain. You start with anticipation and roll easily through the conversation, laughing and hitting highs as it gets better and better. Our energy level looks like this:

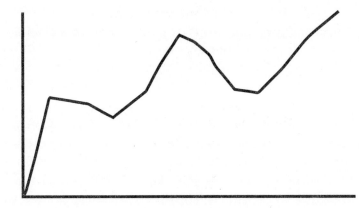

Like a great roller coaster, great conversations leave you feeling both exhilarated and hoping you'll never have to experience small talk again.

Now, the death of small talk requires some effort. Like any good people hack, Big Talk means skirting conversational norms, challenging chitchat status quo, and shirking social scripts. Roller coasters command a little extra height and so does Big Talk.

THE SCIENCE OF SPARKS

The reason why we love roller coasters is because of the peaks. The top of each summit gives us a rush as we await and enjoy the glee of the ride. Big Talk is marked by the same kind of emotional peaks. The best conversations have specific jolts of energy and excitement—I call these star moments "sparks."

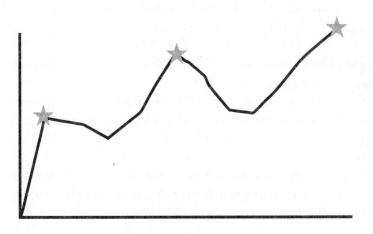

HACK #3: Conversational Sparks
Use unique talking points to create pleasurable and memorable conversations.

Big Talk has tons of sparks—lots of little bursts of pleasure that we remember. Have you ever had a great conversation with someone? Afterward, did you savor it—replaying the high points, rolling around the humorous moments over and over again in your head? This is because conversational sparks make us feel good.

In the brain, sparks are marked by dopamine.[1] Dopamine is a neurotransmitter that is released in the amygdala when we feel pleasure. When we get a birthday gift, praise from our boss, or a reward, dopamine floods our brain. Think about the joy you get when you walk into a store and the clerk tells you, "Free samples!" That feeling of excitement is pure dopamine.

Here's what's interesting about dopamine: It helps your memory. Molecular biologist Dr. John Medina likens dopamine to a mental marker. He says, "Dopamine greatly aids memory and information processing. You can think of it like a Post-it note that reads 'Remember this!' Getting one's brain to put a chemical Post-it note on a given piece of information means that information is going to be more robustly processed."[2] In other words, being memorable boils down to inducing chemical pleasure. **When you produce dopamine during a conversation, you not only give your partner more enjoyment, you are also assigned more significance, which increases your memorability.**

The question is: How do you spark dopamine during a conversation? I would love for you to keep little presents in your pockets like a birthday party magician, but that isn't very practical—and business suits don't have particularly roomy pockets. Instead, you can produce pleasure verbally. Presents don't come only in colorfully wrapped packages. Rewards don't need to have a dollar sign. Gratification doesn't just come from physically feeling good.

There are three ways to hack your conversations to make them both more pleasurable and more memorable. Let's turn your small talk into Big Talk.

Step #1: Conversation Sparkers
One day I was sitting in the green room of a morning news show, nervously awaiting my segment. All of a sudden, in walked one of my favorite

writers—Elizabeth Gilbert, author of *Eat Pray Love* and *Big Magic*. I was stunned and immediately began racking my brain for something interesting to say. I was dying to talk to her, but had no idea what would pique her interest. What does one say to a literary icon, a bestselling author, and a personal hero? Should I ask about her book? No, too obvious. Should I ask where she is from? No, too bland. Should I just blurt out how much I love her books? No, too suck-uppy.

Before I could work up my nerve, the other guest in the green room smiled at both of us and said, "Do you like soup?"

Okay, this is one conversation starter I would never have come up with on my own. But I was grateful. I stared at the other guest, wide-eyed at her courage, and held my breath—how on earth would Ms. Gilbert react? To my amazement, Elizabeth Gilbert ("Call me Liz," she clarified immediately) clapped her hands and began telling us about her favorite winter soup recipes. We reminisced about Grandma-made stews and laughed about the perils of eating healthy while traveling. Who would have thought that a soup conversation starter would spark such a lively and fun discussion?

I found out later that the other guest was a chef publishing a soup cookbook and Liz was on one of her West Coast book tours. I was doing a segment on the science of friendship—and we all had thirty minutes to kill before we went live on air. All we needed was a spark.

Most conversations go something like this:

What do you do?
Oh, that's nice. Where are you from?
Mmm, never been there. So, what brings you here?
Good, good. Well, I'm going to get another drink . . .

Boring! This conversation is the equivalent of sitting on a kiddie ride. There is almost no emotional stimulation, no sparks, no highs, just a slow roll to an anticlimactic ending where you desperately need hand sanitizer. It's time to step up to Space Mountain.

I get it—sometimes we're lazy or plain afraid of tackling new topics. But what's the point of following nearly identical social scripts every time you talk to someone? What's the point of trying to talk to a new client if it's so boring that they won't remember it anyway? What's the point of interacting on autopilot?

Big Talk requires asking fresh questions that cause conversational sparks. I call these conversation "sparkers" in lieu of conversation "starters." They ignite new ideas, introduce topics we have never thought about, and stimulate in-depth discussions.

Why do we get pleasure from novelty?

Neurobiologists Dr. Nico Bunzeck and Dr. Emrah Düzel conducted a study they called "The Oddball Experiments."[3] In this test, experimenters showed participants a series of images while scanning their brains in a functional magnetic resonance imaging (fMRI) machine. Most of the images depicted the same face and the same scene. However, participants were intermittently shown a series of "oddball" images.

The researchers measured blood flow to different areas of the brain as participants observed each image. They found that oddball images activate our brain's "novelty center" (the substantia nigra and ventral tegmental area). Here's why novelty matters:

- **Memory and Learning:** The oddball images activated the area influenced by the hippocampus, which is the brain's learning and memory center. Novelty makes our brain perk up, pay attention, and process the conversation better. Want people to remember *your* name? Spark excitement and novelty.
- **Pleasure:** This novelty center is linked to our dopamine pathways in the amygdala—the almond-shaped bundle of neurons near the base of the brain. New ideas and topics give us a nice bump of dopamine in this region, which makes us feel great.
- **Interest:** Dopamine also encourages us to seek even more rewards. In other words, a little bit of fresh conversation encourages both people to want to go deeper and explore more. Dr. Düzel explains, "When we see something new, we see it has a potential for rewarding us in some way. This potential that lies in new things motivates us to explore our environment for rewards."[4]

If we abandon social scripts and push ourselves to use conversational sparks, we are more likely to enjoy our interactions and remember what was actually said.

In 2016, we partnered with the organizations Mercy Corps, Society for Information Management, and Girls Inc. to run a set of speed networking experiments. In these experiments, we randomly partnered over three hundred participants to test conversation starters. At each chair, participants have seven slips of paper waiting for them. Each card has a different conversation starter and a space for a rating.

Once everyone is seated, we start the speed networking rounds. Each conversation starter gets one three-minute round. At the end of three minutes, we ring a bell and each participant rates the quality of the conversation produced—1 for boring, 5 for stellar. Here are the seven rounds. Can you guess which three were rated the highest?

____ What's your story?
____ How are you?
____ What was the highlight of your day?
____ What do you do?
____ Have anything exciting coming up in your life?
____ What brings you here?
____ What personal passion project are you working on?

There were clear winners. Here they are in order of highest rank to lowest:

1. What was the highlight of your day?
2. What personal passion project are you working on?
3. Have anything exciting coming up in your life?
4. What's your story?
5. What brings you here?
6. What do you do?
7. How are you?

Sometimes, we also do a "Grab Bag" round where we have people choose any of the seven previous conversation starters to ask and write down which one they used. The most popular choices for Grab Bag are "What personal passion project are you working on?" and "What's your story?"

The problem is that the conversation starters we most often use—"What do you do?" and "How are you?"—are rated as the most boring. So why do we keep on using them?

We stick to social scripts out of habit. We use the same dull conversation starters over and over again because they are in our comfort zone. But you know what? Nothing spark-worthy ever happens in your comfort zone. **If you keep using social scripts, you will be stuck in small talk forever.**

I challenge you to try using our top-rated conversation sparkers:*

Instead of ...	Hack ...
How's work?	Working on any exciting projects recently?
How are you?	What was the highlight of your day?
What do you do?	Working on any personal passion projects?
How's the family?	Have any vacations coming up?
Where are you from?	What's your story?
How's it going?	What are you up to this weekend?
Been busy?	What do you do to unwind?

Novelty doesn't just hack your in-person conversations—it also adds spark to interactions both online and off. OkCupid is a dating website with over 3.5 million active users. They do fascinating data analyses on activity on the website to look for patterns of success.[5] One interesting little nugget is that according to the cofounder Sam Yagan, men who begin their online dating messages with "howdy" have a 40 percent higher success rate than singles who open with "hey" or "hi." When it comes to salutations, the more unique the better:

Your typical "hello," "hi," and "hey" get terrible reply rates in direct messages. "Howdy," "hola," and even "yo" rank better. The best greetings, "how's it going" and "what's up," ask a question—even if they are slangy and informal, they do the trick. They ignite some kind of spark.[6]

Don't ask the same old boring questions. Look for topics that get people excited, make people interested, and create sparks.

---

* We are constantly updating our list of favorite conversation sparkers. Check out our current list at www.ScienceofPeople.com/toolbox.

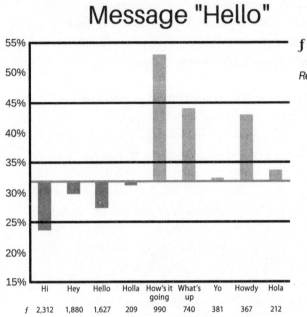

Message "Hello"

$\mathfrak{f}$ = *Frequency per **10,000** messages sent.*
Reply rate of messages containing the keywords in the first 7.

	Hi	Hey	Hello	Holla	How's it going	What's up	Yo	Howdy	Hola
$\mathfrak{f}$	2,312	1,880	1,627	209	990	740	381	367	212

Bonus: Sometimes, if I am nervous about asking a conversation sparker, I will tell people, "I'm on a small-talk diet, can I ask you a new conversation sparker I'm trying out?" This question in itself releases dopamine! I *always* get a positive response when I preface a question this way—in fact, people tend to lean in, raise their eyebrows curiously, and exclaim something like, "Yes please! How interesting!"

Step #2: Push Hot Buttons

One of the ways you can create conversational high points is by looking for someone's hot-button issues. This is a topic, hobby, or activity that lights someone up. You know you have pushed a hot button when the other person:

- Begins nodding their head up and down as if to say, "Yes!"
- Murmurs in agreement with "Mmm-hmm"
- Leans in to hear more
- Writes back a longer e-mail than usual
- Exclaims in surprise with "Huh!" or "Wow!"

- Tells you, "Fascinating!" "Interesting," or "Tell me more!"
- Raises their eyebrows—this is the universal signal of curiosity
- Says, "Ooohh" or "Aahh"
- Smiles and uses more animated gestures

When any of these engagement cues happen, you know that you have just sparked some dopamine and pushed a hot button.

This is what Jeffer Carrillo Toscano is looking for on his tours. He points things out or tells a story and looks to see if he has sparked any interest. If so, he goes into more detail.

You can find hot-button issues by using sparkers that look for specific interests. In the set of studies by OkCupid I discussed earlier, their data scientists found that bringing up specific interests in direct messages also proved to be the most effective. Generic is boring. The more specific you can be, the more likely you are to find a hot button.

The messages that were replied to the most contained words such as "metal," "vegetarian," and "zombie." Why? One of these might be a hot button, but even if they aren't, you at least have something to talk about.

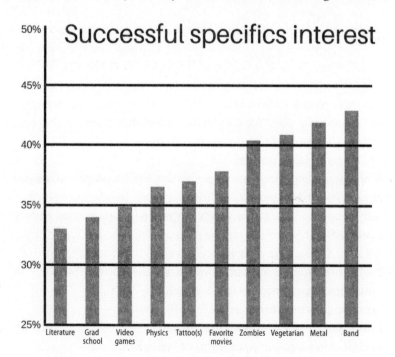

Successful specifics interest

The most successful users actually pointed out potential hot-button issues. They looked at a user's profile and guessed what might be a dopamine-worthy conversation sparker. "You mention," "good taste" and "noticed that" all have great reply rates.

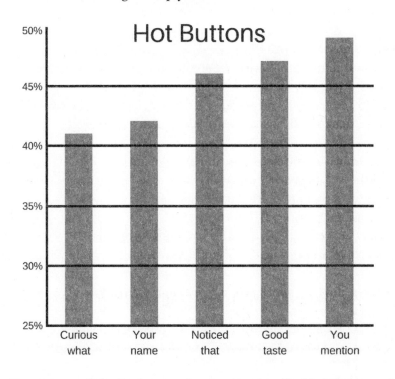

You can search for hot buttons in conversation. I bolded the potential hot buttons in these questions:

- You mentioned that you volunteer with **Big Brothers**—have you always done that?
- You asked for **Argentinian wine**—are you a wine aficionado?
- I noticed that your purse is **handwoven**—did you make it?
- I was curious about your accent—are you **from** here?
- I was just looking at your **bookshelf**—you have great taste in reading materials!
- Your name is beautiful—is it a **family** name?
- I saw you posted some great pictures of your **new dog** on Facebook—what made you decide to get a dog?

The moment someone lights up, you know you have just pushed a hot button. This is when you can ask for background stories, details, and dig deeper. That produces both great conversation and more dopamine, which makes you more memorable. Whether in person, over e-mail, or on the phone, looking for hot buttons is an easy way to spark interest.

Step #3: Wake People Up

You can also use conversational sparks and hot buttons to wake people up.

In 1994, three researchers hired an actor to panhandle on the street asking for money. They ran three trials:

- **Trial 1:** Can you spare any change?
- **Trial 2:** Can you spare a quarter?
- **Trial 3:** Can you spare thirty-seven cents?

Can you guess which question did best? Yup, the third trial got the most people to say yes.

- **Trial 1:** Can you spare any change? (44 percent of people complied)
- **Trial 2:** Can you spare a quarter? (64 percent of people complied)
- **Trial 3:** Can you spare 37 cents? **(75 percent of people complied)**

The researchers found that slightly unusual or surprising requests pique the most interest.[7] It's like coffee for the brain. Unique questions, unexpected stories, and uncommon occurrences keep us alert in conversation. **In other words, being different wakes people up.**

When you try to be the same as everyone else, it's boring. When you try to fit into a mold, you become forgettable. When you try to be "normal," you become dull. Just be yourself, because no one is like you. If you're a little weird, own it. The right people will like you for it.

This is not always easy. It's hard to own being a little unique. Before I started using unique sparks in my conversations, I began experimenting with it on my website. For example, most websites ask you to "Click here!" or "Sign up here" or "Visit this link," so I decided to try something unique. I put a button on my sidebar that says, "Do Not Click Here."

DO NOT CLICK HERE

It is one of the most visited pages on my website simply because it says something different. By the way, I reward clickers of that button with a video of cute baby animals.

Once I got a little more brave, I started to wonder if I could add conversational sparks to my elevator pitch to spice it up a little. My old pitch:

"I'm a writer."

Boring! This is the equivalent of a panhandler asking for some change—you hear it, but it doesn't really register. We have heard it before and we, sadly, pass right by. I decided to do my own version of the panhandling experiment. I came up with three versions of what I do and printed up business cards with a different e-mail address for each one.

- I'm a writer.
- I write about people.
- I'm a professional people watcher.

Over the next few weeks when someone would ask, "What do you do?" I would try out a version and then give them the corresponding card *if they asked for it.* I began to track not only which cards I passed out the most, but also which e-mails got the highest contact rate.

I shouldn't have been surprised to learn that "I'm a writer" did not get many card requests, nor did many people follow up with me after events; my "I'm a professional people watcher" elevator pitch got both laughs and card requests. I even began experimenting with putting unique images and content on my business card and found that those cards always got better feedback and won me more clients:

Vanessa Van Edwards
Author, Behavioral Investigator

Since conversational sparks were working for my pitches, I wondered if they might also work for others. One of my favorite TV shows is ABC's *Shark Tank*. In this show, entrepreneurs pitch their business ideas to a panel of investors called sharks. I wanted to know if there were pitch patterns. So we decided to run a massive *Shark Tank* experiment.

As of January 2016, 495 entrepreneurs have pitched on *Shark Tank*—253 got deals and 242 did not. What's the difference? We analyzed each and every one of the 495 pitches and found distinct differences between the successful and unsuccessful entrepreneurs. One that immediately caught our attention was that standout entrepreneurs used conversational sparks and hot buttons in their pitches. **Entrepreneurs who added a unique request, tried something a little different, or added interactivity to their pitch had a much higher likelihood of getting a deal.**

The majority of successful entrepreneurs—63 percent—used a unique pitch method to get a deal. Some entrepreneurs brought on mascots like the one for Mr. Tod's Pie Factory. Others brought on celebrities like Vincent Pastore from *The Sopranos* for Brocolli Wad. And the Kisstixx pitchers even made sharks Kevin O'Leary and Barbara Corcoran kiss to try out their lip balm.

This is a way that entrepreneurs created sparks or high points in their pitches. Sharks hear dozens of pitches every episode, so when an entrepreneur tries something unique, it sparks dopamine for the investors and wakes them up.*

Conversational sparks add fuel to any interaction. I love to use the element of surprise to pique people's interest. I frequently hand out lollipops with my business cards that say, "Learn how not to suck."

---

* Read all ten patterns we found on *Shark Tank* in your Digital Bonuses at www.Scienceof People.com/toolbox.

When people visit my office, I offer them hot cocoa instead of coffee. At trade shows, I have a bowl of Pop Rocks at my table instead of mints. In my guest bathroom at home, we have an R2D2 Pez dispenser and a gift book welcoming snoopers to our medicine cabinet. I send people air plants instead of flowers. I hide Easter eggs on my website (these are hidden links that once clicked deliver people to a video of me telling a corny joke).

Think about how you can energize different areas of your life. This creates tons of dopamine-worthy moments for the people you encounter. Again, this takes a little bravery, but can supercharge your conversations, pitches, meetings, parties, and social media with a little bit of uniqueness. Here are some more ways you can add conversational sparks to your interactions:

- **Spice up your job title.** Quicken Loans has a "vice president of miscellaneous stuff" who helps with a little bit of everything. Houghton Mifflin Harcourt calls its receptionists "directors of first impressions" since they are typically the company's greeters.
- **Stop posting food pictures and sunsets on Instagram.** Post something people haven't seen before. New mom and photographer Laura Izumikawa started posting (frickin' adorable) pictures of her sleeping newborn baby dressed like different celebrities and characters like Jon Snow, Pikachu, and Beyoncé. As of writing she has over 400,000 followers and her account has been featured on the *Huffington Post*, Buzzfeed, and *Inside Edition*.
- **Put a unique quote in your e-mail signature.** Noah Kagan, creator of an e-mail and analytics software, has a funny sign-off on all of his e-mails: "Ps. Y u NO install the free SumoMe.com to get more e-mail subscribers?" The purposeful misspellings and play on a popular meme makes his ask unique and very clickable.
- **Don't serve coffee to clients; serve vanilla tea, lemonade, or cake pops.** When I checked into San Diego's famous L'Auberge Del Mar hotel, I was given a room key and a s'mores cupcake— talk about a welcome gift! My elevator ride and first few hotel moments were sweet bliss.
- **Stop bringing casserole to potlucks. Whip up a recipe no one has tried before.** Pinterest is a never-ending source of inspiration for rainbow cupcakes, Rice Krispies ice cream, and pickle potato chips.

- **Instead of sending thank-you cards, send thank-you stickers—or pins, or lollipops, or popcorn.** At the Be Sage wedding conference, they gave attendees coloring books and pencils to use during sessions and on the plane ride home. People loved them and shared tons of pictures of their creations on social media with the conference's hashtag.

Don't be afraid to try out a new joke, tell a silly story, or ask a nontypical conversation sparker. You'll spice up your night, add flair to theirs, and have conversations you will never forget.

> *It is not your customer's job to remember you. It is your obligation and responsibility to make sure they don't have the chance to forget you.*
>
> —Patricia Fripp

Bonus: Say My Name

You've probably heard that it's charming to lightly drop someone's name in conversation. You, me, everyone else: We love the sound of our own names.

Dennis Carmody and Michael Lewis found that compared to other people's names, upon hearing our own name we have greater brain activation in the middle frontal and superior temporal cortex—also where the amygdala and hippocampus are located.[8]

This was one of the reasons why Jeffer hits it off so well with his tour groups right away. He makes a point of quickly memorizing every single person's name on the tour.

Not good with names? Not anymore. Here is my three-step Name Game that you can do every time you meet someone new:

1. **Meet and Repeat:** As soon as you hear the name, say it out loud back to them. "It's so nice to meet you, Eliza!" or "Eliza, this is my colleague Jenna." This jangles the audio part of your memory and allows you to hear the name in your own voice. Plus, you give them a nice hit of dopamine.
2. **Spell It Out:** Now we want to give that name a visual hook. Memory expert Dr. Gary Small encourages people to mentally

spell out the name they are trying to remember.[9] You can also pull up a picture of the name in your head.

3. **Associate and Anchor:** Lastly, tie the name to someone else you know with that same name. It can even be a celebrity. This anchors the name to someone else you are familiar with. For example, whenever I meet a Matt, I always seat him at a poker table with all of my other Matt friends.

4. **Bonus:** If it is a unique name or a name you have not heard before, tie it to a word that most closely resembles it. For example, I met a Syder (pronounced very similar to "cider") so I pulled up a mental picture of a steaming glass of cider. He was shocked when I remembered his name at the end of the night.

This exercise takes a bit of practice, but is a fun way to gamify names. I highly recommend teaching this Name Game to your friends or colleagues because you can help each other think of anchors when you meet people.

Insider Tip: If you totally forget a name, set up a system with the people you are with. Anytime you introduce someone to them first, they should ask for the name. For example, if my husband says, "I would love to introduce you to my wife," and does not mention the person's name, it means he does not know it. Then I know to ask, "Lovely to meet you. What was your name?" Easy peasy.

A Safety Net

Worried you won't be able to think of a snazzy conversation sparker when the moment comes? Scared you will be caught tongue-tied during your next interaction? Wish you had "someone" to text on an awkward date? Have no fear—Vanessa is here!

Anytime you don't know what to say, anytime you're awkward, anytime you need a little social help, **just text me. Really.* (Blah, blah, normal text messaging rates apply.)**

- **"Tell me what to say"** and I'll send you a conversation starter.
- **"Give me a pep talk"** and I'll send you an encouraging word.

---

* Find the link and number in your Digital Bonuses at www.ScienceofPeople.com/toolbox.

- **"Send me a joke"** and I'll send you a corny joke to make you laugh.
- **"Send me a tip"** and I'll send you a social skills tip to help pump you up.
- **Bonus:** Want to be daring? Text me: **"Give me a social dare"** and I'll send you a superfun challenge to try wherever you are!

FIND YOUR SPARKS

If you want to have dazzling conversations, it's up to you to create sparks. You can remember someone's name, use conversation sparkers, or push hot buttons to create talking high points. Get out of your own conversational autopilot. Don't use social scripts, ignite conversational sparks. Stop passively listening and push hot buttons. Hack conversations by creating talking high points. Be more memorable by really remembering the people you meet—from their names to their interests. Ending small talk starts big connections.

CHALLENGES

1. Use one conversation sparker this week and see how it completely changes the interaction.
2. Try adding some hot buttons to your pitch, e-mail signature, or next conversation.
3. Turn on the TV and find a show you have never seen before. Every time a new character is introduced, try the three-step Name Game. This is a low-stakes and laid-back way to practice.
4. **Bonus:** Send me a text to say "hi." If you're really brave, ask me for a "social dare."

CHAPTER REVIEW

We don't like, remember, or enjoy being around boring people. The best way to hack into stimulating conversations and create memorable connections is to ignite conversational sparks. We are attracted to people who give us mental pleasure, who push our hot buttons, keep us mentally alert, and learn our names.

- Abandon social scripts to change your small talk to Big Talk.
- Find topics that turn people on.
- Create sparks by using people's names, asking unique questions, and bringing up novel topics.

My biggest takeaway in this chapter is: _____

CHAPTER 4

HIGHLIGHT

How to be the most memorable person in the room

My Vow of Silence lasted for seven days. No talking. No writing. No posting on social media. No responding to e-mail.

That week was one of the hardest, most introspective, soul-wrenching times of my life. I almost lost my mind.

The whole adventure started the day my kind, honest friend dropped an advice bomb. She gave me one of the toughest pieces of constructive feedback I have ever received: "You are an interrupter."

Horrified, I tried to clarify, "What do you mean? Do you think I interrupt you when you speak?"

Gently, she explained, "Yes, and"—another truth grenade—"I've heard you do it to others, too."

Boom! Shock. Embarrassment. And then a little self-exploration: I am terrified of awkward silences. I fear that moment when someone finishes a sentence and no one knows what to say next. To prevent these uncomfortable pauses, I got in the habit of interrupting. Worse, I began to pre-plan my responses while only half listening to the conversation. This is a terrible way to interact—it's disrespectful, inauthentic, and exhausting for all parties.

I realized that if I wanted to learn to be a better listener quickly, I should quit talking cold turkey. Enter: Vow of Silence. On August 10, 2014, I took a pledge and alerted all of my readers and colleagues that I would not be talking. I wanted to be in silence until the silence became less scary.

There was one other hurdle. Even though I couldn't talk, I still wanted to listen. So instead of hiding out in my house reading, I forced myself to attend all of my usual meetings, networking events, and dinners like normal, but just listened. This way, I had to be present. I couldn't think about witty comebacks, funny stories, or follow-ups. My number one goal was simply to listen with my entire brain. I didn't even allow myself to write—then I still would have been dreaming up clever responses instead of listening. My only allowances were four premade flash cards that I could show to people I encountered. They said:

1. "I've taken a Vow of Silence. I'm trying to become a better listener."
2. "Please tell me about yourself."
3. "I'm sorry."
4. "Thank you for allowing my silence."

The first day was the hardest. I walked into my first networking event as a sweaty, jittery mess. What if I freaked people out? What would I do in those horrible long pauses of silent disgust? Can you get kicked out of networking events for not networking?

I completely panicked when a gentleman introduced himself. But I shakily held up my first card: "I've taken a Vow of Silence. I'm trying to become a better listener."

To my delight and surprise, he laughed and told me how he had once lost his voice to laryngitis in college and it was one of the coolest and craziest experiences of his life. Then he spoke about meeting his wife a few weeks later. Then he shared his hope for his children. Then he asked for my card. I didn't say a word. I didn't have to. He just wanted to be listened to.

As humans, we are desperate to be heard. The biggest thing I learned during my Vow of Silence is that **the best conversations aren't about what you say, they are about what you hear**. I made better business connections during my *silent* week than during the fast-paced industry conference I went to the week before. One businesswoman even e-mailed me the day after my Vow of Silence and said:

Hey Vanessa! I have been thinking so much about our conversation last night. I just joined your body language course and can't wait to start it. I would love to take you out to coffee in the next few weeks if you are free.

This e-mail boggled my mind! I hadn't said a single word, but somehow our "conversation" was so memorable that it brought me business. Why?

SILENCE SCIENCE

As much as we hate to admit it, we love to talk about ourselves. In fact, humans spend 30 to 40 percent of their verbal output solely dedicated to self-disclosure. This number balloons to 80 percent on social media sites like Twitter and Facebook.

Harvard neuroscientists Diana Tamir and Jason Mitchell found that something changes in our brain when we talk about ourselves. Activity increases in the brain regions that form the mesolimbic dopamine system. Keyword: dopamine.[1] **Talking about ourselves gives us pleasure.**

In one experiment, participants were even willing to forgo money to disclose more information about themselves. Yup—people will pay for the privilege to express their opinions.

This is the science behind the famous Dale Carnegie phrase "To be interesting, be interested"[2] and why my Vow of Silence worked so well. When you are interested, when you listen, when you let people talk, they feel pleasure.

Before my Vow of Silence, my mind was always spinning trying to think of what I was going to say next. I couldn't really process what people were saying because I was too busy trying to think of witty jokes, dazzling stories, and clever responses. This was a terrible way to interact. I was both distracted and turning people off by my distractedness. Then, to my great surprise, my silence won me more friends than my overeagerness ever had. Does this mean we should all go around being silent during our interactions? Definitely no. Being interested is only the first piece of the puzzle.

Step One: When you ask dopamine-worthy conversation sparkers and listen to people's responses, pleasure is produced. Success! BUT it's what you do next that counts.

Step Two: How do you honor what they say? What are you listening for? How do you respond to their self-disclosure? A great interaction is not one-sided.

Here's the thing: Being quiet didn't just help me learn how to avoid interrupting, it also taught me a new way of listening.

I never learned anything while I was talking.

—Larry King

SILENT SLOAN

When Alfred P. Sloan took the reins as vice president of operations at General Motors, the company was struggling. In 1920, General Motors accounted for only a 12 percent share of car sales in the country. Sloan dreamed bigger. He decided the best way to tackle his industry competitors—namely the Ford motorcar—would be to go directly to his dealers to improve sales. Sloan began to visit each and every dealership personally and listen to the salesmen's ideas. Sloan's unique style was unheard of at this time—borderline heretical. As reported by the *New York Times:*

> "It may surprise you to know," he said at the time, "that I have personally visited, with many of my associates, practically every city in the United States, from the Atlantic to the Pacific and from Canada to Mexico. On these trips I visit from 5 to 10 dealers a day. I meet them in their own places of business, talk with them across their own desks and solicit from them suggestions and criticisms as to their relations with the corporation."

When meeting with dealers, Sloan didn't try to win them over or convince them of his ideas. He once said, "I prefer to appeal to the intelligence of a man rather than attempt to exercise authority over him." He was nicknamed Silent Sloan because "When he listened, it was with the extra intentness of the deaf."

Sloan remained at the helm of General Motors until 1956. During his tenure, he spearheaded major advances in automotive technology including four-wheel brakes, ethyl gasoline, crankcase ventilation, and knee-action front springs. By the time he left in 1956, General Motors was one of the world's most successful companies and had claimed over 52 percent of market share (a big leap from the 12 percent when Sloan first started).[3]

Personal friend of Sloan and leading business author Peter F. Drucker credits Sloan's success not to a fearless vision or to ruthless tactics but to a listening-driven management style. How did Sloan hack the art of listening? Here's how he worked:

- Sloan spent six days a week in meetings, three with formal agendas and three to address problems as they arose.
- Other than stating each meeting's initial purpose, Sloan attended each meeting in silence. He almost never took notes or spoke except to clarify something with a question. According to Drucker, he ended each meeting with a brief pointed summary and thanks.
- Following each meeting, Sloan would pick one executive to be accountable and composed a short memo with a summary of what was said, next steps, work assignments, and a specific deadline. A copy of the memo was sent to everyone in the meeting.[4]

Sloan overturned conventional wisdom on what effective leadership looked like. In 1931, MIT created the first university program for executives called Sloan Fellows. And then the MIT Sloan School of Management was founded in 1950.

For three decades, Silent Sloan **led with what he heard, not with what he said.** He listened with intent and then followed up with action. I call this hack being a highlighter.

> *You bring out the best in yourself by looking for the best in others.*
>
> —Gene Bedley, National Educator of the Year

SKILL #1: BE A HIGHLIGHTER

I have a moderate obsession with office supplies. Nothing gets me going like a fresh pack of snazzy pens, a bunch of little notebooks, and a colorful array of sticky tabs. I remember inheriting my first bright yellow highlighter from my older brother—and by inherited, I do mean stolen from his backpack.

It was such a game changer! That little stick of brightness helped me learn faster, remember more and emphasize important points. The best communicators do the exact same thing—they serve as conversational highlighters. They listen to learn more about a person, to remember what was said and then find the important points to act upon.

So far, you've designed your Social Game Plan, leveraged the Triple Threat, and sparked conversation. Now what? It's time to hack the art—and science—of listening. You can do this by being a highlighter:

HACK #4: Highlighter
Bring out the best in people by highlighting their strengths.

When you know what to listen for, you know exactly how to respond. Highlighting is also a way of practicing more refreshing and honest interactions. Highlighting is not about sugarcoating, it's not about brown-nosing, and it's not about sucking up. It's about honoring what you truly find noteworthy and getting real conversations started.

Emily McDowell has made an entire business out of speaking truth by highlighting people.[5] And, it happened by accident. In 2012, Emily had an idea for a different kind of Valentine's Day card. She wanted to help the people on Valentine's Day who are dating but not officially in a relationship.

So she printed up one hundred copies of this card at a local printer and put it up on Etsy in late January 2013. She called it "The Awkward Dating Card."

I KNOW WE'RE NOT, LIKE, TOGETHER OR ANYTHING BUT IT FELT WEIRD TO JUST NOT SAY ANYTHING SO I GOT YOU THIS CARD. IT'S NOT A BIG DEAL. IT DOESN'T REALLY MEAN ANYTHING. THERE ISN'T EVEN A HEART ON IT. SO BASICALLY IT'S A CARD SAYING HI. FORGET IT.

Talk about a conversation sparker! Her card's raw honesty and humor took the Internet by storm. Three months later, she got an order from Urban Outfitters for 96,000 cards. Emily started creating more honest posters, pins, tote bags, and paper products that help highlight anyone who receives them.

She has ridiculously candid birthday cards that say, "Thinking about you is like remembering I have ice cream in the freezer."

You can get notepads that are "Everyday Achievement Awards" where friends or colleagues can fill in the blanks to highlight a recent task: "Is hereby issued to _____ for the modest yet mighty task of _____. We honor your victory."

I was turned on to Emily's amazing highlighting approach when someone handed me a card that said, "I notice how awesome you are." It made my day! I then got myself a pack of her cards to hand out that say, "I love the shit out of you" and "You don't suck."

Emily's cards are powerful because they give both compliments and truth. Anyone can be a Hallmark card—doling out bland flattery and boring cliches. But highlighting is about more than just giving regular praise. Like Emily McDowell's cards, it is about truly expecting the best from people and helping everyone in your life perform, act, and show up as the best, most honest version of themselves.

The Pygmalion Effect

There is a famous Greek myth about the sculptor Pygmalion. According to legend, Pygmalion used a large piece of ivory to carve his vision of the ideal woman. His statue was so beautiful and realistic that he fell in love with it. Embarrassed and ashamed to admit his desires, Pygmalion made offerings to the love goddess Aphrodite. At her altar, he secretly prayed to meet a woman who would be "the living likeness of my ivory girl."[6]

When Pygmalion got back to his studio, he planted a soft kiss on the statue. To his surprise, he found the ivory lips warm. When he kissed her again, the statue came to life. Pygmalion then married the woman of his own creation.

The Pygmalion myth is about the self-fulfilling power of expectation. Pygmalion created a blueprint of what he wanted and then it came to life. In other words, **great expectations are met with greatness.** Psychologists have found that this idea is no myth. This phenomenon is called the Pygmalion effect.

When voters are told they are more "politically active" than their peers (even if they were actually chosen at random), they have a 15 percent higher turnout rate than the control group.[7]

When donors are told that they are above-average givers (even if they are not), they in turn donate more to become above-average givers.[8]

When hotel maids are told that they have a high-intensity, calorie-burning job, they in turn then burn more calories.[9]

When a computer gives automated compliments to students, those students perform better on tasks—even when students know those compliments are automated.[10]

Positive Labels

Humans love to be given positive labels. They improve our self-image and gently push us to be better versions of ourselves. So as you use conversation sparkers and see what unexpected directions they lead you in, allow yourself to be impressed by the person across from you. Listen for their eloquent ideas. Find ways to emphasize their strengths. Celebrate their excitement.

Take the rather silly example of the Sorting Hat in the Harry Potter series. At the beginning of each school year, Hogwarts students are sorted into different houses by a magical hat that reads their minds, taking full measure of their hidden skills. Each house is known for different strengths, and as they move to the higher grades, students' defining characteristics become more and more pronounced. Students in Slytherin tend to be sly, savvy, and interested in the dark arts, whereas those in Hufflepuff often end up in caretaking magical jobs like herbology and care of magical creatures. For better or for worse, the more clear the labels we're given, the more we embody them.

Here are some examples you could use:

- "You know everyone—you must be a great networker!"
- "I'm amazed by your dedication to this organization—they are lucky to have you."
- "You are so knowledgeable in this subject—thank goodness you are here."

Exponential Excitement

Another way of highlighting is to celebrate the victories of others as if they were your own. Good feelings multiply around other good feelings—and divide when they are not matched. When you see someone who is proud, excited, or passionate—mirror and match it. This associates you with their feelings of pleasure.

You can say something simple:

- "I am so thrilled for you!"
- "How wonderful that must be!"
- "That is just the best news, congrats!"

When I see something—anything, that's awesome, I always take the opportunity to highlight. I tell my barista his latte art is gorgeous. I gush over my friends' new haircuts. I send out postcards telling people they're ballers. Yes, really:

SKILL #2: BE A RAVER

Want to know one of the biggest missed opportunities in social situations? Introductions. I get some version of this e-mail multiple times per week:

Hey Vanessa—I wanted to intro you to Dave. Dave, here is that intro you were asking for. Hope you two connect.

Boring! I have no idea who he is or why I should know him. The same thing happens at networking events, client meetings, and conferences. I am almost always introduced to someone in the most boring, generic way possible:

Vanessa, meet John; John, meet Vanessa.

This is a waste of an opportunity! Seize introductions as the perfect way to highlight people. Even if you have only known them for a few minutes, you can find something to rave about.

- "Vanessa, meet Dave. He is killing it in the software industry and just had a hugely successful launch."
- "Joe, meet Sue. She is an incredible painter and one of the most talented artists I know."
- "Kirk, let me introduce you to Annie. We just met and she is telling me the most fascinating story of her trip to South Africa."

You can even do this when you're the one introducing yourself:

- "It's so nice to meet you! I have heard that you have an incredible blog. Please tell me all about how you got all of your success."
- "Great to know you, a friend of John is a friend of mine. He always knows the most interesting people."
- "It's a pleasure! Your name tag says you work at Ken's Bakery— they are my favorite pizza in town! Have you always been a pizza aficionado?"

Why are raving introductions so powerful? First, you give people positive labels right at the start. Second, you tee up a great conversation and possible discussion topics for the people involved. Third, you get people talking about themselves—what they do and who they are, which produces dopamine. Yes, a raving introduction is ALSO a conversational spark. Boom: win-win-win.

SKILL #3: DON'T BE A GOLEM

Do you know what the opposite of the Pygmalion effect is? The golem effect.[11]
The golem effect is when low expectations lead to poor performance. Major Wilburn Schrank[12] decided to test the golem effect on incoming

United States Air Force Academy freshmen. Schrank randomly assigned labels to a group of one hundred enlisted airmen at the United States Air Force Academy Preparatory School. They were given one of five different made-up "ability levels." The US military is all about labels, rank, and position, so Schrank wanted to know if these labels have any effect on academic performance. Sure enough, for all of the data sets, the airmen who received the worst labels also performed the worst.

The golem effect can have devastating consequences across the board. Dr. Brian McNatt found that the golem effect is especially prevalent in the workplace.[13] Think of bosses who pick favorites. Here's what happens:

Jeff is the boss. He hires a new sales associate from his alma mater, XYZ University. He takes her under his wing, they grab lunch more often, he gives her the best assignments. After all, Jeff thinks anyone from his alma mater has the best possible education, and he wants his fellow alumni to succeed. She benefits from the Pygmalion effect. Jeff expects the best from her and she performs at her best. Other employees see this favoritism and feel left out. One particular manager, Ken, went to ABC University, XYZ's rival. Jeff is constantly ribbing Ken—jokingly, of course. Ken doesn't get invited to watch games at the boss's house on weekends. Jeff teases Ken for not being able to get into XYZ—Ken knows he's kidding, but feels the sting anyway.

Hallway chitchat and watercooler conversations matter. Expecting the best is not just important for new people, but also to build up the existing people in your life. What are you saying about and to your colleagues?

Being a highlighter is about constantly searching for the good in people. When you tell people they are good, they become better. When you search for what's good, you feel great.

BONUS: HELP PEOPLE IMPRESS YOU

Have you ever wanted to impress people with your knowledge? Your experience? Your success? I think highlighting is actually the key to impressing people.

My friend Thursday Bram is an amazing highlighter. She runs a club called PyLadies. This is a group of female coders who use the Python programming language. They meet multiple times a week to socialize, brainstorm, and help on coding projects. When Thursday and her fellow founders got the idea for the group, it was important for them to create a thriving, supportive group of women.

Thursday got the idea to bring gold star stickers. You know the kind teachers gave us when we were little? Everyone, no matter how old, loves getting a gold star. So at meetings and during events, Thursday passes out gold stars to ladies who contribute an idea, help fix a problem, or are just all-around awesome. Not surprisingly, people love it. And as more and more PyLadies receive gold stars, they act in more and more gold-star-worthy ways. The cycle creates an upward spiral of behavior.

You don't actually have to carry around gold star stickers to highlight people—although it would be a fun experiment to try! Instead, highlighting is about giving people emotional gold stars by assigning positive labels, capitalizing on their excitement, and calling out their good deeds.

Being memorable is not about bringing up your high points. It's about highlighting theirs. **Don't try to impress people, let them impress you.**

HACKING LISTENING

I have made my Vow of Silence an annual tradition. It reminds me to pause, stop interrupting, and listen intently. Now, hundreds of my readers join me on these quiet adventures with the hashtag #vowofsilence. We quit social media, turn off e-mail, and just practice listening.

Every time, I am astounded by how many people yell at me during my vow—as if my not speaking somehow also turns off my hearing. Each time, I am shocked when people attempt to use elaborate hand gestures and dramatic dance as they talk to me—quiet is not deaf. Most importantly, after each vow, I am reminded that while listening is an amazing tool to get people to open up, it's only the first step. Real connection comes from interaction.*

I once had dinner with a former fashion model. Genevieve is stunning—shiny auburn hair, milky skin, and superlong legs. During our meal, she was demure, pleasant, and attentive, but barely spoke. When asked a question she would smile, answer quickly, and take a sip of wine. I didn't think much of the experience and probably wouldn't have remembered it all until something interesting happened a few weeks later.

---

* Want to do a vow of silence with me? Join us! When you sign up for the Digital Bonuses we will send you a reminder when we have our next one. Register at www.ScienceofPeople .com/toolbox.

I was at a party, talking to a few friends, when Genevieve sauntered up. I turned and introduced her—trying as best as I could to rave. Even though we had spent an evening together, I didn't have much to go on. So, I kept it simple: "Everyone, meet the lovely Genevieve. We had dinner at that amazing new Italian restaurant on Twenty-third last month."

She shook hands with the group, stayed for a few minutes, and then asked if I wanted to grab another glass of champagne with her. As we walked away, she huffed in exasperation. "Ugh!" she exclaimed. "I have met your friend Chris at least a dozen times. Every time I see him he doesn't remember me. What's his problem?"

This didn't surprise me in the least. Here's the hard truth: It wasn't Chris's fault, it was hers. Genevieve doesn't give people a reason to remember her. **Being an amazing listener is not just about what you hear, it's how you respond to what you hear.**

In every conversation, every interaction, every meeting we have, we want to give people a reason to remember us. Genevieve has supermodel looks and a very pleasant demeanor. But that's not enough! I can't help but compare my experience with Genevieve to a daily interaction I have with the parking lot attendant at my gym.

George directs the traffic in the insanely small parking lot at my local gym. Despite people grumbling at him all day, he always greets everyone happily and asks them the same question: "Want to know the daily fun fact?"

The first time he asked me this, I was lost in my own thoughts charging across the lot. It stopped me dead in my tracks. "Daily fun fact?" I was delighted, dopamine pumping in promise of a mental reward. "Of course I want to know the daily fun fact!"

Then he recited his fun fact of the day—which is always something titillating or laugh-worthy like "Did you know Scotland's national animal is the unicorn?"

Or "You can see an owl's eyeball when you look in its ear."

Or, the one from today, "Russia has a larger surface area than Pluto."

Here's the best part. Do you know where he gets his fun facts? Us! After he delivers his fact of the day, he asks each person, "Do you have a fun fact for me?" And he waits and listens as people tell him all kinds of obscure tidbits—some real facts and some just fun facts about all aspects of life—talk about using Hack #3: Conversational Sparks.

Inevitably, they end up laughing (and checking Google for verification on most). Secretly, I hoard fun facts for him and always hope he will pick mine the next day.

I used to pull into that lot stressed and miserable trying to squeeze into a parking space. Now, I look for George.

CHALLENGES

1. Introduce a colleague or friend to someone you think they should know. Practice making two raving introductions.
2. Who impresses you? Who is an amazing friend? Who is the best networker you know? Go tell them.
3. Bonus: Take a one-day Vow of Silence to be a better listener.

CHAPTER REVIEW

We remember people who make us feel good and who make us want to be the best version of ourselves. You can optimize an interaction by expecting optimal outcomes. Elevate people by hacking listening, highlighting, and expecting the best in those around you. **Being a highlighter helps you be the highlight.**

- Listen with purpose—always search for the good.
- Be the high point of every interaction by giving people a reason to remember you.
- When you expect the worst, that's exactly what you will get.

My biggest takeaway in this chapter is: _____

CHAPTER 5

INTRIGUE

How to be ridiculously likable

In 2007, Lewis Howes was at the top of his game. As a six-foot-four wide receiver for the Arena Football League and an All-American decathlete, Howes was poised to go all the way to the NFL.

Then he snapped his wrist on a diving catch, and his dream of professional football was over in a matter of seconds. "It wasn't pretty. I was 24 years old, washed up, broke, and sleeping on my sister's couch with my arm in a cast and a mountain of credit card debt staring me in the face," said Howes.[1]

Howes had to start a new career track from scratch and accidentally discovered a powerful way to connect with people. In 2008, LinkedIn was a small social media website for business professionals, but Howes saw an opportunity to stay in touch with people in athletics—even though he could no longer play, he still had a passion for sports.

He began to construct his contact list from scratch. Next, he started testing what kind of messages worked best on cold contacts. "It was easy to track which messages were working and which were not based on the replies in my LinkedIn inbox," explained Howes.[2] He found that his most successful messages mentioned at least three commonalities he had with the person.

"I would try to find at least three things we shared—usually a mutual connection, a mutual interest, and a mutual organization, like a school, league, or sports team," said Howes. These messages were short and to the point. Howes composed a sample for me using this method:

Hi Vanessa! My name is Lewis and I wanted to reach out because I saw you're also friends with Nick Onken, we do work with Pencils of Promise together. I'm based in LA and saw you're from here. Do you ever get back in town? Would love to connect.

Howes crafted a strategy for his follow-up messages, too. "I told them I loved their work and wanted to learn from them. I was direct and said, 'My goal is to learn about you and your success,'" said Howes. He ended every interaction with a specific question they could answer.

Amazingly, this approach landed Howes phone calls, one-on-one meetings, and mentorships with some of the most powerful people in sports over and over again. One of his most impressive cold messages landed him a meeting with the cofounder of ESPN, Bill Rasmussen. "I was this kid with no job and no money, but I reached out to Bill and was able to get a sit-down meeting and interview him," recalled Howes.

After the first year of reaching out to important people and learning from them, Howes hit a turning point. He realized what he was doing wasn't enough. "At this point, I understood that I couldn't just take, I had to give. But how do you give to someone like Bill Rasmussen?" explained Howes.

As his contact list grew, Howes realized he finally had something to offer his connections—his own network. "I enjoyed helping people and relished becoming what Malcolm Gladwell calls a 'connector,'" said Howes.[3] He asked his VIPs who they wanted to meet and then worked to get them that connection.

"I would ask people, 'What's your biggest challenge right now?' and then would connect them with at least three people who I thought could help. I would literally take out my phone over our cups of coffee, make the call, and hand the person my phone," said Howes.

Howes also applied the Triple Threat to all of his interactions without even realizing it—and it worked like a charm. "I show people I'm listening to them and only them. I make eye contact, take them in, and pay attention to nothing else," said Howes.

By January 2010, his company had over $5 million in sales. Eventually, he sold his business for seven figures. Now, Howes runs a successful lifestyle blog and podcast called *The School of Greatness*, where he interviews VIPs, experts, and luminaries on a wide variety of subjects. He uses his connection skills to find the most interesting, remarkable, and fascinating people to interview—I should know, I was one of them! (Insert self-deprecating laugh here.) Yes, he did use the exact template above to reach out to me to be on his podcast.

This chapter is about the powerful human behavior principle that makes Howes so socially attractive.

THE SIMILARITY-ATTRACTION EFFECT

One night I was having dinner with a few friends when someone pulled a Pilot G-2 pen out of her purse to take some notes. My friend Tyler spotted it instantly and asked, "Does your G-2 pen have a point-seven-millimeter tip?"

She didn't even have to look. "Well, of course it does. Point-seven-millimeter tips are the only sensible choice for Pilot G-2s."

Tyler smiled knowingly. "We are going to be friends," he said simply.

Now, I am no pen expert, but according to Tyler, the Pilot G-2 .7mm pen is simply the best. So good, in fact, that Tyler not only fiercely guards his against borrowing thieves, but also uses it as a sign. "If someone has a G-2 pen, I know we are going to get along," Tyler explains.

What's going on here? As humans, we are constantly on the lookout for people who are similar to us. "Birds of a feather flock together" is a far more accurate cliché than "opposites attract." This is called the **similarity-attraction effect.** It says that "people like and are attracted to others who are similar, rather than dissimilar, to themselves."[4]

Researchers Dr. Ellen Berscheid and Dr. Elaine Walster believe we enjoy spending time with people who are similar to us for combinations of the following reasons:

- It is easier to get along with someone who enjoys the same activities and conversation topics. Spouses and friends are more likely to have similar personality types than randomly assigned pairs.
- When someone agrees with us, it makes us feel less alone and more right in our own opinions.
- If we can relate to someone strongly, we might be able to better predict their behavior and future decisions, making us feel more in control.

- We hope that if someone is similar to us, then there is a greater likelihood they will be attracted to us—like begets like.[5]

A "like" on Facebook or a "heart" on Instagram or a "retweet" on Twitter are all digital forms of the similarity-attraction effect in action. When you give someone some link love, you are telling them, "I like this, too!" That is why we are so addicted to checking our social media—we like to know that our friends and followers both like us and are like us.

Without realizing it, we are **constantly searching for reasons to think, feel, or say, "Me too!"** In a good meeting or great coffee date, you hear phrases like this:

- Wow—you like *Orange Is the New Black*? I'm an addict!
- You're gluten free? Join the club!
- Oh, I love Thailand! Maybe we were there at the same time?
- Are you kidding? I'm a huge 49ers fan.
- You're into rock climbing? Me too!

On the other hand, one of the biggest mistakes I see people make is inadvertently pointing out differences while trying to connect. **Whenever you say a version of "Not me!" you are handicapping your connection from the start.** "Not me!" phrases sound like this:

- You know, I never really got into *Orange Is the New Black*. I thought it was kinda boring.
- You're one of those gluten-free people? Don't you think that's a fad?
- I'm not a big traveler.
- Sports? No, thank you! I would rather read a book or watch the news.
- You're into rock climbing? Not me! I'm afraid of heights.

These kinds of "Not me!" comments tend to push people away and shut down a conversation. Does this mean you constantly have to blindly agree with people you meet? No, of course not! But it does mean you have to put effort into searching for real similarities and shared interests.

When someone posts something on social media that isn't relevant to you, you just keep scrolling. You don't share the post with a huffy comment like "This isn't relevant to me!" But we sometimes imply as much in our responses. So if someone mentions they went to private school growing up, don't say, "Ugh! I hated those preppy kids. I went to good old public school." Instead, note it and resume looking for something you do have in common. (You might say, "Interesting! Did you play any sports?" or "Wow, I didn't know that, tell me more!")

Don't fall into the "Not me!" trap; instead, find a way to say "Me too!"

SEARCHING FOR "ME TOO"

My friend Allon Freiman sells raffle tickets at sporting events for charity. He messaged me with an interesting question:

> Hey Vanessa! I was wondering if you could use your human behavior knowledge to help me out with something I have been wondering. When I sell raffle tickets at games I often dress in a suit to be more professional. But recently I have been thinking that I should dress in team colors—maybe my tie or something? Let me know if there is any science to this or if you think it is a good idea.
>
> Best, Allon

Allon's intuition was absolutely right. We like people who look like us. One study found that we are more likely to help people who are dressed like us.[6] Someone dressed casually is more likely to help someone else who is also dressed casually over someone in a business suit. This is counterintuitive—one would think that someone in a business suit would be helped more often, period. Not so.

I advised Allon to not only wear the team's colors but also to dress exactly like the fans he was trying to sell to—jeans, jersey, sneakers, hat and all. Guess what? He immediately began to sell more raffle tickets. This is the similarity-attraction effect in action.

We don't just have a soft spot for people who *look* like us, we are also drawn to people who *think* like us. There is an admittedly terrible (and addictive) MTV show that I watch "for work" to "observe human behavior." *Are You the One?* is a reality show where ten men and ten women are brought into a house to find their soul mate. But, of course, there's a catch. Each of the contestants has taken a battery of personality tests with "love experts" who have picked one ideal mate for them. Their goal is to find their ideal match from the batch of singles.

In season three, two of the singles, Connor Smith and Kayla Brackett, try to get a feel for their compatibility. Here's how that conversation goes (note the constant searching for similarity):

KAYLA: I want someone who is close to their family.

CONNOR: I'm a total mama's boy. But can you keep someone's attention?

KAYLA: Are you kidding me, that is all me. I whip my man into shape. That's my thing.

CONNOR: Huh, that's what I ask for!

KAYLA: I want someone who is big and strong, because I like to feel protected. (Note: Connor is over six foot five and calls himself the Gentle Giant.)

CONNOR: I always want to sleep on the side of the bed closest to the door.

KAYLA: Oh good, I like to be closer to the wall!

SUMMARY: You're like me. I like what you like. I like you.

We engage in the exact same behavior as Connor and Kayla even in nonromantic situations. We do it with potential clients—aligning interests and work methods. We do it with new friends—comparing music taste and weekend activities. We even do it in line with strangers—commiserating over the long wait.

You can hack the similarity-attraction effect for your benefit with what I call:

HACK #5: Thread Theory
Find and follow threads of similarity to be more socially attractive.

Every interaction should be about finding threads of commonalities. Every thread that binds you brings you closer to a person. The more threads you have, the more socially attractive you become. Here's how you can use thread theory to connect with the people you meet instantly:

Step #1: Search for Threads

Thread Theory is the ultimate tool for opening any conversation. Whether you are cold-calling, e-mailing a new contact, or meeting someone for the first time, the Thread Theory can help you blast through the dialogue door.

Imagine that each person is walking around carrying a big knotted ball of string. All of these strings are their thoughts, ideas, and opinions. We often wish our thoughts were more organized, but they are usually in a jumble—especially when we first walk into an event. We might be thinking about our to-do list, our parking meter, what we want for dinner, that good-looking person across the room, our neck ache, where to hang our coat—you get the idea. So we are all walking around carrying this mass of thoughts.

The Thread Theory is an incredibly easy way to both open conversations and never run out of things to say. When you first begin in an interaction, I want you to try to tease out some thoughts you both share. The more threads you share, the more you will be able to talk about—and the more ridiculously likable you will be.

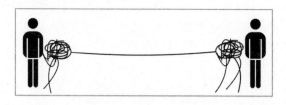

There are three main categories of commonalities that you can pull from at any time:

- **People:** Mutual contacts are the best way to find threads of similarity. You can also liven up the conversation by searching for mutual friends.

- **Context:** Think you don't have anything in common? Think about the context of your meeting. Maybe you're both on LinkedIn or both at the same conference. All you have to do is ask about it to get the conversational ball rolling.
- **Interests:** Common interests are the best kind of threads because they introduce a topic you both invariably know a lot about, ripe territory for great stories and interesting conversation.

Here are a few openers and ideas for tapping into each type of commonality:

Category	Opener	Possible Threads
People	How do you know the host?	You work at ____, do you know ____?
	I saw we are mutually connected through _____	You went to ____ school, do you know ____?
	I saw you speaking to ____, have you known each other for very long?	Are you a friend of the bride or groom / roommate A or roommate B / an employee or the boss?
Context	How long have you been a part of this group?	Do you usually come to these types of events?
	Great venue, right?	Have you ever been to this conference / restaurant / event before?
	How long have you been living here?	I saw you are also a part of _____ LinkedIn group.
Interests	Love your pen / keychain / bumper sticker / shirt / hat. I am also a fan of _____	How long have you been a ____fan?
	I'm a fellow member of ____; how long have you been a part?	What are you up to this weekend?
	I saw you also went to / studied / are a part of ____.	Wasn't that speaker / presentation / raffle interesting?

These Thread Theory questions can be used in groups, with new people and even in e-mails and cold messages. Every time you discover a common thread, it links you together:

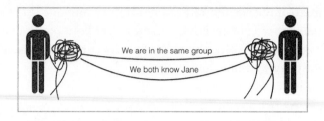

You might have noticed that some of these Thread Theory questions are also my favorite conversation sparkers—that's no coincidence! Simple questions can lead you into exciting conversational territory when you ask strategically and follow up with good listening.

If you ask one of these questions and don't find a similarity, it's totally okay. For example, if someone says, "Oh, I don't know her," or "Nope, never been here before." No worries! Use that as an opener. You can say, "Yeah, it is a pretty big school. I think she studied political science. What did you study?" or "Me neither! Do you have any favorite local watering holes you go to?" Every answer you hear is one more step in getting to know them and being further along in conversation. **Don't let it faze you, let it fuel you**.

Be on the lookout for physical examples of similarities, too. For example, if you notice someone's USC keychain you can say, "Go Trojans!" Or if someone is driving a car you like, you can comment, "I was thinking about buying that car, how do you like it?" It can even be as simple as noticing what someone is drinking: "The red wine isn't bad, huh?"

Making conversation has never been so easy.

FAST FACT BOX

83 percent of our Twitter poll voters said that they overthink what they say—this section will help!

> **Vanessa Van Edwards**
> @vvanedwards
>
> [POLL] I often overthink what I want to say.
>
> 83% True
> 17% False
>
> 129 votes • Final results

Step #2: Follow the Thread

The Thread Theory is not about simply pointing out similarities; it is about exploring them. Once you have found a common thread, you can make it stronger by following it.

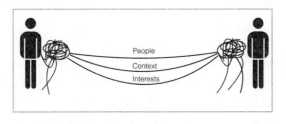

How do you follow a common thread? Easy. Ask for why.

Revolutionary Japanese inventor Sakichi Toyoda founded Toyota Motor Company in 1937. He is also known for his innovative managerial techniques, one of which is called the Five Whys.

Toyota employees use the Five Whys to problem solve and get to the bottom of issues. This technique is now used across industries to quickly and effectively find solutions and root causes of problems. You might use the Five Whys to figure out why a colleague is late on a project:

1. Why? I couldn't get the numbers on time.
2. Why? I didn't know the right person to talk to.
3. Why? I have never worked with that department before.
4. Why? I usually go through my manager.
5. Why? Interdepartmental communications only go through managers, which causes a bottleneck. (Root cause)

Of course, in day-to-day conversations you can't ask why over and over again, but **you can get a conversation to go much deeper much faster if you use the spirit of the Five Whys.**

When you find a commonality, don't let it pass by, ask the other person why it's important to them. When you stumble upon a similarity, don't jump to the next topic; take it a step further and find out how they got started. If you hear a shared interest, don't let it hang without comment; dig a little deeper.

Let's say, through the Thread Theory, you find out the person you are speaking with is also an entrepreneur. If you follow that thread, you get a much deeper interaction:

YOU: **Why** did you decide to become an entrepreneur?

THEM: I always wanted to start my own business.

YOU: Interesting! **Why** did that appeal to you?

THEM: I really wanted flexibility and freedom in work hours, and I knew I could never get that with a boss.

YOU: I feel the same way! **Why** were you looking for more flexibility?

THEM: Oh, I love to travel so I wanted to be able to work from anywhere.

YOU: That's wonderful—I'm also a huge traveler, I just came back from Chile! **Why** do you love to travel?

THEM: I have been dying to go to Chile! You know, I think I love travel so much because I think it's so important to get out of your comfort zone and learn from people around the world.

YOU: That's so true! I have met the most interesting people on my travels. **Why** do you think being out of our comfort zone is so important?

THEM: Hmmm, good question. I guess I think true happiness comes from trying new things, seeing new things, experiencing new things. How about you? Where do you think happiness comes from?

This is a synthesized version of the kind of robust, deep conversations that come when you ask more whys. "Why" gets you beyond small talk into an exploration of motivations, dreams, and interests. And every why helps you find more threads.

In this way, the Thread Theory ensures you will never run out of things to talk about. Nor will you ever have to be worried that you won't have something to say. Just search for the commonality and follow the thread with why.

FAST FACT BOX

We had 1,049 participants tell us who they have the hardest time communicating with. As you can see, we all have someone we have a hard time communicating with and the results are all over the board! You can use the Thread Theory with anyone in your life to make communication easier. Who is your person? How can you find a tie with them?

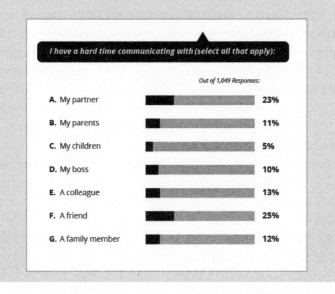

I have a hard time communicating with (select all that apply):

Out of 1,049 Responses:

A. My partner	23%
B. My parents	11%
C. My children	5%
D. My boss	10%
E. A colleague	13%
F. A friend	25%
G. A family member	12%

Step #3: Create Ties

The last step of the Thread Theory is optional and reserved only for special interactions. When you are having a really great discussion and clicking with someone, you can take your connection to the next level by using your common threads to tie you together. Let's look at how Lewis Howes did this.

After he searched for commonalities and followed the threads he found, he asked people what they needed and how he could help. In other words, **he tied his abilities to their needs**. When you say, "You have a problem, I'm going to help you fix it," you create the ultimate similarity.

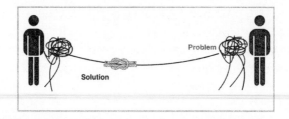

Every time you offer help, support, and advice, you create a deeper bond with someone and a permanent similarity.

Most of the time, opportunities to help people find solutions come up organically. You hear someone has a need and know you can help. Here are some examples:

- Since you're new in town, I can send you a list of my favorite local restaurants.
- I'm sure I know someone in that industry—connect with me on LinkedIn and I can introduce you.
- I frequently get extra tickets to the game; I'll text you next time!
- It sounds like that is a real problem. Let's set up a consult call and I can see if my company can help.
- Yeah, going vegan is so hard. I have a few recipes I can send you.

If nothing comes up during a conversation, you can also end with a tie. I typically end most of my great meetings with a single question:

Can I help you with anything?

This is my favorite Thread Theory question. Not only does it give me a chance to create a tie, but also I usually end up learning something new about them. It's a tiny hack that goes a long way.

In fact, every step of Thread Theory is others oriented in that it helps people untangle their own bundles of thoughts. For example, going through the Five Whys with a friend can help them figure out why things aren't working at their job. Following a thread with a partner could help you both figure out vacation plans.

Remember: Since step three of the Thread Theory is optional, you actually have to mean it when you use it. Don't offer help you can't give.

Don't make hollow promises. Create ties only with people who you genuinely want to be connected to.

Bonus: Teach Me?

What if you can't find a thread? What if there are no authentic opportunities for "Me too"?

Lewis Howes frequently interviews experts on his podcast in new areas of business or life, and when he can't say "Me too," he says, "Teach me." This produces incredible content for his listeners *and* deep connections between him and his experts. If someone mentions something that you don't know about or are unfamiliar with, ask for more information. "Teach me?" is still a thread!

Here are some ways you can make "Teach me?" a thread:

- I have never heard of that book—what is it about?
- What an interesting career—I have never met anyone in your line of work before. Tell me about it!
- I've actually never been out of the country, but would love to travel more. Have any insider tips for a beginner?

Bottom Line: "Me too!" and "Teach me?" are two of the most powerful and underutilized phrases we have. Use them whenever possible.

CHALLENGES

1. Next time you talk to someone, try finding three commonalities in the first three minutes.
2. Practice asking "why?" five times and see if you learn something new.
3. Create a tie by asking a colleague or friend if you can help them with anything.

CHAPTER REVIEW

The more you have in common with someone, the more likable you become. We like people like us. The Thread Theory is an easy way to captivate attraction by simply searching for shared interests, asking why, and then offering to help. Always be on the lookout for ways to say, "Me too!"

- Don't overthink what you are going to say, just search for commonalities.
- Go deeper by asking the Five Whys.
- Tie yourself to someone by making their problem your own.

My biggest takeaway in this chapter is: _____

PART II

THE FIRST FIVE HOURS

Dr. Mike Cruz is the new head of the ER at All Saints Hospital in Manhattan. He's headstrong, direct, and a little intimidating.

Dr. Cruz needs the support of his staff in turning the All Saints ER into a premier trauma center. But shaking up systems and changing protocols has led to an all-out battle with longtime doctors and nurses.

Finally, a sympathetic nurse, Zoey, goes into his office with a pink notebook.

"It's kind of like a passport," she explains, "It's a map to the people who work for you."

Dr. Cruz eyes it suspiciously as Zoey continues. "It has their birthdays, anniversaries, things that make them sad, things that make them happy. Who cries when a patient dies, who makes a joke and then cries in private. It's the things you should know."

Dr. Cruz flips through the book halfheartedly. Finally he asks, "Why are you giving me this?"

Zoey tries again to explain. "You expect us to be good at our job. We expect the same of you."

This scene appears in *Nurse Jackie*, season 4, episode 10, "Handle Your Scandal." In Part II, you'll get a map to navigating people much like the one Nurse Zoey gave Dr. Cruz—a guide to decoding, understanding, and predicting behavior. Nurse Zoey calls it a people passport. I call it your matrix. **This section will help you solve puzzles like:**

- How do you speed-read someone?
- How can you predict someone's behavior?
- How can you prevent miscommunications?

While Part I helped you hack the first five minutes of an interaction, this section will help you take your connection one step further. How do you get the next date? How do you nail the next interview? How do you make a deeper connection in your next meeting? This section will help you advance your relationship during those first five hours.

CHAPTER 6

DECODE

How to uncover hidden emotions

I have a sad story to tell you—but don't worry, it has a happy ending.

In the 1970s, there was a forty-two-year-old housewife who was having a midlife crisis. To protect her identity, we will call her Mary. Upon reaching her fortieth birthday, Mary found herself alone most of the time. Her children had grown and moved out of the house, and her husband was a busy professional. At night she had difficulty sleeping, and during the day she had a harder and harder time managing the house. Frequently, she spent most of the day crying. She complained of feeling overwhelmingly "useless." Finally, she began to contemplate suicide.

Luckily, Mary knew she needed help. Her family admitted her to a local hospital for extra care. The first three weeks of treatment went well—a combination of group therapy and medication seemed successful. During one of Mary's filmed sessions with her psychiatrist, Mary insisted she was feeling significantly better. Given her improved mood, Mary asked, perhaps she could get a weekend pass to visit her family? After consulting with the staff, the doctor agreed with the team: Mary was better.

Fortunately, right before checking out, Mary came clean. She went to her doctor and admitted that she had been lying in her interview and faking it in group therapy sessions. She was still desperately depressed. The coming weekend, she'd planned to do something drastic away from the hospital. But her confession marked a true turning point in her recovery, and after many months of treatment—overcoming a few relapses—Mary went on to lead a normal life with her family.

Despite this happy ending, the Mary incident left the hospital's medical team rattled. **How had she deceived so many people in the facility?** The hospital staff reviewed a video recording of the doctor's interview with Mary—what had they missed? In fact, medical deception is a worrying dilemma—patients frequently lie to their doctors, and psychologists dread being fooled by patients who hide their real health needs.

After multiple experienced psychologists reviewed Mary's film without answers, the team decided to get more help. They enlisted Dr. Paul Ekman, a young psychologist who had been conducting experiments on human lie detection with patients.[1]

Dr. Ekman and his team spent hundreds of hours reviewing Mary's footage. It wasn't until he put the video in slow motion that clues began to emerge. When the doctor asked Mary about her plans for the weekend, a frightening emotion leaked out. You just had to know where to look.

"We saw in slow-motion a fleeting facial expression of despair, so quick that we had missed seeing it the first few times we examined the film," explained Dr. Ekman.[2]

This flicker of sorrow was the break that Ekman and his team needed. They began to re-examine the footage looking for these microgestures. After a few rounds, they started spotting them consistently—always right before a lie, and often covered by a fake smile. Dr. Ekman came to call these flickering facial gestures "microexpressions."

Genius is only a superior power of seeing.

—John Ruskin

FACE SCIENCE

Doctors once thought babies learned to smile by mimicking the doting expressions of their mothers and fathers. This is a myth.

Congenitally blind babies make the same facial expressions as other babies—despite having never seen a face.[3] Our instinct to make certain expressions derives from nature, not nurture.[4] **Microexpressions are an innate universal human behavior.**

Fascinated by this idea, Dr. Paul Ekman conducted a series of studies in a remote part of New Guinea.[5] He brought with him photos of Americans expressing different emotions—showing everything from smiles to grimaces to frowns. The tribe he was visiting was especially disconnected from the Western world. They'd never seen a movie, much less a TV.

With a translator's help, Dr. Ekman asked the New Guineans to examine the Americans' facial expressions and guess what they thought each American was feeling in the picture. Dr. Ekman was shocked to find that their guesses were extremely accurate.[6] They could even perform the experiment in reverse. As Ekman named an emotion, participants quickly mimed the corresponding facial expression.

After repeating this experiment with participants all around the world, Dr. Ekman was able to identify seven universal microexpressions.

Microexpression: *n.* A brief, involuntary facial expression that humans make when they feel an intense emotion.

We make these expressions regardless of culture, sex, or race. This is why reading microexpressions is such a valuable people hack. **Since everyone falls prey to the same seven facial tells, we can study them, spot them, and decode them.**

HOW TO DECODE FACES

While my husband watches *Monday Night Football* on ESPN, I am glued to ABC for my weekly Monday dose of *The Bachelorette*. It's trashy TV that I insist is "for work" to "observe human behavior." Really, I just want to win my Bachelorette Fantasy League.

In one particularly notable season, bachelorette Emily Maynard meets Arie Luyendyk Jr., a dreamy race car driver from Arizona. There are twenty-five men competing to win Emily's heart and propose to her at the end of the season. Tall with a big smile and blue eyes, Arie has potential to go all the way. There is only one problem. Emily's former fiancé was also a race car driver and tragically died on the way to a race. Could Arie's profession hit too close to home? Let me tell you, viewers like me were on the edge of our seats to find out.

The night of the confession, Arie sits Emily down to "tell her something." Emily smiles demurely, waiting for the potential bomb to drop. Here's a recap of just the verbal exchange:

Speaker	Verbal
Arie	I'm a little nervous about one thing, I'm going to admit.
Emily	Tell me.
Arie	So my background is in racing . . . so I don't know if you knew that about me but I have been in race cars since I was fourteen years old. Are you okay with that?
Emily	Yeah I am. Totally. I love racing. I love being at the race track, I have so many good memories there. And it's a part of who I am and it's really the only sport I know about.
Arie	That's so cool.
Emily	I know it like the back of my hand. I can tell you about racing. I can tell you about cars.

Whew, sounds good right? Nope. It sounded good, but it looked pretty bad.

This twenty-second moment spoke volumes. Emily's facial expressions told us a totally different story. Here's what happened behind the words:

Speaker	Verbal	Emily's Nonverbal
Arie	I'm a little nervous about one thing, I'm going to admit.	
Emily	Tell me.	Happiness Microexpression
Arie	So my background is in racing . . . so I don't know if you knew that about me but I have been in race cars since I was fourteen years old. Are you okay with that?	Sadness Microexpression Fear Microexpression
Emily	Yeah I am. Totally. I love racing. I love being at the race track, I have so many good memories there. And it's a part of who I am and it's really the only sport I know about.	Shakes her head "no" Loss of Volume Contempt Microexpression
Arie	That's so cool.	Hair Touch
Emily	I know it like the back of my hand. I can tell you about racing. I can tell you about cars.	Contempt Microexpression

During this interaction, Emily showed three crucial microexpressions: sadness, fear, and contempt. These were key because they were incongruent with her words. Even though her words said she was fine, her true emotions were displayed on her face.

Emily didn't choose Arie in the end. He made it to the final two before being cut. Anyone who could read microexpressions would not have been surprised by Arie's fate. His profession was a deal breaker. All you had to do was look at her face to see it—perhaps this could have saved Arie. If he had noticed her hidden emotions and addressed them, he could have reassured her. Instead, he missed the nonverbal clues of what was to come.

I call this hack "The Decoder":

HACK #6: The Decoder
Spot the seven microexpressions during interactions to uncover truth.

Decoding is all about looking for the emotional intent behind the words. It's about listening by hearing *and* looking.

First, here's how to use the Decoder hack:

- **Congruency**: Look to see if someone's stated emotions match their visible emotions. If your client says he is happy to see you, he should have a happy microexpression. If your wife says she is "fine," but has an angry microexpression, she probably isn't "fine."
- **Connection:** People make microexpressions while they are talking *and* while they are listening. Facial expressiveness is never "off." While this can be a lot to take in, paying consistent attention to someone's face also helps you with Hack #2—the eye contact piece of the Triple Threat. If you thought your average eye contact was below 60 percent, then reading microexpressions is an easy way to incentivize more gazing.
- **Speed**: Microexpressions happen incredibly quickly—in less than a second. Anything longer than a second is simply a facial expression. Why is this important? Microexpressions (less than a second) cannot be controlled, so they are honest views into emotions. Facial expressions (longer than a second) can be faked and are less honest. Therefore, you should look at brief flashes of facial responsiveness for the most accurate reading.

Step #1: Spotting

According to Dr. Paul Ekman, when you are speaking with someone, these are the seven reactions you should look out for:[7] *

Anger

We flash signs of anger when we feel displeasure at others or annoyance with a situation.

The anger microexpression is marked by:

- Lowered eyebrows that are pinched together
- Two vertical creases in between the eyebrows
- Tensing of the lower eyelids
- Tightening of the lips—either pressed firmly together or in a position to yell

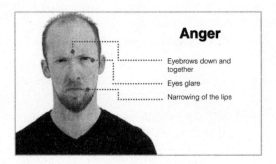

Anger

Eyebrows down and together

Eyes glare

Narrowing of the lips

You often see an anger microexpression in the following situations:

- During a confrontation
- When delivering bad news
- Before an argument or fight
- Photo alert: Accidentally in a profile photo when someone is squinting into the sun or does not like being in front of the camera

---

* Watch videos of all of the microexpressions in action in your Digital Bonuses at www .ScienceofPeople.com/toolbox.

Contempt

Contempt—scorn, disdain, or disrespect—is quite a powerful and complex emotion that is marked by an extremely simple facial gesture. Contempt is often called "smirking" because it is a one-sided mouth raise.

Here's what's interesting about contempt: It confuses us. We offer a microexpression quiz for you to take in our Digital Bonuses at www .ScienceofPeople.com/toolbox. Over 22,000 people have taken this quiz. Contempt is the one that gets the most wrong answers. Of all the emotions, contempt seems to stump 40 percent of people (followed closely by fear, which 35 percent of people get wrong).

Contempt confuses us because we mistake the smirk for a partial smile or boredom, but that could not be further from the truth. Contempt is a cue of serious dislike and scorn. We often show contempt when we feel that someone or something is beneath our attention.

The contempt microexpression is marked by:

- A one-sided cheek lift
- Pulling up the right or left corner of the mouth

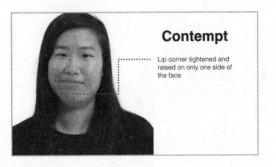

Contempt

Lip corner tightened and raised on only one side of the face

You often see a contempt microexpression in the following situations:

- If you tell someone no
- When someone hears or encounters something they don't like
- During a disagreement or after being put down
- Photo alert: Accidentally in a profile picture where someone thinks it means a partial smile

Happiness

Woo-hoo! We have already learned the microexpression for happiness in Chapter 1. Genuine happiness is marked by the lifting of the upper cheek muscles, officially called the orbicularis oculi and zygomaticus major muscles. You know you are seeing a real smile when you see those lovely crow's-feet wrinkles around the eyes.

The happiness microexpression is marked by:

- Corners of the lips equally pulled up
- Possible lip parting with teeth visible
- Engaged upper cheek muscles
- Wrinkling along the sides of the eyes

You often see a happiness microexpression in the following situations:

- When celebrating with someone
- Delivering good news
- In a pleasant or positive experience

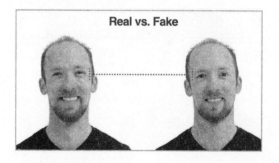

You might see fake happiness as well. This often happens when:

- Someone is trying to cover up real feelings
- They're feeling tired or overwhelmed but trying to look positive
- Photo alert: Accidentally in a profile picture when trying to look relaxed

Fear

When we are afraid, our body often goes into fight-or-flight response. Our facial expression actually helps us respond quickly and accurately to threats. As soon as we are afraid, our eyes widen and our eyebrows go up our forehead—this way we can take in as much of our environment as possible to look for potential escapes or more threats. Then, our mouth opens and we gasp for breath—taking in oxygen in case we have to yell for help or flee.

The fear microexpression is marked by:

- Widened eyes
- Lifting of the upper eyelids
- Elevated eyebrows with horizontal lines in the center of the forehead
- Slightly opened mouth

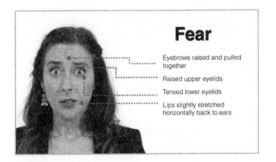

You often see a fear microexpression in the following situations:

- During a dangerous situation
- When you give someone difficult information
- In an unknown or confusing interaction
- Photo alert: In a picture when a flash blinds someone or they're nervous being photographed

Surprise

Surprise is a great truth-telling emotion. For example, if you ask a colleague, "Did you know I was going to be taken off the project?" surprise will tell you instantly that they had no idea. If they show fear, it can be a clue of their previous knowledge.

Surprise is easy to spot because it is the longest of the microexpressions. The mouth drops open and the eyebrows shoot up the forehead.

The surprise microexpression is marked by:

- Raised, rounded eyebrows
- Widened eyes
- Dropped-open jaw
- Intake of breath

You often see a surprise microexpression in the following situations:

- Delivering unexpected news
- Sharing a story with a shocking ending
- When someone is amazed or in awe
- Photo alert: In a picture when someone is ambushed by a camera

Special Tip: The easiest way to tell the difference between fear and surprise is the shape of the eyebrows. Fear is marked by flat eyebrows with horizontal lines across the forehead. In surprise, the eyebrows are rounded like upside-down *U*s.

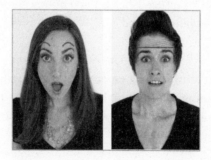

Disgust

When we experience something unpleasant, revolting, or repulsive, we show disgust. It is the face you make when you smell something bad. Imagine a kid eating spinach for the first time: "Ewwwww" they say, with their nose crinkled up and a flash of their upper teeth.

The disgust microexpression is marked by:

- Wrinkling of the upper nose
- Lifting of the upper lip
- Raising of the cheeks
- Tightening of the lower lid

You often see a disgust microexpression in the following situations:

- When someone smells or tastes something bad
- If they don't like a person or an idea
- During an unpleasant interaction
- Photo alert: In a picture if they're trying to force themselves to look happy but hate being photographed

Sadness

This is the expression most accurately portrayed by emoticons. A frowny face really does mean that someone is in a downy place. Sadness is the hardest microexpression to fake, so when you see it you know that you have hit a deep feeling. It is also the precursor expression to crying, so it can help you predict when someone is going to burst into tears.

The sadness microexpression is marked by:

- Corners of the eyebrows pinched together
- Drooping of the eyelids
- Puffing or pouting of the lower lip
- Pulling the corners of the mouth down into a frown

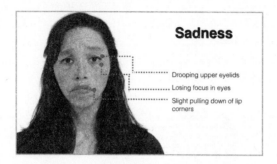

You often see a sadness microexpression in the following situations:

- When someone is disappointed
- Right before they're about to cry
- If they're overwhelmed or upset

Step #2: Responding

While microexpressions give you tremendous insight into someone's emotional state, spotting them is only the first step of the Decoder hack. Choosing a response comes next. Here are a few strategies.

Anger

When I see anger, I think **opportunity**. Why? If you spot anger, you know that you have the opportunity to explain, dispel, and get to the truth.

Let's say, for example, you are pitching a project to a new client. The presentation is going swimmingly—they seem very engaged, are asking great questions, and nodding along with your points. Then you get to the price. Right as you mention the cost of the project, your client flashes anger at you—across the boardroom table you can easily see those two vertical lines appear between their eyebrows.

Typical Response: If you continue with your pitch, you leave questions unanswered. Yet the typical response is to just barrel through the rest of the material you planned to present and hope the anger evaporates. At the end of your talk, you'd be lucky if your client brought up his or her suspicions on pricing. Most wouldn't. Then you'd be stuck wondering why they said no.

Using the Decoder: Immediately pause and explain the reasons you arrived at your price—so your client has the full context and understands your perspective. Then, before moving on to your next slide, ask if there are any remaining questions about the price. Once you have finished the pitch, circle back to the price and see if you still spot the anger.

How to Respond:
- Explore—where is the anger coming from and how can you oust it?
- Stay Calm—not offensive or defensive.
- Explain—what information can you give them to feel less threatened?

Contempt

When I see contempt, I think **red flag**. Contempt is a devious little emotion. When it isn't addressed, it festers and grows into deep disrespect and hatred. This is why you need to tackle it the moment you see it.

Remember that spotting contempt doesn't mean that someone is a contemptuous person or that they think *you* are a contemptuous person. People can have disdain for an idea or a situation while still having a great relationship with you. This is why it is important to identify the trigger and talk it through so you can use it to strengthen your relationship and learn more about them.

Let's say you are working with a colleague on a new project. You sit down over coffee to hammer out the details. You easily agree on a fair way to divvy up the project tasks and move on to the timeline. When you mention your six-week goal, you spot a microexpression of contempt.

Typical Response: Ignore it—you know it's a tight turnaround, but it's all hands on deck for this one. Six weeks later, you are surprised when your colleague says he is at least two weeks behind. Now it's up to you to pick up the slack.

A Hacker's Response: Go into information-seeking mode and figure out exactly what your colleague is worried about. What are his expectations for deliverables? How can you re-evaluate to help him (and you) get this project done on time? Either decide on a new timeline or change the deliverables to be more equitable.

  How to Respond:
- Find the source—what exactly is causing this contempt?
- Re-evaluate—how can you address the contemptuous issue?
- Build rapport—where can you agree?

Happiness

Fake happiness (above) sends completely different social signals than real happiness.

When I see happiness, I think **celebration!** Happiness is one of the most beautiful and joyous emotions—savor it, capitalize on it, celebrate it! Don't let happiness go unnoticed.

Let's say your partner had an amazing day at work. He bursts through the door right as you are cooking dinner. He whistles as he takes off his coat and saunters into the kitchen shouting, "Hey, honey, I have great news!" Hugging you from behind, he asks if there is any champagne to celebrate. You turn and see he is beaming with a huge smile.

Typical Response: You have pasta on boil, veggies sautéing, and wine already open—"No, we can't chill champagne, I just opened this bottle of red!" you say. Then, "Babe, watch out, the pasta is hot, I have to keep stirring." As you try to finish making dinner, you say to your partner, "Tell me the good news as you set the table." Your partner is a little deflated. He still shares the news, but doesn't feel nearly as excited as he did when he came home. You have a normal dinner.

A Hacker's Response: "Tell me! Tell me! Let me turn this heat down so you can tell me everything," you exclaim. He shares his major win at work while you put a cork in your wine and throw a bottle of champagne into the fridge. "We have to celebrate," you say. Dinner takes a little bit longer, but you get to clink glasses and ride the high of his work win together.

How to Respond:

- Celebrate—smile with them, savor the moment.
- Capitalize—ask for details, jump into the joy with them.
- Express gratitude—tell them you are so excited they wanted to share their happiness with you.

Fear

When I see fear, I think **there must be more**.

It's your mother's birthday and you have a big family get-together planned. It's going to be a fun party—she's turning sixty, so you and your siblings saved up to get her an iPad for her to watch her favorite shows while she cooks.

After dinner, your mom begins opening presents. She gets to yours and goes all teary-eyed while reading the card from you and your siblings. After ripping off the wrapping paper, she looks down at the brand-new iPad and leather case. She flashes a microexpression of fear before gushing about how generous her children are. Then she rushes off to serve the cake.

Typical Response: Nailed it! You and your siblings are very proud of your gift. You can't wait for your mom to use it. A few weeks later, she still hasn't taken it out of the box. A few months later, she has opened it and put it in the case, but refuses to do more than play Scrabble on the free app you downloaded for her. Why did you get her this nice gift if she isn't going to use it!?

A Hacker's Response: After cake, you take your mom aside and ask her if she is excited about the iPad. "Of course!" she says. But you spot that fear again. You offer to come over in the next few days and give her a tutorial on the iPad. She sighs with relief.

After a few sessions, she has figured out Netflix and her e-mail. You also sign her up for a free iPad class offered at the Apple Store. She comes back with a list of cool new apps she thinks *you* would like. Nailed it!

How to Respond:

- Address—what's the threat? What is the source of discomfort?
- Soothe—how can you make it safer?
- Comfort—can you reassure, re-evaluate, or remove the threat?

Surprise

When I see surprise, **I hope we are on the same page**. Sometimes, you mean to evoke surprise—using a conversation sparker or delivering good news. Other times, their surprise surprises you.

You're having lunch with an old friend. It's been forever since you have been able to catch up, so you spend the first twenty minutes just updating each other on what's been going on in your lives. The appetizers finally come and you begin to reminisce about college.

"Can you believe," you ask, "that Robby just got engaged?!" Your friend flashes a look of surprise.

Typical Response: You assume she knows—doesn't everyone? Sure, Robby didn't post about it on Facebook (he doesn't use Facebook because of his job). But you figure it's common knowledge. You breeze past the topic. A few days later, you hear through the grapevine that you spilled the beans. Robby was waiting to tell his parents before sending out announcements to everyone—your leak got back to them before he could share his news. Oops. You are definitely not invited to the wedding.

A Hacker's Response: You spot the surprise and clarify, "Didn't you know?" Your friend shakes her head and says, "I had no idea!" Thinking quickly, you say, "Hey, I'm sure he'll want to tell everyone himself—if you can keep it under wraps until he announces, that would be great." Crisis averted. Wedding open bar is in your future.

How to Respond:

- Clarify—do they know what you know?
- Qualify—what needs to happen next?
- Equate—how can you get on the same page?

Disgust

When I see disgust, I think **we better get to the bottom of this**. People often flash disgust when they are trying to think of a polite way to say they don't like something. When we are worried about offending people, we keep our true feelings of disgust under wraps. However, if you want to get to the truth, you have to give people permission to express their real feelings.

Let's say you are hiring a new employee. Everything in the interview is going great—he has a solid résumé and a positive attitude. As you explain the different parts of the job, you notice that your interviewee flashes disgust when bringing up that the job is paperwork heavy. There is a lot of filing, alphabetizing, and photocopying that happens at the end of each week.

Typical Response: Hope for the best. Everything looks good and you really think he is a great candidate for the position. You are shocked when at the end of his first month, none of your client invoices have been sent out. Why? There was a bottleneck in the filing system. He had been pushing off his weekly paperwork tasks and now all of your payments are late.

A Hacker's Response: Noticing the disgust, you ask the candidate if he did much paperwork in the past. "Oh no," he says, "I am great with strategy and ideas, but not great at organization." He tells you in his last job he had an office assistant help with those tasks. After the interview, you go back to your boss to approve budget to hire him a secretary. He's worth it, so you want to focus on his strengths and delegate his weaknesses.

Once he joins the staff, the entire office increases efficiency and you're able to double production.

How to Respond:

- Permission—let them tell you how they really feel.
- Openness—everyone is entitled to his or her opinion.
- Solve—how can you fix the dislike?

Sadness

When I see sadness, I think **empathy**.

Let's say you are working with a contractor to redesign a bathroom in your house. The contractor comes highly recommended from your neighbors and you love his work. You have talked on the phone, but today the contractor is going to evaluate the scope of the project and give you a bid. When he comes up to the front door, you shake hands and say, "Nice to meet you. How are you?" He says, "I'm all right," but you notice a micro-expression of sadness.

Typical Response: You have work to do! You are hoping and praying the project is within your budget. You offer the contractor some water and then tour the bathroom. After a few minutes, the contractor says he has all he needs. You are shocked—he spent no more than ten minutes in the space and barely measured anything! As he is gathering his stuff, you ask for an estimated price. He gives you a number double what you expected. There is no way you can do it. Looks like you will be stuck with the old bathroom or have to start from scratch finding a new contractor.

A Hacker's Response: You spot the sadness so you ask, "Yeah? Everything ok?" The contractor sighs and says, "Long day, you know those?" You get him a glass of water and say, "Those are rough. Is anything wrong?" He tells you that he just found out his father's in the hospital. He can't run over and check on him until after your appointment. You immediately tell him that you can reschedule. He should definitely be with his father.

The next day, he calls to say everything is fine—it was just a false alarm, but he is so grateful for your understanding. He comes back that afternoon in a great mood and gives you an excellent price on the project.

How to Respond:
- Understanding—what is causing the sadness?
- Empathy—how can you help?
- Space—how much time do they need to recover?

Step #3: Understand Outliers

While the seven microexpressions are universal, there are a few special exceptions I want you to keep in mind before diving into the world of facial responsiveness.

The Eyebrow Raise

An isolated eyebrow raise might look like partial surprise, but it is actually an indication of interest. We raise our eyebrows as if to say, "Oh really?" or "Fascinating!" Offering affirmation like this is an excellent addition to the Triple Threat.

You can also use the eyebrow raise to highlight something important you're saying. For example, teachers often raise their eyebrows when they get to a particularly important part of their lesson. This is a subconscious way we call attention to our words. And, frequently, the most engaged student listeners will raise their eyebrows right back to show that they find it interesting, too.

Eyebrow raises show:
- Engagement
- Attention
- Curiosity

Facial Punctuators

Just as we use our hands to emphasize our words, we use rapid facial movements to accent or punctuate what's being said.[8] For example, we might bite our lips to show nervousness or puff out our cheeks to show frustration. This is a way we add dimension or expressiveness to our verbal communication.

Facial punctuators are a normal part of interaction. Occasionally, people will use one of the seven microexpressions as their facial punctuator. For example, Simon Cowell, the infamous *American Idol* judge who rips contestants to shreds, uses contempt as his facial punctuator. No wonder he's stereotyped as the critical one. Yet for him, contempt is a means of accenting his statements, and isn't necessarily a sign of inner derision.

If you notice someone using one of the seven microexpressions frequently along with their words, it might just be their facial punctuator.

Facial punctuators:
- Highlight ideas
- Accent words
- Can be one of the seven microexpressions

Squelching

Squelching is the result of trying to hide a microexpression, which creates a mishmash of facial gestures.

Have you ever tried to suppress a yawn? Your body has a really hard time stopping itself, so you make a crazy expression—squishing your eyes closed, cranking your mouth shut and tensing your cheek muscles. It's a very similar feeling and look when someone tries to hide or contain a microexpression. It can be an indication of embarrassment or a concealed lie.

If you notice someone make a squelched expression, be sure to dig deeper to find the source of the disguise.

Squelching can be seen if someone is:

- Lying
- Embarrassed of their reaction
- Hiding their true feelings

THE SCIENCE OF SELFIES

These days, we very rarely have the luxury of making a first impression in person. An interviewer Googles you before your interview, a potential client adds you on LinkedIn after getting your e-mail, or you meet someone on Tinder before going out on a real date. The question is: **What does your digital microexpression say?**

When making a first impression, you get the luxury of a few seconds in real life—online it's not so cushy. Princeton University researcher Dr. Alexander Todorov found that you make a snap judgment about someone online within 100 milliseconds of seeing their picture.[9]

The good news is that you're in control of the messages you send in your photo. Whether you have an e-mail avatar, a social media profile picture, or a business head shot, you can use the seven microexpressions to send the right signals.

In another experiment, Dr. Todorov found that different images of the same person can create drastically different first impressions. Participants changed their minds about a person's intelligence, trustworthiness, and attractiveness depending on what picture they were looking at.[10]

We did a mini-experiment in our lab that we called Hot or Not, indeed using the website HotorNot.com. If you're unfamiliar, visitors to the website "rate" pictures of strangers. We coded four hundred photos of men and women and found that the "hottest" photos had different patterns than the photos with the lowest scores.*

Specifically in regard to microexpressions—photos with fake smiles or closed mouth smiles got lower ratings. Be sure your profile pictures

---

* We created a free guide for you as a Digital Bonus called "How to Take the Perfect Selfie." Get it at www.ScienceofPeople.com/toolbox.

aren't accidentally showing negative microexpressions. Common mistakes are:

- Showing contempt in an attempt to look casual
- Flashing fake happiness in lieu of a real smile
- Squinting in the sun, which looks like an anger microexpression
- Blinking or reacting to a flash, causing an accidental look of fear

Check your online photos to make sure you're projecting a strong digital first impression.

MICROEXPRESSION CHALLENGE

A book can teach you only so much about microexpressions. The best way to exercise your Decoder muscles is with video—you can slow it down, pause it, and speed it up.

We have created Watch Guides for some of our favorite TV shows so you can practice spotting, decoding, and exercising your facial-reading muscles. The Watch Guides are like *Where's Waldo?* for facial expressions. All you have to do is follow along with each episode and see if you can spot all of the clues. It's super addictive! It's also the best way to see facial expressions "in the wild."

We have all these free for you in your Digital Bonuses at www .ScienceofPeople.com/toolbox. Just download the Watch Guide and see if you can spot all of the expressions. I also frequently tweet about microexpressions I see during debates, newscasts, and recent events. So be sure to follow me @Vvanedwards on social media.

FOLLOW YOUR INSTINCT

One final reminder: Follow your instincts.

Just as we are wired to show microexpressions, we are also wired to read them. This hack teaches you the names for what you already know. If you ever forget what a facial expression means or can't recognize an expression, try to mimic it. When you copy a facial expression, you will often feel the emotion it portrays. This is because of something called the facial feedback hypothesis.[11]

The hypothesis is that our facial expressions and our emotions are connected in a loop. When you feel an emotion, it is expressed on your face. On the other hand, when you have an expression on your face, you also feel that emotion. This is a great ninja tip—if you want to really feel as someone else feels, copy their expression to glimpse their inner state.

CHALLENGES

1. Use the tear-out flash cards in the microexpression appendix in the back of this book to practice facial reading on the go.
2. Take our Science of People microexpression quiz to test your facial reading skills.
3. Watch shows like *Lie to Me*, *Survivor*, and *The Bachelorette* to practice spotting facial expressions. We have a full list of shows and Watch Guides in our Digital Bonuses at www.ScienceofPeople .com/toolbox.

CHAPTER REVIEW

There are seven universal facial microexpressions that humans display. Once you know how to read them, you can spot hidden emotions behind words. The Decoder is the ultimate hack for speeding up connection by getting to the truth and understanding emotional needs.

- Always look for the seven microexpressions as you listen.
- Don't confuse eyebrow raises or facial punctuators for universal emotions.
- If you don't recognize an expression, mimic it and see how it makes you feel.

My biggest takeaway in this chapter is: _____

CHAPTER 7

SOLVE

How to crack someone's personality

In 1984, Procter & Gamble, once the go-to brand for everything from soap to paper towels to vegetable oil, was thrown into crisis by the creeping encroachment of rival companies.[1]

Something had to change. Out of the blue, Richard Nicolosi, a shift foreman at Procter & Gamble, was approached by a P&G marketing executive about joining their team. "I didn't even know how to spell marketing at the time," said Nicolosi. But executives recognized his unique ability. They hoped his engineering mind could solve some of the company's biggest problems.

Nicolosi began doing what he knew best as a chemical engineer: solving puzzles. He applied this methodical way of thinking to his dealings with people, too. "**Getting the best out of people is like solving a puzzle,**" Nicolosi explained to me.

He was given authority to carry out a massive reorganization and began dismantling division teams and assigning new leadership roles. But he knew he couldn't assemble new teams from scratch based on nothing but résumé printouts. He believed the key was to assign the right person to the right team in the right category.

Nicolosi had to find the best matchups, and find them fast. He developed a rigorous process that he still follows today. First, he sits down with each person and uses probing, insightful questions to seek to understand them. He both watches and listens—looking for body language tells, facial expressions, and behavioral traits.

Second, he spends time with them—and not two arms' lengths

removed. He tries to see them in action. "There is a world of difference between what people say and what people do," said Nicolosi.

Third, he listens to the words they use and then speaks their language back to them. This allows him to align what he wants to accomplish with what they want to accomplish.

Armed with this intel about each of his employees, Nicolosi set up effective teams and new workflows that carried the company out of the 1984 slump and through many crises in years to come. By the end of 1988, profits were up 68 percent.

Nicolosi began to teach his philosophy of people to many of P&G's other leading businesses: soaps, detergents, cleaning products, and soft drinks. He was the youngest-ever sector president, youngest-ever group vice president, and the youngest-ever corporate vice president. Eventually, he was asked to restructure Scott Paper, where he was able to double both operating profit to $700 million and increase return on investment to 23 percent in less than two years.

When I asked Nicolosi what his secret was, he replied: "People come in a host of flavors, and understanding what flavor they are—and therefore what their hot buttons are—is necessary to lead and motivate them."

Nicolosi solves people puzzles, and so can you.

SOLVING THE PEOPLE PUZZLE

I used to find people intimidating. I couldn't keep personality differences straight. And I found it impossible to figure out behavior—let alone predict needs. Why did one friend love to chat while another never called me back? Why did some bosses encourage an open-door policy, while others used their secretary as a gatekeeper?

Then, one day, I stumbled upon something called the five-factor model. This psychological principle posits that all humans have five basic personality traits: openness, conscientiousness, extroversion, agreeableness, and neuroticism (easily remembered as OCEAN). And each and every person ranks either high or low for each trait. Here's a summary:[2]

> **Openness:** This trait reflects how you approach new ideas. It also describes how curious you are, your level of creativity, and how much you appreciate variety and originality.

High: Enjoys novelty, change, and adventure.
Low: Savors traditions, routines, and habits.

Conscientiousness: This trait describes your approach to getting things done. It measures your self-discipline, organization, and reliability.
High: Loves to-do lists, organization, and schedules. Enjoys digging into the details and making things "perfect."
Low: Typically prefers big ideas and strategy. Might find lists and schedules stifling and overwhelming.

Extroversion: This trait describes how you approach people. Do you get energy from social situations, or do they drain you? This probably affects your talkativeness and optimism.
High: Gets energy from being with people. Tends to be cheerful and seeks out social time.
Low: Craves alone time and finds being with people draining.

Agreeableness: This trait describes how you approach cooperation and working with others. It also speaks to how empathetic and quick to forgive you are, and how much attention you pay to the mental states of others.
High: Easy to get along with, very empathetic, and enjoys caring for others.
Low: More analytical, practical, and skeptical—prefers to keep emotions out of decisions.

Neuroticism: This trait describes how you approach worry. It also explains how emotionally reactive you are to your environment.
High: Tends to be a worrier. Frequently experiences mood swings.
Low: Typically calm, stable, and has very little mood fluctuation.

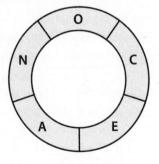

These traits gave me a starting point. I began to "solve" each of the important people in my life by looking at their behavioral patterns. For fun, I created small ciphers for each person, like this:
Then I would guess, based on their choices,

attitudes, and behaviors, where they fell in each category. Here was one I made for my boss at the time:

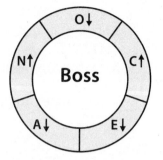

I came to call each of these little ciphers a matrix. After a few weeks of making a matrix for everyone in my life, something interesting happened. I noticed that many of my relationships and conversations were beginning to change.

First, my conversations were flowing much more smoothly. I finally had a guide for easy banter—I just asked people questions that helped me solve their matrix. For example, I was no longer anxious when I ran into my boss in the break room. When trying to figure out if he was high open (likes trying new things), I asked about his most recent vacations and then his career path. This led to a great rapport, and, eventually, his asking me to grab lunch "to continue this great conversation."

Second, I was arriving at a much deeper and more accurate understanding of the people in my life. Once I learned my boss was a low extrovert (preferred to work and brainstorm alone), I got in the habit of sending him my ideas before our office meetings so he could review them on his own time—he always got back to me first and prioritized my ideas.

Finally, I was getting faster at decoding new personalities. After only a few minutes of chitchat, I could guess how someone would rank. When I met my boss's wife, I was able to instantly connect with her by asking about her favorite restaurants. Her answer helped me predict which topics of conversation she might enjoy most, leading to a lively discussion over drinks.

Without realizing it, I was following Nicolosi's guide to figuring people out. I was asking purposeful questions. I was listening and watching for behavioral clues. Then, I was using their individual cipher, or personality matrix, to predict and optimize for their behavior.

This led me to one of my most powerful people hacks: speed-reading. Before you learn to master it yourself, let's talk about where personality comes from.

FAST FACT BOX

Most people in our survey felt their personality was their best asset.

Times taken			
1673			

1. My best asset is: (select one)

		Responses %	Responses
A.	my body	8%	140
B.	my personality	31%	515
C.	my sense of humor	21%	354
D.	my intelligence	20%	337
E.	my empathy	20%	327

PERSONALITY SCIENCE

Researchers have long been interested in personality, but it wasn't until the 1980s that Dr. Lewis Goldberg cultivated the first major breakthrough, finding that the five-factor model, which Dr. Goldberg nicknamed "the Big Five," was the most accurate.[3] Since then, the Big Five has been used as the standard in academia and has been found to be more reliable than Myers-Briggs, DiSC, or Enneagram personality measures.

Personalities play a huge role in how we make decisions, form goals, and balance work and relationships. And we usually can't control them. About 35 to 50 percent of your personality is wired into your genetic makeup. Your upbringing, another factor you have zero say in, also shapes you considerably.

Ever wish your colleague was more organized? Ever try to make your partner less of a homebody? Ever try to calm your friend down from worrying so much? This never works! We can't alter people's nature. Instead of trying to change the people in your life, learn how to decode, optimize, and predict their behavior.

First, let's start with a self-assessment.[4] Be as honest as you can:

Openness
This trait describes your curiosity and affinity for new ideas. Check off the statements that sound like you:

If you are high in openness you:

____ Are very curious

____ Love to try new things

____ Are adventurous and a bit of a dreamer

____ Can be seen as unrealistic or not focused

If you are low in openness you:

____ Love habits, rituals, and routines

____ Honor and follow traditions

____ Are more pragmatic and data driven

____ Can be seen as closed-minded and inflexible

Based on your answers, where do you think you fall on the openness scale? Put a line where you are:

LOW ◆- ➤ HIGH

Conscientiousness

This trait involves the way you get things done. Check off the statements that sound like you:

If you are high in conscientiousness you:

____ Are very organized and detail-oriented

____ Love to-do lists, plans, and schedules

____ Are a perfectionist

____ Can be seen as controlling and rigid

If you are low in conscientiousness you:

____ Love broad ideas and don't get bogged down in details

____ Are very flexible

____ Hate being boxed in with a plan or schedule

____ Can be seen as sloppy and unreliable

Based on your answers, where do you think you fall on the conscientiousness scale? Put a line where you are:

LOW ◆- ➤ HIGH

Extroversion

This trait is all about how you relate to people. Check off the statements that sound like you:

If you are high in extroversion you:

____ Are very talkative and tend to initiate conversations

____ Are assertive and expressive with your opinions

____ Feel energized and refreshed being around other people

____ Can be seen as opinionated and attention seeking

If you are low in extroversion you:

____ Are more shy and reserved

____ Enjoy alone time; being with lots of people can feel draining

____ Like your privacy and are more hesitant to share personal information

____ Can be seen as aloof

Based on your answers, where do you think you fall on the extroversion scale? Put a line where you are.

LOW ◄-------------------------------------► **HIGH**

Agreeableness

This trait taps into your attitudes toward teamwork and decision-making. Check off the statements that sound like you:

If you are high in agreeableness you:

____ Tend to get along with people easily

____ Are trusting of others and love being on teams

____ Default to saying yes when someone asks you to do something

____ Can be seen as a pushover or passive

If you are low in agreeableness you:

____ Have a harder time working in groups

____ Are frequently suspicious of others' motives

____ Default to saying no when someone asks you to do something

____ Can be seen as competitive or challenging

Based on your answers, where do you think you fall on the agreeableness scale? Put a line where you are:

LOW ←- →**HIGH**

Neuroticism

This trait speaks to your emotional stability and tendency to worry. Check off the statements that sound like you:

If you are high in neuroticism you:
____ Are a worrier
____ Tend to be moody
____ Are sensitive
____ Can be seen as too emotional or insecure

If you are low in neuroticism you:
____ Are stable and balanced
____ Are usually calm
____ Have faith that everything always "works out in the end"
____ Can be seen as unemotional or cold

Based on your answers, where do you think you fall on the neuroticism scale? Put a line where you are:

LOW ←- →**HIGH**

A note about the middle: Did you notice you tended to fall in the middle of some of the spectrums? This is totally normal. You belong in the middle if you can see yourself having both high and low qualities at different times. For example, those who fall in the middle of the extroversion scale are "ambiverts," meaning some situations make them feel outgoing and others make them feel closed up. (This has a lot to do with your thrive and survive locations.) For our purposes, think of the personality you express the majority of the time. You might even limit your rankings to the way you feel professionally or socially, depending on your goals from this book.

If you had trouble with these self-statements or feel all of your traits are in the middle, you might need to take the official forty-four-question personality test to verify your rankings.*

SPEED-READING THE MATRIX

By the end of 2014, our lab was booming. I was swamped with new projects, my speaking calendar was completely full, and we had just enrolled over 40,000 students in our online courses. We needed help.

Luckily, three new interns were starting in our lab. I couldn't wait to get more hands on deck. Everything started out peachy. By their fourth day, the interns were helping manage our active social media accounts.

About two weeks in, we hit a snag. One of the interns—I'll call her Eva—was struggling to complete tasks. No worries, I thought, I'll just send her more-detailed instructions.

But the following week, her incomplete projects were still backing up the rest of my team. No worries, I thought, I'll check in with her and ask her what she'd personally prefer to work on. Over lunch, we sat down together and I suggested some new projects she might like. She was on board! We were looking good.

A week later, I found out she hadn't even started on the tasks we'd talked about. No worries, I thought, I'll just pair her with an older team member as a mentor.

A week later, Eva sent me an e-mail saying she wanted to quit. I was flummoxed: What went wrong?

The answer was simple: I had failed to decode her matrix. I was interacting with Eva according to my personality traits, not hers. Since then, I have developed a system for solving someone's matrix.

HACK #7: Speed-Read
Use the matrix to solve people's Big Five personality traits.

Speed-reading is a three-step hack—first you must decipher your own personality, then quickly figure out the person you are interacting with, then decide whether to compromise or optimize.

I have taught this method to over 12,500 students all over the world.

---

* You can take the full personality quiz in our Digital Bonuses at www.ScienceofPeople .com/toolbox.

We have had over 18,000 people take our personality test in our lab. Of all of the people hacks I teach, this is the one I get the most excited e-mails about.

Speed-reading is a relationship game changer. When used correctly, it clears up miscommunications, prevents arguments, spices up chitchat, and accelerates bonding.

While speed-reading is one of my most powerful hacks, it is also extremely advanced. If you have to read this section a few times, do it. If this hack takes you a little longer than others, embrace it. If it's a little out of your comfort zone, do a little energizing jig and keep moving forward. I promise, it will change your relationships.

Step #1: You

Decoding your own matrix is the first step to speed-reading.

Based on your scores earlier in this chapter, fill out the blank matrix below. Put a down arrow next to the traits you rank low in, an up arrow in the traits you rank high in, and an equal sign on the traits where you fall in the middle.

Special Note: Some people find their personality traits are slightly different personally or professionally. If this is you, feel free to mark these two areas of your life in separate colors.

Here is my matrix and explanations to give you an idea of how self-decoding works. Put your answers next to mine.

My matrix was almost the opposite of my intern Eva's. This is one reason we had such a hard time getting along. I tried to impose my personality onto her—and that never works out well:

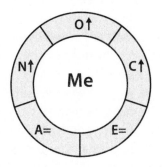

- I am high open, so I'm incredibly curious and love experimenting. I assumed Eva would also like being assigned fun new tasks at work and learning new skills. I picked her projects based on what I would have wanted, not what she would have wanted.
- I am high conscientious so I love details, plans, and to-do lists. I kept sending Eva more details in the hope they'd reassure and guide her.

- I am a high neurotic, so I'm overly eager to make sure everyone on my team is happy. I was constantly checking in on Eva—which made her feel pressured.
- I am medium agreeable and medium extroversion, so I like working with people in the right circumstances—or in my thrive locations. I did not take Eva's into account.

This approach didn't work—**in fact, it was a selfish way to interact.** I was seeing Eva through my personality instead of optimizing for hers.

Step #2: Them

I realized a little too late that I was not using Eva's matrix. Upon receiving her e-mail, I quickly pulled out a sheet of paper to decode her personality—which I should have done when I first hired her.

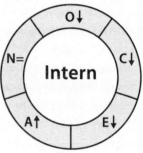

- Eva is low open, so she was overwhelmed by my flood of suggested projects.
- Eva is low conscientiousness, so my long, detailed e-mails intimidated her. She did not know how to start—so she didn't start at all.
- Eva is highly agreeable, so she said yes to all my questions and projects, even though they scared her a bit. She was afraid to mess up the team flow or disappoint me, but wasn't sure how to make it work.
- Eva is a low extrovert, so pairing her with a mentor *and* putting her on a team of three new interns thrust her into a survive scenario. Worse yet, she was uncomfortable asking for help.
- Eva is a medium neurotic, so she had trouble understanding my worry and got a little frustrated with my constant check-ins.

Finally, her behavior and the failures in productivity made sense! Looking at her matrix next to mine not only cleared up previous misfires, but also let me know what steps to take next.

The Direct Approach

Begin to practice guessing the personality traits of people you meet. I highly recommend the direct approach for this. I frequently ask new friends, new hires, and new colleagues directly about their personality traits. This is the easiest and most straightforward way to decode someone's matrix. Here are a few strategies:

- **As a Conversation Starter:** "I'm reading this book about the five personality types—have you ever heard of them?" If they have, great—ask where they rank. If they haven't, explain each one and guess each other's on the spot.
- **As a Game:** "Hey, friend! I just stumbled upon this personality test at ScienceofPeople.com/personality. Here are my scores. I would love to see yours!" You can use this direct approach with new hires and partners as well. People love taking quizzes!
- **As a Formal Process:** These days, I make it a point to formally give the personality test to each of my interns the week they start. This also produces great office conversation.
- **As a Virtual Process:** There are many tools online that can also help you decipher people's personality traits. The University of Cambridge created a free tool called Apply Magic Sauce that will scan your Facebook profile for cues to your personality using your posts, pictures, friends, and communication patterns as indicators.
- **As a Communication Process:** A tool called Crystal* uses your e-mail history and people's LinkedIn profiles to give you suggestions on their Big Five personality needs and how to communicate with them. For example, when I e-mail my colleague Danielle, it gives me e-mail templates on how best to communicate with her based on her personality and ideas on how to work well together:

---

* We have links to both personality tools in your Digtial Bonuses at www.ScienceofPeople .com/toolbox.

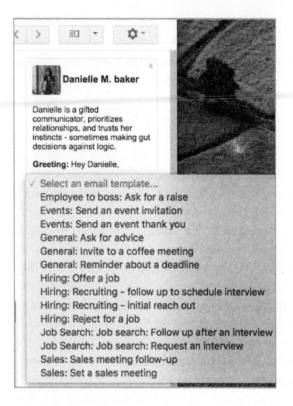

The Speed-Reading Approach

If you don't have time to directly ask people about their personalities—or feel you can't—you can speed-read them. You'll crunch data from their body language, verbal cues, and behavior to decode their personality matrix. **Every hack I have taught you so far was building up to this one.** As you speak with someone, listen for verbal cues and look for nonverbal clues. For example:

- Asking an introvert, "Do you know anyone else here?" might make her nervous so that she flashes fear.
- Encouraging a low open friend to try a new restaurant or order something different might make them irritated so that they flash an anger microexpression at you.
- Pitching a low conscientious client with a long, detailed proposal might overwhelm them so they flash contempt when you hand them a large packet.

You can also use clues to decipher personality with what researcher Sam Gosling calls behavioral evidence. In a series of fascinating studies, Gosling analyzed participants' personal belongings, rooms, and cubicles to decipher their personality types.[5] Using his findings, here is a list of casual questions to help you gauge personality traits, plus behaviors that are reliable personality evidence.

OPENNESS

Possible Questions:
- Have any big vacations coming up?
- I just tried _____ for the first time. Have you ever done that?
- Tried any new restaurants lately?

Behavior:
- **High:** This is a great way to find out if someone goes to new places, restaurants, and tends to travel—or has the desire to experience more new things.
- **Low:** If someone goes to the same vacation spots or restaurants every year or prefers to stay home, they could be low open.

Clues:
- Highs might have knickknacks from trips scattered around their living space and post pictures of exotic food on social media.
- Highs have diverse taste in books and music.
- Highs are very inquisitive.
- Lows have lots of routines and habits.
- Lows might know the server at their favorite restaurant and order the same dishes over and over.

CONSCIENTIOUSNESS

Possible Questions:
- Have any big projects coming up?
- What's the plan?
- Did you make any goals or New Year's resolutions this year?

Behavior:
- **High:** Highs usually know exactly what's coming up in their lives, and will typically be much more descriptive about upcoming projects, as if they're reading off a to-do list.
- **Low:** Lows are much more easygoing. They might have difficulty making plans. They want to "play it by ear," "see how it goes," and "go with the flow."

Clues:
- Highs usually put great care into their appearance and property.
- Highs often have alphabetized bookshelves, a personalized filing system, and a detailed planner.
- Interestingly, Sam Gosling also found that they tend to have good lighting in their rooms.
- Lows are usually the ones to ask to borrow a pen, forget to charge their phones, and tend to show up a little late. This also doesn't bother them much—after all, "it'll all work out in the end."
- Lows tend to let the laundry go until they're down to the last pair of underwear.
- A low might not notice a messy desk covered with stacks of papers and unopened mail.

EXTROVERSION

Possible Questions:
- Know anyone else here?
- What are you up to this weekend?
- What's your ideal day look like?

Behavior:
- Though a low might know just as many people as a high, highs might want to know more about the people around them and make a point to "work the room."
- **High:** Typically, an extrovert will want to spend more time with people, and won't need recovery time between social activities. Alone time might not be essential to them.
- **Low:** An introvert might have fewer social events planned—or might intersperse people activities with solo activities.

Clues:

- Highs tend to smile more often and more broadly, as they tend to be more optimistic.
- Highs engage more comfortably with big groups of people and often stand with broad, confident body language.
- Highs love sharing details of their life and accomplishments with others. They reach out more often via text and use more words in e-mails.
- Lows prefer one-on-one conversations.
- Lows prefer to bond with others in quiet environments, or to do activities that don't require talking at all.
- Sam Gosling found that extroverts have more decorations in their offices or cubicles because they want to make their spaces more inviting. In other words, they set out trinkets, games, and candy to lure people in. Interestingly, this does not apply to their bedrooms!

AGREEABLENESS

Possible Questions:

- What do you want for dinner?
- Are you usually the peacemaker? (This question can come up naturally. For example, if talking about siblings, ask if they were the troublemaker, the goofball, or the peacemaker. When talking about friend drama, ask if they're usually the one stuck in the middle.)
- Want to join us later? (This question can also help you gauge extroversion.)

Behavior:

- **High:** Agreeable people typically default to a yes, so they will usually respond with something like, "Sure, whatever everyone else is doing!" or "What did you have in mind?"
- **Low:** Low agreeable people typically default to a no. They will often turn down all your suggestions before weighing the pros and cons of a decision themselves.

Clues:

- According to Sam Gosling, highs tend to have a more relaxed walk with more arm swinging.

- Highs take the world's problems on their shoulders. They want to help, fix, and care for everyone in their life—and sometimes this means they don't take care of themselves.
- Lows are less driven by emotions than facts. Cooperation is less important to them than being right, or simply getting to the right answer.
- Lows don't want to know how you *feel* about something. They want to know what Google says.

NEUROTICISM

Possible Questions:
- How has your week been?
- Is this your busy season?
- Anything else I should know?

Behavior:
- **High:** High neurotics are usually stressed and busy. (It sounds awful to say, but worriers often think that if they don't have something to stress about, they aren't doing enough. I should know—I am one.)
- **Low:** Low neurotics have a higher capacity for stress and difficulty, so even if they are busy, their *attitude* toward their busyness will be less anxious.

Clues:
- According to Gosling, high neurotics tend to have more self-help quotes and inspirational messages in their office space and homes. They use them to self-calm and self-regulate.
- Highs usually have *one more thing* they want to tell you, just in case. They're planning and preparing for every eventuality.
- According to Sam Gosling, high neurotics tend to wear darker colors of clothing.
- High neurotics are good at *preventing* crises. They think through every possible what-if scenario so they're prepared for the worst.
- Low neurotics are great to have around during a crisis—they can think clearly, stay calm, and act as everyone's rock.

- Lows typically think about what's going right instead of what's going wrong. So they have a harder time commiserating about stress and being busy.*

Not only can you ask the questions above to decipher personalities, but you can also listen to questions you're being asked. For example, take this brief e-mail I got from my friend Sarah a few days before a party I was hosting:

Hi Vanessa!

I can't wait for the party on Saturday!!! I'm bringing a chicken recipe I've never made before so advance notice we might have to order pizza =).

Your invite didn't have an ending time on it. Do you know what time the party will be over so I can tell the babysitter?

XO—Sarah

PS—Last time you mentioned wanting more chairs. Let me know if you want us to bring our extra folding chairs.

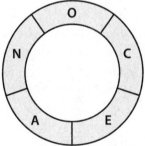

Can you guess Sarah's matrix from this e-mail?

I would always encourage you to do more digging before completing someone's matrix, but if we had to speed-read Sarah, here's what I would infer from her statements. Let's break it down by parts:

Evidence	Guess	Clues
Hi Vanessa! *I can't wait for the party on Saturday!!!*	High Extroversion	• Statement expressing excitement for a social interaction • Lots of exclamation points, indicating energy and optimism

---

* Read our full "How to Snoop" exposé in your Digital Bonuses at www.ScienceofPeople .com/toolbox.

Evidence	Guess	Clues
I'm bringing a chicken recipe I've never made before so advance notice we might have to order pizza =).	High Openness	• Desire to try a new dish • Possible failure is acceptable (perhaps even positive)
Your invite didn't have an ending time on it. Do you know what time the party will be over so I can tell the babysitter?	High Neuroticism High Conscientiousness	• Concern for babysitter • Notice of details and desire to know end time • Need for control
XO—Sarah *PS- Last time you mentioned wanting more chairs. Let me know if you want us to bring our extra folding chairs.*	High Agreeableness High Conscientiousness	• Remembers an emotional need • Willing to go out of her way • Planning ahead

Again, I can't be 100 percent sure of these traits, but I can make an educated guess about them, and that helps me write an e-mail in response:

- Since she's a high conscientiousness person, I would want to send her an exact time and exact chair count.
- Since she's a high neurotic, I should give her this information as soon as possible.
- Since she's a high open, I want to encourage her desire to try a new recipe (and have the pizza guy on speed dial).
- Since she's a high agreeable person and high extrovert, I can be pretty sure she will enjoy the party no matter what.

Learning to quickly and accurately decipher where people fall on each personality trait will take practice. Luckily, we already talked about the importance of your first impression in Hack #2: The Triple Threat. Our own first impressions of others are just as important.[6]

Here's the good news: **Your first impressions are 76 percent accurate.**[7] Do you know why? A study from the November 2014 journal *Trends in Cognitive Sciences* indicates that we can guess personality and general traits based on face shape and attributes.[8] For example, we tend to think extroverts and introverts look different. Here are a few spectrums from the research. Can you match the descriptions to the correct row? The images are computer generated, but they're representative of what each personality trait tends to look like.

___ Introverted to Extroverted
___ Unreliable to Trustworthy
___ Incompetent to Competent
___ Nondominant to Dominant

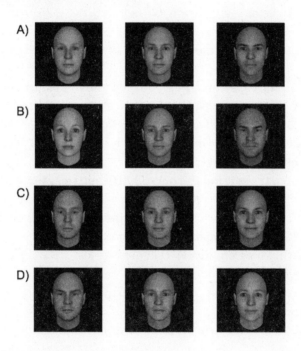

Answer Key:
_C_ Introverted to Extroverted
_D_ Unreliable to Trustworthy
_A_ Incompetent to Competent
_B_ Nondominant to Dominant

Somehow our brains recognize the "look" of a trait. Some studies indicate that we can subconsciously draw conclusions about personality based on face shape and bone structure. So here's what you do when you first meet someone:

- **Gut Check:** We are most accurate at speed-guessing extroversion, conscientiousness, and agreeableness—try to go with your first impression when assessing people in these areas.[9] Openness can be discerned best from someone's physical space or face shape.
- **Verbal Check:** We are least accurate when assessing someone's neuroticism—this is where following up with questions and observations becomes most important.
- **Digital Check:** We can even draw conclusions about someone's personality based on their online pictures and profiles. Researcher Simine Vazire found that Facebook profiles reflect people's actual personalities, not merely their idealized selves.[10]

When you start speed-reading, you might be able to guess only two or three traits. This is a great place to start! Next time you have a friend over, ask if you can pull up old Facebook photos of their sibling or childhood friend. Try to guess their matrix before you have your friend spill the beans on their personality.

Just for fun, **try solving the personality matrices for some of your favorite TV characters as practice:**

- Ricky Ricardo from *I Love Lucy*
- Velma Dinkley from *Scooby-Doo*
- Phil Dunphy from *Modern Family**

Ethical Speed-Reading
Three final points to keep in mind while speed-reading:

1. **Speed-reading is about empathy.** Even attempting to speed-read someone gets you leagues ahead in the people game. Solving people's matrices requires asking intentional questions, listening deeply, and trying to connect with someone on their terms. We want to be solved—it makes us feel heard and understood.
2. **There is no "best" or "normal" personality orientation.** When you assign people trait labels, do so with no assumptions about what's "right" or "wrong." My goal is to help you diagnose and honor

---

* We have answer key matrices for you in your Digital Bonuses at www.ScienceofPeople .com/toolbox.

someone's natural tendencies and find out who someone really is, not who you want them to be. When you accept and optimize for who someone really is instead of trying to change or judge them, your interactions become much deeper, your conversations become smoother, and you are better able to predict behavior.

3. **Personality traits are not stereotypes.** Don't let assumptions about someone's gender, race, or age block your ability to accurately decode someone. This is just one more reason to abandon any and all prejudice—it never helps you get along with or decode people.

Step #3: Us

Once you have begun decoding someone's personality, begin thinking about which of your traits are complementary and which put you in conflict.

When your traits match, awesome. You'll typically have smooth and well-balanced communication. When they don't match, you have two options: You can optimize or you can compromise.

Tactic	Explanation	Questions to Ask
Compromise	When you compromise, you acknowledge that you can't completely change either of your personality traits, but you can find a middle ground.	Based on your needs and their requirements, how can you make it work with a little movement from both sides?
Optimize	When you optimize, you decide to get out of your comfort zone for the sake of greater harmony. This might mean going against your natural inclinations to support the other person. Sometimes in tough work projects, arguments with our partner, and long-term friendships, we have to give a little more than we take.	Where are your boundaries—what's not on the table for change? What are their boundaries—where can they give and take?

I experience the compromise-optimize decision on a daily basis with different personalities in my life. For example, I am high in conscientiousness and my husband is low. I love for the sock drawer to be organized by color, shape, and occasion. My husband doesn't care if he is wearing two different socks, Teenage Mutant Ninja Turtles' shells, or bonsai trees on his feet. We tried to optimize—I attempted to teach him my method of advanced sock organization. This lasted precisely two days. Now we have two separate sock drawers on opposite sides of the closet. This has saved us a lot of headache.

Here's how the compromise-optimize method might have worked with Eva:

Openness: We are opposites on the openness spectrum.
Optimize: Instead of assigning her new learning projects, I should have looked at her previous work history on her résumé and assigned her projects to build on her existing skill set—not start her on a totally new track.

Conscientiousness: We were also opposites in conscientiousness.
Compromise: Since Eva was low in conscientiousness, I should have emphasized the big goals of each project, and then given her freedom to try tasks on her own before bombarding her with details.

Extroversion: As a low extrovert, Eva prefers to work on her own. In-person meetings are too overwhelming for her. I should have sent her work assignments in writing before our meetings.
Optimize: It would have been no hassle for Eva to work on projects solo instead of sitting with the other interns. I also should have asked her to take our Science of People tutorials before her in-person training. She needed time to prepare questions and learn at her own speed.

Agreeableness: Yet another reason to have more e-mail contact and fewer in-person meetings was Eva's level of agreeableness. She so wanted to please her new manager and coworkers.
Optimize: Instead of sitting down together for weekly reviews, I should have arranged a more formal written review where she could give me feedback. She needed a safe space to state needs and set boundaries.

Neuroticism: As a high neurotic, I was freaking Eva out with all of my worries. She took it personally that I seemed to be micromanaging her.

Compromise: Even though I can't be less of a worrier (I wish!), I could have let Eva know that my check-ins were nothing personal. She had no idea that I do the same with everyone on my team. And I could have minimized her frustration by standardizing their timing (every Friday afternoon, for example), so she would've known what was coming.

In sum, my difficulties with Eva were probably preventable. But it's nice to know that wrinkles like these can easily be ironed out in the future.

Bonus: The Personality Advantage

Knowing someone's personality gives a tremendous boost to your persuasive powers. Whether you are pitching an idea to a client or trying to convince your partner to choose your favorite restaurant for dinner, you should tailor your pitch to their personality. This will not only make your pitch more likely to succeed, but also will make the entire process more enjoyable.

Openness Advantage

- **High**: If you know you are pitching a high open person, lead with all the exciting new benefits and give them time to brainstorm ideas with you.
  - *Personal:* "I have heard this Indian fusion place combines ingredients that we've never tried before!"
  - *Professional:* "This new water system will give you better water pressure, a lower water bill—and new shower heads are included!"
- **Low**: If you're pitching a low open person, lead by describing what you're *not* changing. Then present a rational, evidence-based case for your new idea to help them overcome their apprehension about trying something new.
  - *Personal:* "I know they still have our favorites, naan and saag paneer, but they do a new take on chicken tikka, which might be good. They have great reviews on Yelp."
  - *Professional:* "This system is easy to put in—you won't have to change water companies or do anything different with your water meter. Our clients say they didn't notice any change except suddenly having great water pressure."

Conscientiousness Advantage

- **High**: A highly conscientious person will want to hear a long, in-depth proposal without missing details. Be prepared for lots of questions.
  - *Personal:* "I think we should go to Hawaii. For one, the flights are direct, and we'll have all kinds of activities within reach. I went ahead and put together a list of ways to spend time on the Big Island. Here's a sample itinerary I printed and a basic budget of what we need to save up."
  - *Professional:* "I have prepared a twenty-page document of each phase. Let's review it together and then I can answer all of your questions."
- **Low**: A low conscientious person is most interested in your executive summary or brief overview. You'll want to give a short, punchy synopsis—the details would only bore them.
  - *Personal:* "Hawaii is the most cost-effective option with the most activities for the kids. It should cost ___ dollars."
  - *Professional:* "Let me give you the three most important points of this proposal and the immediate next step."

Extroversion Advantage

- **High**: An extrovert is listening for social proof in a pitch—what do other team members think? They also won't mind an impromptu group brainstorm session.
  - *Personal:* "Okay, everyone! What do we want to do for New Year's? Any ideas? I hear that a bunch of people are going to see Pink Martini at the Crystal Ballroom—thoughts?"
  - *Professional:* "I am going to throw some ideas on the board for our next work retreat. Call out whatever you have in mind and then we can vote."
- **Low**: An introvert won't like being put on the spot for questions. They'd prefer to have time to review your proposal on their own before making a decision.
  - *Personal:* "Hey, what did you have in mind for New Year's? Want to start a text chain with some ideas? Let me know if you come up with anything."

- *Professional:* "I want us all to start thinking about the work retreat in the summer. Please send me your suggestions so I can do a quick e-mail poll."

Agreeableness Advantage
- **High**: A high agreeable person might say yes to your face, but no later on. They typically want to avoid confrontation and protect everyone's feelings—which might make them hesitant to bring up the real issues on their mind.
  - *Personal:* "Are you sure you're okay? I know this is awkward to talk about, but it is really important that I know how you feel. Tell me whatever's on your mind."
  - *Professional:* "I'm going to pause at the end of each section to get everyone's thoughts. Trust me, you won't offend me—be sure to bring up all of your concerns. At this stage, it's best to get everything on the table."
- **Low**: A person who is low agreeable might be skeptical of your claims until they get their hands on evidence. Be prepared for tough questions!
  - *Personal:* "Before you say anything, let me explain my side of the story and tell you what happened. I think it will make sense in context."
  - *Professional:* "I am going to go through the entire presentation—so please hold your questions until the end. I've saved plenty of time for Q and A after we cover everything."

Neuroticism Advantage
- **High**: A high neurotic likes to hear that *you're* worrying about everything for him. In other words, to keep a neurotic calm, convince them you've thought about and solved every potentiality so they don't have to. This builds trust. Pro and con lists help show you have thought about both sides.
  - *Personal:* "I know you're worried about what we should do. I think we should move. But let's sit down and make a big pro and con list together. We should discuss backup plans, too."
  - *Professional:* "Let's begin with the safeguards built into our proposal. If anything is late or something doesn't work, we've built in time cushions and have extra staff on standby."

- **Low**: A low neurotic isn't as concerned with what-ifs, so bringing them up could worry them unnecessarily. Within reason, they will take your word for it. So do your due dilligence, mention you did your due dilligence, and leave it at that.
  - *Personal:* "I've thought long and hard about it and I'm sure we should move. If you're on board, I'll talk to the Realtor and keep you informed on my progress."
  - *Professional:* "We also know that unexpected snags are a possibility, and our staff is well equipped to handle any hiccups. I can assure you of that."

Different personalities require drastically different approaches—and this is a good thing! When you cater to people's unspoken preferences, you put yourself way ahead of the curve.

Speed-Reading Challenge

Like learning to read, learning to speed-read doesn't happen overnight. The best way to get good is to practice with people you know and always review past experiences.

Go through the following challenge. If you forget a trait, use the Personality Cheat Sheet in our Digital Bonuses.

- Start identifying the personality traits of people in your life by putting an equal sign or up or down arrow in each column below. Leave the space blank if you aren't sure.
- Highlight or circle the traits where you match.
- Name some of your relationship or communication challenges. Are they related to personality differences?
- Can you optimize or compromise on any of these issues?

	O	C	E	A	N	What are your biggest challenges?	Optimize or compromise?
Your Riser							
Your Target							
Your Best Friend							

	O	C	E	A	N	What are your biggest challenges?	Optimize or compromise?
Your Partner (or a previous partner)							
Your Boss (or a previous boss)							
Your Colleague							
Your Parent							

As you complete the challenge for people in your life, you might notice some interesting patterns.

- **Geography:** Depending on where you're located, you might notice a high concentration of traits or personality patterns. Since a large part of personality is genetic, we see blooms of traits in certain areas. We also know that culture exerts a strong influence on traits. For example, Southern California and New York City are hubs of entrepreneurship, adventure, and living in the moment. Not surprisingly, more high open people live in these areas, so these areas attract more high open people to them.
- **Self-Selection:** I tend to get along better with high conscientious friends because they show up on time and are easier to plan with. In this way, I self-select my friends and favor certain personality types. You, your boss, and your friends might have similar personality types because that helps you get along and understand each other. Don't be surprised if the important people in your life have similar matrices.
- **Workplace Culture:** When I was giving a presentation at Intel, an audience participant noted that Intel attracts and hires people with similar personality traits—typically high conscientious introverts. Certain corporations can attract a specific mix of personality types. A creative agency might hire high open, high extrovert *Mad Men* types, whereas a highly technical boss might hire and retain highly conscientious and highly agreeable employees. Your workplace might have people with similar matrices because they have either been hired by the same person or your corporate culture attracts a certain kind of individual.

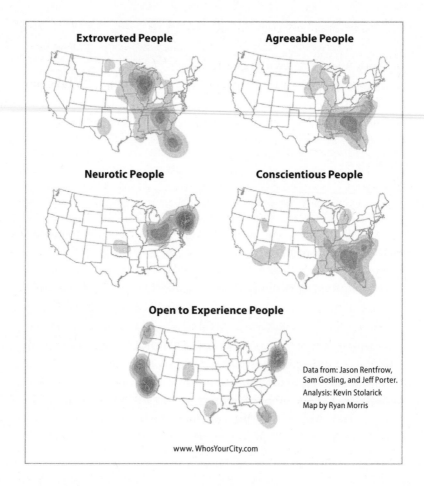

Data from: Jason Rentfrow,
Sam Gosling, and Jeff Porter.
Analysis: Kevin Stolarick
Map by Ryan Morris

www. WhosYourCity.com

Deciphering matrices is an enjoyable process. In the words of Richard Nicolosi, "I discovered that my real love was not marketing, but getting a visceral sense of who people are and what they want and why. It became my passion to get into other people's mind-set." Now it's time for you to hack into other people's mind-sets to help them—and you—succeed.

CHALLENGES

1. Take the official personality test at our website to make sure your matrix is accurate. Get it at www.ScienceofPeople.com/toolbox.

2. Fill in any blank columns in your speed-reading challenge by getting together with the people in your life and asking purposeful (and sparking) questions.

3. **Bonus:** Have your partner, best friend, and parents take our official personality test *as you.* Yes, I want you to test your self-perception by having the people who know you best rank you, too.

CHAPTER REVIEW

The matrix is my most powerful tool. First, honestly examine your own personality. Then learn to decode others' personalities by asking the right questions and observing their behaviors. Lastly, make sure you optimize or compromise for differences.

- Don't impose your personality traits on others.
- Learn to speed-read each of the Big Five personality traits.
- Endeavor to combine your personalities so they work with each other not against each other.

My biggest takeaway in this chapter is: _____

CHAPTER 8

APPRECIATE

How to get the best from people

Every time I see Paige Hendrix Buckner, she pulls a present for me out of her pocket or purse. Sometimes it's herbs from her garden that she's wrapped lovingly in a damp paper towel. Sometimes it's my favorite kind of candy. Basically, she's a younger, spunkier version of my grandma. She has a special talent for finding the perfect gift for each person she meets.

A few years ago, she started capitalizing on her talent for gift giving. Local businesspeople told her they wanted to one-up the generic fruit basket when they sent presents to clients, employees, and business partners. Luckily, there is no better place than Paige's home state of Oregon to find talented local artisans. This became her unique angle—working solely with the best Oregon products she could find and packaging them in distinctive handmade boxes with catchy themes. She named her company ClientJoy.

In her Night on the Town box, she has Masala Spiced Popcorn, The Bitter Housewife's cardamom bitters, Raft Lemon Ginger Syrup, flake salt by Jacobsen Salt Co., and hazelnuts by Albina City Nuts.

In her Sweet and Spicy box, she has local honey from Bee Local, Tracy's Small-Batch Granola, Marshall's Gin Roasted Pepper Haute Sauce, and Olympia Provisions Pepperettes jerky.

Following her passion had its challenges, but she has kept it alive by modeling on the side to pay for groceries and rent. (Paige is the stunning raven-haired model in many of the microexpression photos in this book!) Luckily, in the spring of 2014 Paige got her big break. ClientJoy boxes found their way into the hands of some serious influencers at TEDxPortland. "Speakers were blown away with authentically custom gift boxes filled with love and creativity," said the executive producer of the event, David Rae.

The word got out. Now ClientJoy boxes are being sent to companies around the country, from the Dallas Cowboys to Twitter to *Time* magazine—everyone is getting a taste of Oregon.

What has driven Paige's success? ClientJoy makes curated gifts that don't feel obligatory. "For me, gifting is about showing gratitude. It's about making an easier way to give appreciation to someone. I think appreciation is one of the most powerful tools we have," said Paige.

ClientJoy taps into a deep human need—the desire to be genuinely appreciated.

> *According to the U.S. Department of Labor, the number-one reason people leave their jobs is because they "do not feel appreciated."*
>
> —Tom Rath

THE PSYCHOLOGY OF APPRECIATION

My dad's birthday is November 4. This means that every August while growing up, I began the painstaking process of coming up with a spectacular gift idea.

One year, I hand knit him a tie from yarn that I spun myself. Another year, I made an exact replica of his office in miniature using matchsticks, jewelry boxes, and buttons. Another year, I gave him a painting of a watermelon (his favorite food) covered in over 2,000 sequins (placed by hand one at a time). One year, I gave him a book of over thirty personalized coupons for things I knew he enjoyed, like hugs, Coffee Bean lattes, and Lakers games.

At his birthday dinner, I would place my latest contraption in front of my dad and wait expectantly. Every year, he had about the same reaction: "Oh," he would say cautiously. He would poke it, lift it up, and turn it around a few times. "I love it." But he said this with the kind of voice tone reserved for telling a small child her imaginary friend had died or that the Christmas tree was infested with aphids. And then, a few weeks later, my loving creation would be moved to the attic. And eventually, I suspect, it was secretly placed in the alley garbage cans.

Year after year, no matter how hard I tried, I missed the mark on my dad's gifts. Then one fall, I got mono (don't ask). That year on November 4, I dragged my sick, lymph-swollen, pale body to the couch and told my dad, "This year for your birthday I only have the energy to watch Sunday football with you. I hope that's okay."

For the next four hours, we ate cheesy pretzels and chatted about team mascots. I finally learned how the whole yardage thing works. Sitting down to his birthday dinner, my dad clapped me on the back and said it was the best present I had ever given him.

What the what? I watched a few football games and ate junk food—how could that have possibly been better than his own personalized scented candle collection? What I learned that day is that everyone has different ways of showing and feeling love.

Dr. Gary Chapman has been helping couples as a marriage and family therapist for over fifty years. During the scope of his career, he began to notice patterns in the way couples showed (or didn't show) affection toward each other. He found that there were five different ways people tended to express love—what he calls the 5 Love Languages. If you haven't heard of these before, here's the quick and dirty summary:[1]

1. **Words of Affirmation:** People with this love language express their care through spoken or written word—love letters, texts, and verbal expressions of love.
2. **Gifts:** People with this love language express their care through small gifts or tokens of appreciation—jewelry, candy, or flowers.
3. **Physical Touch:** People with this love language express their care through touch—hugs, cuddles, pats on the back, loving embraces.
4. **Acts of Service:** People with this love language express their care by doing things for others—cooking their spouse dinner, running errands, or crafting something for them. (If you couldn't tell from the story about my dad, this is mine.)
5. **Quality Time:** People with this love language express their care with their time. They want to simply be in the presence of the people they care about.

Dr. Chapman argues that most relationship difficulties arise when we're speaking different languages. For example, if a wife's love language is Words of Affirmation, she lights up when her husband tells her he misses her. However, her husband's love language is Physical Touch, so when he gets home from work, he doesn't want to talk, he just wants to snuggle with her on the couch. When she pulls away, he feels hurt, and when he doesn't ask about her day, she feels stung. Over time, this eats away at the couple.

Dr. Chapman worked with fellow psychologist Dr. Paul White to adapt the love languages for the professional environment. Their collaboration produced the five "appreciation languages." Behavior hackers, take note.

JUST SAYING THANKS ISN'T ENOUGH

Feeling underappreciated eats away at employees who shoulder hard projects on their own, moms who aren't thanked for cleaning up after kids, and friends who feel like they always end up hosting.

Lack of appreciation is an especially pernicious problem in the workplace—and it's often overlooked. In fact, 65 percent of Americans say they received no recognition in the workplace in the last year.[2]

When you ask managers why most employees leave their jobs, 88 percent of them believe **money** is at the root of most job turnover.[3] In fact, only 12 percent of employees leave for financial reasons. The other 88 percent boils down to job satisfaction.

What makes someone love their job? That question is not so simple, but the Society for Human Resource Management feels that job satisfaction boils down to **employee recognition and engagement**.[4] However, one recent Gallup study found that almost **70 percent of US employees say they receive no praise or recognition in the workplace**.[5]

When we feel underappreciated we:

- Are less productive
- Have a harder time working on teams
- Are less motivated
- Feel more discouraged
- Complain more
- Have lower life satisfaction
- Have lower job satisfaction

Appreciation is essential for a happy life, happy relationships, and a happy workplace. But it's not that simple. As Dr. Chapman discovered, we each express and feel appreciation in different ways.

While filming my Master Your People Skills course, I had our studio audience members write love letters to someone important to them. As always with most of my activities, there was a catch. I told the students they had to write the letter with their nondominant hand. In a matter of minutes, all of the students were moaning of hand cramps and their letters were barely legible. **Asking someone to use their nonnatural appreciation language is like asking someone to write with their nondominant hand—it's difficult, sloppy, and frequently causes misunderstandings.**

Until you learn how to hack the appreciation languages.

> *Next to physical survival, the greatest need of a human being is psychological survival—to be understood, to be affirmed, to be validated, to be appreciated.*
>
> —Stephen Covey

HACK #8: THE APPRECIATION MATRIX

After a few years of using the matrix for personality traits, I found there was something missing. Solving someone's five personality traits could only get me so far. I definitely could better understand and predict behavior, and casual conversations were easier, but it didn't help with some of the deeper parts of connection.

When I found Dr. Chapman and Dr. White's five appreciation languages, it clicked. The matrix isn't a key to accessing a single piece of information; it is more like an onion. Each layer you uncover about someone reveals something new about how they operate.

The first layer, as we already learned, is how someone falls on each of the five personality traits. The second layer is how someone expresses appreciation, and how they feel it.

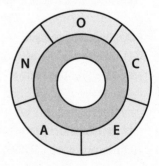

#1: You

Dr. Chapman found that most people have a primary and a secondary appreciation language. Before I give you the official quiz, think about your answers to these questions:

- Let's pretend your best friend just got a big promotion at work. How would you celebrate them?
- When did someone last surprise you with how much they care? What did they do for you?
- What was the best birthday celebration, gift, or experience you have ever had?
- What's one thing you wish your partner did more of? Less of?
- If you had $1,000 to spend on a treat for yourself, what would you do with it?

Do you notice any patterns? Since our appreciation language stays with us, it often plays out in all of our relationships throughout our life—with parents, colleagues, friends, and partners.

Now let's take the quiz based on Dr. Chapman's research.[6] Use the following statements to decipher your appreciation language:

For each pair of statements, check the **ONE** answer that fits best with your relationships (partner, family, friends, colleagues).

1. I like to receive encouraging notes. ____
2. I like to be hugged. ____

3. I like to spend one-on-one time with close friends. ____
4. I feel cared for when a friend helps me out. ____

5. I like it when people give me gifts. ____
6. Compliments are important to me. ____

7. I feel appreciated when someone I care for puts his or her arm around me. ____
8. I feel close to someone when we are doing an activity together. __

9. I feel appreciated when a colleague offers to help me with a job or project. ____
10. I appreciate it when someone remembers special days with a gift. ____

Answer Key:
Words of Affirmation: 1 and 6
Physical Touch: 2 and 7
Quality Time: 3 and 8
Acts of Service: 4 and 9
Gifts: 5 and 10
Your primary appreciation is: _____
Your secondary appreciation is: _____

You can write these into your matrix along with your personality rankings. I like to put the primary language on the top part of the circle and the secondary language on the bottom half.

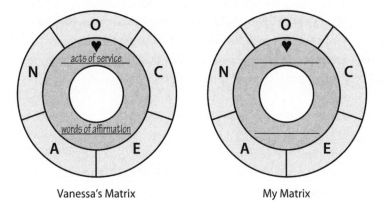

Vanessa's Matrix   My Matrix

This information is not to be taken lightly. It has a huge impact on your overall happiness. When you know your appreciation language, you are able to:

- **Know What to Ask For:** Your partner cannot read your mind. Neither can your boss, your friends, or your colleagues. Understanding your love language can help you know what to ask for when you need support. If your language is Words of Affirmation, you can ask your boss for more verbal feedback and plan catch-up meetings at the end of long weeks. If your language is Quality Time, you know that long-distance relationships or working virtually might not be a good choice for you. Set the people in your life up for success by telling them how you best feel appreciated by them.

- **Understand What's Missing:** Whenever I teach the appreciation languages, the majority of my students have some kind of relationship aha moment. They realize that a fight they have been having with someone in their life has been caused by a difference in appreciation languages. For example, one of my students, Leila, whose primary appreciation language is Acts of Service, is constantly hosting her girlfriend for martini nights, cooking clubs, and brunches. Leila feels like she is the only one who ever does anything and has been feeling bad about the friendship. However, after this lesson, Leila realized her friend's language is Words of Affirmation and always writes her long thank-you text messages and gushes about how much she loves these get-togethers. While this expression of appreciation doesn't mean as much to Leila, she now knows what to ask for and where her friend is coming from.

When you pair your appreciation language with your personality rankings, you'll have doubly powerful insights. For example, if you are low open and your primary appreciation language is Quality Time, you would be better off asking a colleague to a monthly coffee date at your favorite place. If you are high open with Quality Time, you might ask your colleague to try a new coffee place once a month. **When you get to know yourself, you know what makes you happy, what to ask for, and how to have smooth interactions.**

#2: Them

Now comes the fun part! I love to guess other people's appreciation languages. It helps me understand how to make them happy and gauge what our relationship will be like.

As with personality rankings, I always prefer a direct approach like this:

- **As a Conversation Starter:** "Have you ever heard about the 5 Love Languages? I'm reading this book about it and was curious if you had heard of them." Then you can get into a great conversation about which they think they are. I love to try to guess my friends' and colleagues' and have them guess mine.
- **Quiz:** We have a free appreciation language quiz on our website that you can send to a partner or friend and ask to share results. Find this at www.ScienceofPeople.com/toolbox.

If you don't feel comfortable with the direct approach, you can use behavioral evidence to decode someone's appreciation language.

What They Do For You

The easiest way to know how someone likes to be treated is to see how they treat their favorite people.

- Do they love to come around your office and hang out together? (Quality Time)
- Are they leaving little notes all over the house for you? (Words of Affirmation)
- Do they touch your arm during conversations and hug instead of shaking hands? (Physical Touch)
- Do they volunteer to make your favorite dessert for your birthday instead of ordering something premade? (Acts of Service)
- Do they bring little trinkets home from their travels to give you? (Gifts)

Discussion Questions

Another decoding method is to ask about old memories, favorite stories, and recent experiences. These are some of my go-to questions:

- What's the nicest thing someone has ever done for you?
- How do you celebrate your successes?
- I really want to do something nice for our colleague who just had a new baby. What do you think we should do for them?
- What's your favorite thing to do on the weekends?
- What's the most interesting gift you have ever received? Given?
- What's your favorite activity to do with your friends?
- Growing up, what did your parents do to celebrate your birthdays or your successes?

These questions can be surprisingly revealing. If you ask a non-gift-giver about the best gift they have ever given, they might tell you about something they *did* for someone else or a letter they *wrote* to someone else.

I recently asked one of my friends this question. He said the best gift he ever gave was writing his grandmother's life story in a handmade book for her. I instantly guessed his primary and secondary appreciation languages—Words of Affirmation and Acts of Service. He was a great sport and agreed to confirm my guesses with my online quiz. Sure enough, those were his two.

Decoding Microexpressions
Microexpressions can greatly help you in uncovering appreciation languages.

- **Anger:** Getting the wrong form of appreciation can be tiring or downright aggravating. For example, an employee who enjoys gifts might be disappointed at a grand office party thrown in his honor. Why? He didn't want to burden his colleagues with a party. He would have been way happier with a gift card or that new snowboard he has been talking about.
- **Happiness:** A genuine happiness microexpression clues you in when you've truly delighted someone—whether they really like your idea, gift, or praise, or if you're not speaking their appreciation language.
- **Contempt:** Contempt is a clue that someone feels disconnected from your method of appreciation. For example, someone who doesn't like physical touch might betray a half smirk when you try to hug them.
- **Disgust:** Remember that disgust is the microexpression we show when we are trying to think of a polite way to say we don't like something. Get someone a gift they don't like or suggest a quality time experience that they are not into, and they will flash disgust before they answer.

Spotting these microexpressions is only half the battle—how you respond is just as important. How can you use appreciation languages to get on the same page? That's step #3.

#3: Us
Dr. John Gottman and Dr. Robert Levenson were looking for patterns in relationship happiness when they interviewed couples about their personal histories, arguments, and family life.[7]

At the end of these interviews, Dr. Levenson went back over the transcript to see which pronouns each couple favored. **He found that the couples who used more "I, me, mine" had lower rates of relationship happiness and satisfaction than the couples who used more "we, our, us."**[8]

Dr. Gottman calls this pattern the we-ness versus me-ness mentality split. "Couples with a high degree of 'we-ness' emphasized their ability to communicate well with each other. They also emphasized unity and togetherness as well as having the same beliefs, values, and goals in life." On the other side of the spectrum, couples who used more "me," "I," and "my" in their responses had self-oriented goals and long-term ideals. Not surprisingly, these couples were less happy in their marriages.[9]

While Gottman and Levenson were focused on romantic relationships, the same principle applies to all of our relationships. This is where the Appreciation Language hack can really help you level up. When you know the appreciation languages of people in your life, you switch into the "we-ness" mentality. You begin to think about how your needs are being met *and* how you can best meet theirs.

Below are some ideas for how you might honor different appreciation languages in small ways that feel natural. For each language, write the name of someone in your life you suspect speaks it dominantly.

Words of Affirmation

Professional:
- Write check-in e-mails
- Create positive feedback reports
- Do daily or weekly check-in meetings
- Offer to write recommendation letters
- Give public praise

Romantic:
- Send supportive texts
- Leave love notes
- Do catch-up time before bed
- Go phone-free during meals so you are not interrupted

Example Person: _____

Gifts

Professional:
- Birthday gifts
- Holiday gifts
- Desk trinkets
- Thank-you gifts
- Gift baskets or boxes

Romantic:
- Birthday/anniversary gifts
- Flowers
- Travel souvenirs
- "Thinking of you" tokens

Example Person: _____
Note: Holidays are a great excuse to celebrate people with this language

Acts of Service

Professional:
- Helping with task completion
- Party planning
- Organizing or joining a project

Romantic:
- Honey-do List
- Cleaning
- Completing errands or chores
- Cooking or making something

Example Person: _____

Physical Touch

Professional:
- Handshakes

- Arm pats
- High fives

Romantic:
- Holding hands
- Cuddling
- Bow-chic-a-wow-wow
- Massages

Example Person: _____

Quality Time

Professional:
- Lunches or drinks
- Coming in early or staying late
- Weekly check-in times

Romantic:
- Phone-free time
- Weekly dates
- Trips
- Car rides

Example Person: _____

There is one thing I want to mention about physical touch in the workplace: **Proceed with caution.**

From a nonverbal perspective, touch is wonderful for rapport, but you have to make sure you are keeping it appropriate. A good rule of thumb is to know that the farther up the arm you go, the more intimate the touch becomes. And the head and trunk are considered intimate zones.

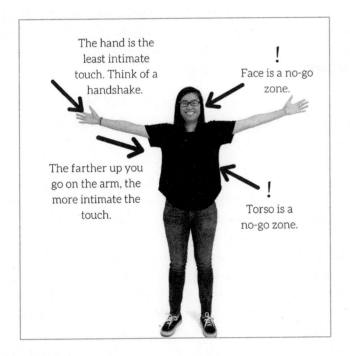

The hand is the least intimate touch. Think of a handshake.

Face is a no-go zone.

The farther up you go on the arm, the more intimate the touch.

Torso is a no-go zone.

Zone One Touch

- Handshakes
- Fist bumps
- High fives

Zone Two Touch

- Back-of-the-hand tap
- Forearm touch
- Shoulder touch

Zone Three Touch

- Hug
- Back pat
- Arm over the shoulder

Hopefully it goes without saying that with physical touch, it is important to follow your workplace etiquette. If you are unsure if your touch is welcome, pay attention to microexpressions as you move through the zones. For example, start with a handshake and see if you get a genuine smile. Next time you meet, give a handshake and a shoulder touch—still smiling? Notice any contempt or anger? Finally, you can try the hug if you feel comfortable and they don't show any negative facial gestures.

BONUS: DON'T BE BORING

Hey! I brought you a pen from my trip to Niagara Falls. We should hang out some time. Honey, I did the laundry.

These are all nice, but they are also boring, predictable, and expected. In Hack #3: Conversational Sparks, I talked about escaping the average and creating dopamine with the unexpected. I want to challenge you to do the same for the Appreciation Language hack.

- Don't get Gifters standard presents—get them something personally meaningful. Leslie Knope, the beloved blond *Parks and Recreation* character played by Amy Poehler, installed an automatic door closer for her boss Ron and creates "Galentine" gifts for each of her female friends every Valentine's Day.
- Don't invite Quality Time people to do boring activities. Forget coffee—ask them to go on a hike or to a grilled cheese shop. My friend Stephen Scott is a triathlete, and he asks people to go on walks or runs in lieu of the typical lunch.
- Have a physical touch partner or friend? Learn how to give massages or do reflexology. Samantha Hess is a professional cuddler who has created an entire business around the physical touch love language. She has created over seventy-one cuddle positions and claims to be a master cuddler—yes, really. In the name of research, I even booked a session with her and filmed it for my YouTube channel—it ended up being both awkward and informative, to say the least! (Watch the full video at www.Scienceof People.com/toolbox.)
- You can always write a thank-you note, but can you jazz it up a little? On NBC's *The Office*, Jim Halpert draws the name of his not-so-secret crush, Pam Beesly, in Secret Santa. He writes down all of their favorite memories and inside jokes and puts them in a teapot. Well played.
- I have an Acts of Service friend who constantly overworks herself. So I send her funny videos to watch during lunch and make her

custom playlists on Spotify to listen to while she drives. Last time she was sick, I made her a little care package with my special vegetable juice blend (the only thing that cures a cold), cough drops, and chicken noodle soup.

THE APPRECIATION LANGUAGE CHALLENGE

How can you better appreciate the people in your life? Fill out the chart below:

	Primary	Secondary	What's one thing they would appreciate if you did more of?
Your Riser			
Your Best Friend			
Your Partner (or a previous partner)			
Your Boss (or a previous boss)			
Your Colleague			
Your Parents			

The bonus part of this challenge is to ask one of the most powerful questions for any relationship:

What is one way I can show you more appreciation?

This is the question that consumes Paige on a daily basis. As she builds ClientJoy boxes and handwrites thank-you notes (to cover those who also love Words of Affirmation), she remembers certain presents that rocked her world as a child. When her dad returned to their home in rural southwest Missouri after work trips, he'd bring her and her five siblings bizarre gifts, like XXL T-shirts from a canceled Disney show. "It didn't matter. We were thrilled to get something," she told me.

Now, as an adult, she sees a grander meaning behind gifting: "I hope that with each gift box people feel that someone, somewhere really cares about them, whatever the reason is. Gifting is about appreciation. And appreciation is how we build real connection."

CHALLENGES

1. Fill in any gaps in your Appreciation Language Challenge chart.
2. Do three appreciative acts for three people in your life.
3. **Bonus:** Ask for more of what *you* need from the people in your life based on your appreciation language.

CHAPTER REVIEW

Appreciation is the key to life and job satisfaction. We can hack connection by using the five appreciation languages. Know what you need, learn what the people around you need, and find ways to show them you care.

- Learn and stand up for your primary and secondary appreciation languages.
- Use the second level of the matrix to decode appreciation languages of the people you meet.
- Honor and engage the appreciation languages of the important people in your life.

My biggest takeaway in this chapter is: _____

CHAPTER 9

VALUE

How to get along with anyone

Boyd Varty and his family own and operate Londolozi, one of the best luxury safari camps in South Africa, perennially ranked as one of the top one hundred hotels in the world. His guests have high expectations. Some expect the height of extravagance in the middle of the wild African bush. Some want to see the full cornucopia of wildlife Londolozi has to offer. Varty's challenge is to understand his guest's idea of a perfect vacation, and deliver it seamlessly. The only problem? Londolozi is located in one of the most dangerous and inhospitable private game reserves in South Africa.

"I've also discovered that people have more phobias than you would ever imagine: buffaloes, worms, feathers, spiders, insects, loud noises, skulls, teeth, dung—any or all of which are very likely encountered on a game drive," Varty wrote in his book *Cathedral of the Wild*.[1]

Over breakfast Varty told me about one particular guest that called on all of his experience.[2] Martin, an elderly British gentleman, had previously been on safari more than a dozen times in exotic locations around the world. He told Varty he had saved the best for last, and that this would be his final safari. Wanting to live up to the expectations of a safari aficionado, Varty decided he would personally take Martin on his game tour to ensure everything went according to plan. Unfortunately, Varty and Martin would both encounter an unpleasant surprise.

On the second day of cruising around in an open-air Land Rover, Varty spotted some leopard tracks. He departed the vehicle on foot to investigate, leaving Martin in the safety of the vehicle until he returned.

Martin hadn't been alone for long when a huge male bull elephant came trotting out of the brush to inspect the vehicle—and Martin.

Martin hoped the elephant would get bored and walk away so he remained as still and silent as possible. All of a sudden the two-way radio installed in the roofless Land Rover started crackling with traffic between other drivers on the property. The elephant became rattled and then agitated as the radio continued to blare. Soon the elephant began pounding his trunk on the hood of the Rover and started spraying it with dirt.

Eventually the elephant stalked away, but when Varty returned he found Martin white-knuckled, ashen faced, and furious that he had been left to fend for himself in the face of a house-sized pachyderm. Martin bellowed from the back of the truck, "I'm very angry with you! Take me back to the camp!"

For the next two days, Martin refused to talk to Varty—but insisted on completing his last few game drives. "I tried everything I could to win him back over the next couple of days, but he would have none of it," said Varty.

Then Varty had a fresh idea. Martin thought of himself as an adventurer. What if Varty could redefine his experience as a feat of daring? Calling in some favors, Varty asked all of the ladies in the camp to go up to Martin and congratulate him on being brave enough to stare down that big bull elephant all on his own. Bingo!

"In no time Martin began to feel like he was the main man, even to the point where he began to expound on the story to any person who walked past the bar. By the time he left Londolozi, he felt like the king of Africa," said Varty. Martin told Varty at the end of the trip that his elephant encounter would be his greatest memory.[3*]

Varty's genius move was to tap into Martin's ideals. I call this finding someone's primary value.

THE SCIENCE OF VALUE EXCHANGE

In Africa, I learned that animals give and take what they need to survive. Humans are not so different.

---

* See videos from Londolozi in your Digital Bonuses at www.ScienceofPeople.com/toolbox.

Social psychologist Dr. Uriel G. Foa discovered the resource theory of human relationships.[4] **He argues that all interactions are actually transactions.** That people cooperate simply to give and take resources from each other. "A resource is defined as anything that can be transmitted from one person to another."[5]

Special Note: When I talk about "transactions" here, I'm not insinuating that all intimate relationships are actually cold and businesslike. Many transactions are aimed toward finding people who truly fulfill us and building relationships that are mutually beneficial.

Resources include physical items like money and food as well as emotional resources like love, advice, and status. As humans, we need both kinds of resources to survive and thrive.[6] Foa and his research team proposed that each of us have a hierarchy of six needs that originate in our childhood. If these needs are met, we are able to grow up, gain independence, and feel secure in our surroundings and relationships:

Resource	Meaning	Give	Take
Love	Affection, acceptance, and likability		
Service	Support, care, and warmth to provide comfort		
Status	Responsibility, praise, and titles to evoke pride		
Money	Coin, currency, or tokens that have been assigned value		
Goods	Tangible products, objects, or materials		
Information	Advice, ideas, opinions, and teaching		

In the Give column, put a check mark next to the resources you think you give frequently. In the Take column, put a check mark next to the resources you think you take frequently.

We both *give* each of these resources and *take* them during interactions. For example, we might buy a friend lunch to ask for their advice (giving Money and taking Information). Or we might give a colleague praise after they help us finish a project on time (giving Status and taking Service).

We need all six of these resources, but we typically take what we need more of and give what we have in abundance. Looking at your selections, is this true for you?

Occasionally, especially with the nonphysical resources like Love, Service, and Information, **we give what we most want**. We might crave Love, so we give it to everyone around us—even if they don't deserve it. Or we might desire to be in the know, so we gossip in hopes of people telling us more. Does this ring true for you?

This exchange of resources is a core dynamic of every relationship. Misunderstandings here can cause needless tension, even breakups. Here's why:

- **Power:** Foa argues that power can be measured as the amount of resources you have to give others. Having a lot of Money is obviously an element of power, but having a lot of Love to give others is also an element of power.
- **Needs:** We can use resource theory to better meet people's needs. If you need to motivate a colleague, for example, you'd best consider whether they value Information—learning, applying new job skills, and maybe even insider knowledge—or Status—getting respect, a high title, and esteem from peers—or whether they're just in it for the Money—a higher salary, bonuses, and financial incentives.
- **Security:** Relationships become more difficult when there's consistently an unequal exchange of resources. Anxiety, guilt, and resentment bubble up. We all know a romantic relationship is doomed when one person gives more Love and begins to feel resentful. Meanwhile, the person doing all the taking might feel smothered. You can even understand workplace tensions in these terms: When a factory foreman gives the resource of Money to her employees, she expects employees to give back the Goods they make in the factory. If the boss doesn't pay enough, employees get angry. If employees don't produce enough, the foreman gets angry.

Whether we are in personal or professional environments, establishing equilibrium in our relationships is essential. However, other people's resource needs might not always be what you expect.

FINDING VALUE

One day, a man was walking down the street with his eight-year-old daughter. They turned a corner and saw a little boy sitting next to a large wicker basket. He held a sign that said, "Puppies 4 Sale."

Before the man could stop his daughter, she ran up to the basket and clutched a tiny dog to her chest. "Oh dear, I'm in trouble," he thought.

He turned to the boy, "Son, how much does this puppy cost?"

"Well, sir, this puppy is the best, most adorable puppy in the entire world. He costs one thousand dollars," the little boy replied.

"One thousand dollars!" the man exclaimed. "That's crazy! Now, be reasonable and give me a better price and I'll buy this puppy from you."

"Sorry, sir, this puppy is the best in the world. It is one thousand dollars," the boy said.

The man haggled with the boy for another twenty minutes, but he wouldn't budge on the price. The man decided he would have a much better negotiating position if he came back without his daughter, who was crying hysterically.

The next day, the man returned without his daughter, and sure enough, the boy was still sitting with his wicker basket and a napping puppy inside. The man said, "Well, well, well, looks like no one has taken you up on your offer of one thousand dollars for that puppy. Now that you have had a day to think about it, can you cut me a better deal?"

"No, sir, the puppy is still one thousand dollars because it is the best puppy in the entire world," the boy said.

After another ten minutes of negotiations, the man left empty-handed. A few weeks later, the man saw the boy playing basketball with his friends on the local playground. He called over, "Hey, kid! Did you ever sell that puppy?"

The boy trotted over. "I sure did!" he said.

The man was surprised. "Really? Did you sell it for one thousand dollars?"

"Yes!" he replied. "A girl traded me two five-hundred-dollar kitties." [7]

This parable demonstrates that **value is in the eye of the beholder.**

We typically think of valuable assets in terms of their monetary value, but there are other, more subjective currencies. To the little boy, two five-hundred-dollar kitties were much more valuable than ten hundred-dollar bills. Which leads me to this simple and intuitive hack: When you know what drives someone, interactions become much easier.

Each of us is oriented toward one of the six categories of resources. I call this a primary value, and it is the last layer of the matrix.

HACK #9: Primary Value
The underlying motivation that drives a person's decisions, actions, and desires.

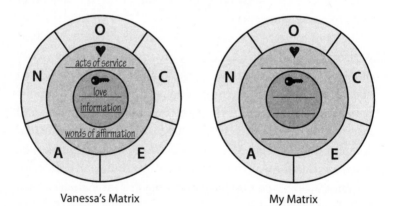

Vanessa's Matrix   My Matrix

Level One: Do they rank high or low in the five personality traits?
Level Two: Which of the five appreciation languages do they speak?
Level Three: Which primary value language drives them?

When you can answer each of these questions, you have "unlocked" someone's cipher. I have one of these for every person in my life—and most of them have one for me as well. **These matrices are like Cliffs-Notes to relationships. They give you an instant, accurate snapshot of a person to guide your interactions.**

Now, let's learn how to solve the last level.

FINDING PRIMARY VALUES

A few years ago, I was conducting an experiment in our lab called Fifty Shades of Awkward. I was hoping to research where, why, and how awkwardness is caused in our social interactions.

The setup was simple. We recruited one hundred participants—fifty men and fifty women from all over the country and of varying ages—to keep "social diaries." For seven days, the participants jotted down brief summaries of their social interactions in a simple chart:

Event	+ = −	Description

We wanted the diaries to be done on the go, so they had only enough room for essential pieces of information. In the first column, participants entered a brief description of the event. We wanted to know if it was romantic, professional, familial, or social. The second column asked for a single symbol:

"+" means it was an overall good experience.

"=" means it was only ok.

"-" means it was an overall negative experience.

The final column, "Description," recorded the feelings that popped up during interactions. A participant might write, "Fun! Met lots of people" or "Super awkward, didn't know anyone."

At the end of the seven days, our researchers coded the diaries for patterns. We were looking for syntax changes, feeling repetitions, and word usage after each type of event. We then compared these notes to each participant's Big Five personality traits.

It was quite easy to predict extroversion, agreeableness, conscientiousness, and neuroticism based on a participant's notes. Openness was the only pesky one we found harder to detect. But the most interesting part of this experiment was the discovery of people's primary values.

Until this experiment, my matrix had only two layers—personality and appreciation language. This research added the final layer. We noticed that each person's notes focused on one resource, whether to complain about its absence or to extol its presence. It was as if participants were looking to gain something from each of their social interactions. If they got it, it was a positive interaction. If they didn't get it, it was a negative interaction.

For example, here's a snippet from one of our participants, who we'll call Subject 57:

Event	+ = –	Description
Coffee meeting with colleague	+	Laughed until my face hurt. She is hilarious!
First date	–	Such a drag! He was so boring. Conversation was painful.
Leadership workshop	=	Interesting to do the team activities, but not sure how relevant the tips were.

Can you guess Subject 57's primary value? What is this person looking for in these interactions? Subject 57's primary value is Information. She wanted to be entertained, taught, and informed by her interactions.

Each of us wants all of the resources on some level, but we tend to have a primary choice. **All of us have a cherished need that we are looking to fill during interactions.**

#1: You

Have you ever played *Super Mario Bros.*? According to my nonscientific, completely personal, emotion-based fact-finding mission, this is the best video game of all time.

In it, Mario runs, flies, and leaps through the Mushroom Kingdom to rescue Princess Toadstool from the enemy known as Bowser. Mario has to collect coins, special bricks, and rare items throughout each level. Coins make him richer. Red and yellow Super Mushrooms make him bigger. Some secret bricks give him special powers. Fireballs protect him against enemies like Goombas and Koopa Troopa shells.

Imagine that you are Mario. What do you want to collect more of in your life? Do you want to feel richer? Bigger? Invincible? And the big question: Do you know what drives you?

- **Filling a Missing Need:** Foa and his team argue that we often try to seek from others what we have been denied earlier in life. For example, someone who didn't grow up in a loving household may seek Love, validation, and belonging from their friends and colleagues later in life. They might become people pleasers in their desperation to feel liked. Or someone who grew up short on Money might cut coupons and haggle over a few cents at garage sales even after they have plenty to pay the bills. It's hard to feel sated when the memory of resource deprivation is old and ingrained.
- **Finding What We Lack:** We also tend to seek out what we can't provide ourselves. If someone has low self-esteem, they are more likely to seek the Status resource from others. We all know someone who incessantly posts selfies on social media. They need likes, comments, and shares to feel good about themselves.
- **Giving Us Purpose:** Researcher Dan P. McAdams at Northwestern University studied our self-narratives—the stories we tell ourselves *about* ourselves. He found that knowing what we value can impart a sense of purpose on our life and work.[8] Hoarders might tell themselves that having a home full of Goods is absolutely necessary to having a secure, adult life. Nurses might tell themselves that taking care of others is part of their personal mission to give Service.

Value extraction and identification is hard work. It's a journey that people spend years on. This exercise will help get you thinking about the values that drive you. Go through the following statements and give each a numerical rating:

0 = This does not describe me at all.
1 = This describes me somewhat.
2 = This describes me well.

Resource	Meaning	Total
Love	___ It's important to me to feel accepted. ___ It's important to me to be liked by others. ___ It's important to me to feel like I belong.	
Service	___ It's important to feel the people in my life support me. ___ It makes me feel special when someone does a favor for me. ___ It's important to me to feel cared for.	
Status	___ It makes me feel great when someone praises me. ___ I like to be in charge. ___ It's important for me to feel respected by others.	
Money	___ It is important to me to be financial stable. ___ I do my job mostly for the money. ___ I think you have to have money to be completely happy.	
Goods	___ I like to collect things. ___ I often buy and give gifts. ___ I can think of many objects in my home that have emotional meaning.	
Information	___ I like to be in the know. ___ I like to give advice. ___ I enjoy teaching and learning.	

Add up each section and put the totals in the far right-hand side. Which one gets the highest number? This could be your primary (or possibly secondary) value.

The next exercise is designed to tell you if you have a different primary value for each area of your life—social, professional, and romantic. Go through the following prompts and put down the first answers that pop into your head. This is a free-flowing exercise to get you to tap into your values. There are no right or wrong answers:

Professional Primary Value:
- What gives you a sense of purpose at work?
- What do you hope to get from the work you do?
- During the workday, I feel most worthy when:

Your professional primary value might be: _____

Social Primary Value:
- What is your favorite thing about being with your closest friends?

- What would you add to your social interactions to make them even better?
- When I am with my closest friends, I feel most content when:

Your social primary value might be: _____

Romantic Primary Value:
- If you had to describe the best part of your relationship, what would it be?
- What is the greatest gift your partner could give you, tell you, or do for you?
- When you are with your partner, you feel most worthy when:

Your romantic primary value might be: _____

My professional primary value is Information. I'm constantly teaching and reading every book, blog, and study I can get my hands on. My social and romantic primary value is Love. I did not feel very liked or accepted growing up and never had a great group of friends in school. As an adult, I am incredibly lucky. I finally have a wonderfully supportive partner and loving friend group. But I still consistently try to give Love and take Love with these important people.

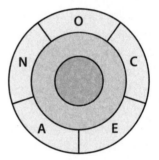

You can write your own answers in the middle of your now completed matrix along with your personality rankings and appreciation language.

There's a reason your value language belongs right at the heart of the matrix. Tapping into your values is one of the most powerful things you can know about yourself and the people around you. Why? **Knowing your primary value is the key to contentment.**

Want to know why you're in a funk? Your primary value isn't being met. Want to know why a relationship isn't working for you? It's probably a value misalignment. Want to understand why you made a poor choice? Your primary value was driving you in a different direction.

Many of my students say that decoding their own matrix was just as powerful as learning how to decode others'. **Our primary value is at the heart of who we are, the choices we make, and what drives us.**

#2: Them

Here's a nice, fat human behavior truth for you: **Most people's choices make sense to them.** When they don't make sense to you, it's usually because you are being driven by a different primary value.

Knowing primary value differences with the people in your life can help explain:

1. Why some people drive you absolutely crazy
2. Most relationship misunderstandings
3. Unpredictable choices and behavior from the people you care about

Do you need to motivate someone at work? Tap into what they value. Do you need to understand a partner's baffling choice? Figure out how it met their value needs. Want to know what gets someone up in the morning? Decode their primary value.

Killer social skills require seeing the world through someone's lens besides your own. **Appeal to someone by focusing on what they value, not what you value.**

Be warned: I think uncovering someone's value language is the most difficult layer of the matrix. I use three tactics:

1. **Complaints and Brags:** Does someone complain about not being paid enough at work? (Money) Not being recognized for an achievement? (Status) Not having a nice enough car? (Goods) Or do they brag about how they took care of a sick parent? (Service) How much the new boss likes them? (Love) How much they know about the new corporate partner? (Information) We're usually proud of obtaining our primary resource and upset about not having enough of it. This comes out in boasts, grumbles, and brags.
2. **Nonverbal Cues:** Body language can also help you figure out if you are tapping into or refusing someone's primary value. Think of our good friend Mario. When he gets a Fire Flower or Super Mushroom, he jumps into the air, gets bigger, or runs faster. But when he hits a Koopa shell or a Goomba, he shrinks or loses a life. It's the

same in real life (minus the overalls and mustache). When someone gets a primary value met, they are delighted! Watch for genuine happiness microexpressions, leans, nods, and winner body language. When someone does not get their primary value met, they show disgust, anger, contempt, or defeated body language.

3. **Behavioral Cues:** Once you start looking for it, someone's behavior can tell you a lot about needs they are trying to fill. Here is how this might look in the workplace:

   - Colleague A always stays late to suck up to the boss. You can tell they're constantly looking for praise or more responsibility. Their primary value might be Status.

   - Colleague B leaves promptly every day at five p.m., but always gets their projects done in time for the raise review. They are the first to ask about year-end bonuses. Their primary value might be Money.

   - Colleague C is an office butterfly, making friends with colleagues and leaving supportive notes on people's desks. Their primary value might be Love.

   - Colleague D always remembers people's birthdays, loves to plan office parties, and always organizes the corporate softball team. Their primary value might be Service.

   - Colleague E desperately wants the corner office and the best parking space in the lot. They love all the corporate perks and never forget to bring everyone souvenirs from vacations. Their primary value might be Goods.

   - Colleague F is a bit of an office gossip, so they always know what's going on behind the scenes. They also play golf with all the partners. Their primary value might be Information.

4. **Worries:** What keeps someone up at night? What do they stress out about? This can clue you into their primary value. Do you have a friend who is constantly moaning about feeling out of the loop? Her primary value might be Information. Do you have a colleague who freaks out over people's titles and is always stressing about who will get the next promotion? His primary value might be Status.

   - Listen to the kinds of things someone worries about.

   - Ask them what they worry about or the biggest worries in their life.

   - Match it with a primary value.

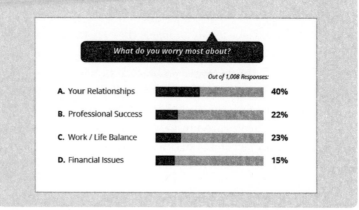

FAST FACT BOX

We asked over 1,000 participants what they worry about—the answers are very evenly distributed. Why? Our unique primary values inform our different kinds of worries.

What do you worry most about?

Out of 1,008 Responses:

A. Your Relationships   40%

B. Professional Success   22%

C. Work / Life Balance   23%

D. Financial Issues   15%

These can be hard to pick up on at first, but analyzing someone's past behavior can help point you in the right direction toward their primary value.

Special Note: I love the direct approach, but primary values are hard to talk about honestly. Most people who are driven by Money are ashamed to admit it—even though this is a legit and necessary resource. Others feel embarrassed to say that they need to be liked or please people. Be aware that what someone says about their value language might not match the way they actually behave.

#3: Us

Once you think you know someone's primary value language, what do you do with that information?

First, your predictions about their future behavior and choices will improve. This is extremely helpful when trying to decide how a colleague will perform on a new project or if someone would be a good potential romantic partner.

Second, you can use it to motivate the people in your life. Want to encourage your child to do more chores? More allowance might not be the best option. Want to impress your boss? Support their primary value, not yours, with the behavior *they* will appreciate. Want to incentivize your teammate to do better? Give more of what they value and take less of what matters most to them.

Lastly, you can adopt a primary value to help people feel worthy. I think the greatest gift we can give our fellow human beings is to meet their resource needs. If I can give someone more of their primary value, I always do.

> *No act of kindness, no matter how small, is ever wasted.*
>
> —Aesop

Here is a breakdown of each primary value and how it can be used to provide worth. "Example Person" is for someone in your life who you think might have that primary value.

Primary Value: Love

Feel Worthy When:
- They are included
- They feel liked
- Someone appreciates them

Example Person: _____

Primary Value: Service

Feel Worthy When:
- They don't have to ask for help
- Someone is assisting them with tasks or chores
- Someone does a favor for them

Example Person: _____

Primary Value: Status

Feel Worthy When:
- They are praised

- They are given power or credit
- Their accomplishments are recognized

Example Person: _____

Primary Value: Money

Feel Worthy When:
- They have a "full" bank account
- They can afford what they desire
- They are earning money

Example Person: _____

Primary Value: Goods

Feel Worthy When:
- They have a comfortable home or office
- They have lots of assets
- They are surrounded by tokens or objects from their past

Example Person: _____

Primary Value: Information

Feel Worthy When:
- They are in the know
- They are told information first
- They are asked to give an opinion

Example Person: _____

The best way to harness the power of primary values is to give the right resource right away. For example, one of my good friends, John Boylston, ran for state representative in Oregon. He reached out to a mutual friend of ours, Matthew Scott, about a campaign coordinator opening. (Thank you to both of them for letting me use this example.)

John wanted Matt's help, but was also hoping to make it a win-win interaction. I have a hunch John's professional primary value is Service. He needed help with coordinating his entire campaign—calling donors, making fliers, knocking on doors, and answering phones.

Before reaching out to Matt, John had to figure out Matt's primary value. Was Matt's primary value Money—would he want to get paid hourly? Was it Status? Did Matt want to be listed on his website and campaign materials? Was it Information? Would Matt want to get an insider's view into politics? After talking to a few friends in our circle, John found out that Matt had been wanting to get experience running a political campaign. Guessing that Matt's primary value was Information, here's how John reached out via e-mail (edited slightly for length):

Hi Matt,

I heard that you were thinking about getting more involved in politics and potentially helping out on a campaign, is that right?

If so, I think you would be an awesome fit for a project that I'm working on. This spring I am going to run for state representative for House District 26. When I run I will need a good campaign team around me. I have already gathered a team of professional consultants, fundraisers, a data manager, and compliance and accounting individuals. What I really need, though, is someone who can be director of voter contact and volunteer manager.

This is more than the entry-level volunteer position and I think it could be a chance for you to get inside a campaign and really see how campaigns work while also getting to make decisions, be creative, and do more than stuff envelopes (though we will have to pitch in on that stuff from time to time).

I would be able to guide you through this, and we have an awesome team coming together who will help as well. So, we will have tons of support for you, but I need someone who can be the engine for the campaign when it comes to making sure that we're actually talking with voters.

As I was setting up my team, you were the first person I thought of for this job and I think you would be awesome at it.

—John

Later, I learned that Matt was ecstatic to get this e-mail from John. It was exactly what he had been wanting. He replied right away:

> I'd absolutely love to help out in any way, shape, or form and this sounds like something that I'd be very interested in for sure. I believe my weekends and nights are usually fairly calm, with the exception of I'm out at a trade show, so those times would work great for me. Thank you so much for thinking of me for this position and I'd love to help out. When would be a good time for you to meet so we could talk through everything? Once again, thank you so much!

To put this in perspective, **Matt thanked John for asking him to work for free**. At first glance this seems counterintuitive, but if you know that Matt's primary value is Information, it makes sense. Matt wanted to know more about running a campaign and was happy to join for an insider's look. This e-mail was the start of a powerful working relationship because both men had their primary values being met.

Special Note: Some of my students have found the need to occasionally add a situational value. This is when someone's primary value is different in a specific situation. For example, you might know that a colleague's primary value is Money. However, you notice that projects where he takes the lead, he craves praise, recognition, and likes to claim credit: a situational value of Status.

The Hunt for the Heart

One of Boyd Varty's biggest challenges arrived when a king decided to visit Londolozi. "We've had our share of visiting celebrities, dignitaries, and politicians . . . but handling this royal entourage would require an unprecedented level of coordination," recalled Varty.[9]

Not only did major logistics have to be taken care of—like extending a small runway to accommodate royal jets—but Varty had to figure out what would make His Highness's experience special.

Luckily, Varty and his team got their clue right away—Goods seemed paramount to the king and his entourage. By talking to the king's staff, Varty learned that the princesses enjoyed shopping. "Our small gift shop had to be hugely overstocked so that the royal retinue of twenty women accompanying the king could discover fresh merchandise should they choose to shop once, twice, or three times a day."

The Varty team flew in the king's Clarins face wash, his favorite vibrating workout machine, and papaya hand lotion. By the day of the king's arrival, Londolozi had been totally customized to his primary value.

Aside from the natural beauty of their surroundings, this basic human insight is how Boyd Varty and his family have turned Londolozi into a world-renowned resort. Varty taps into primary values every day, with every person he meets—whether a safari guide, front desk concierge, or cook. He can quickly discern whether someone is on safari for the luxury experience (Service), the all-inclusive five-star dining (Goods), or a sense of oneness with nature (Love).

At the end of the day, Boyd is hunting for heart. He is searching for ways to bring meaning to the people who come to Londolozi. Your goal as a hacker is to do the same thing. Hunt for people's values, hunt to give them meaning, hunt for heart.

CHALLENGES

1. Think of the five most important people in your life. What are their primary values?
2. Identify your Riser's primary value. How can you better serve them?
3. **Bonus:** Do the primary value exercise with your partner or best friend. What do they think drives you?

CHAPTER REVIEW

Interactions are about transferring resources to each other. There are six categories of resources that we give and take with each other. We are driven by one main category, also known as your primary value. Each of us has a primary value that drives our behaviors, actions, and decisions. Hacking into someone's primary value is the final step to decoding them.

- Understand how you give and take resources.
- Know what your primary value is.
- Tap into the value layer of the matrix to know what drives people.

My biggest takeaway in this chapter is: _____

PART III

THE FIRST FIVE DAYS

How do you turn casual acquaintances into lifelong friends? How do you make it easier to have "the talk" and make it official with the person you are dating?

In Part I of this book you learned how to capture attention in the first five minutes. In Part II you figured out how to capture understanding by learning how to speed-read people's behavior and personality. In this final section you'll master the art of leveling up your relationships.

You already know how to make a killer first impression and analyze an inscrutable personality. Here's how to increase your influence—how to turn teammates into partners, clients into raving fans, and good friends into best friends.

CHAPTER 10

CONNECT

How to speak so people listen

On May 18, 1926, Aimee Semple McPherson went missing.

The day started off quite normally. McPherson and her secretary went for a swim near Venice Beach. Only a few minutes after diving into the water, McPherson disappeared. Searchers combed the nearby beaches. The city of Los Angeles went on high alert. Nothing.

Then something odd happened. All over the country, people began reporting sightings of McPherson—impossible sightings. Several would come in on the same day, thousands of miles apart. The police received ransom notes from a variety of sources.

No one could find McPherson, yet everyone could find her. And then, a month after her disappearance, McPherson emerged unharmed from the Mexican desert, claiming she had been kidnapped and held hostage in a shack.

The media was quick to point out that some aspects of McPherson's story did not add up. (How did she get to Mexico? Why was she unharmed? Who kidnapped her?) The public was enthralled. When she arrived in Los Angeles, over 30,000 people greeted her as a hero at the train station.

McPherson fanned the flames of fame and funneled her new followers into the Angelus Temple—a church that still runs in Los Angeles today. At one point, 10 percent of Los Angelenos were members at McPherson's temple.[1]

"And that's why I want to fake my own kidnapping and start a cult," said Nicol Paone. The comedian is standing on top of a double-decker bus outside the Angelus Temple, speaking to a rapt group of tourists. The Angelus Temple is only one of many bizarre and hilarious stops on Paone's alternative comedy show, *The Last Show I Do Before I Go on Medication*.[2]

The concept behind the tour is personal, telling of her life in Los Angeles—the breakups, the walks of shame, the drunken stumblings. At one point during the show, Paone pulls the giant bus up in front of her ex-girlfriend's house and leads the entire bus in singing a rendition of Adele's song "Hello" as loud as possible. "Occasionally my ex pops her head out of a window and sings with us . . . it depends on what kind of mood she is in," explained Paone.

In between stops, Paone ducks tree branches, gives quirky tidbits about Hollywood murders, and points out hidden hangouts. At a particularly long red light, Paone encourages riders to "Get out your phones, post a picture of me on your Instagram, and then hook me up with your most successful friend." After her fourteenth tour or so, she figured out which blocks to avoid and how to effectively catcall pedestrians.

Paone never imagined her tour would become a local Hollywood highlight, that she would have a waitlist for shows, or that she'd be approached by TV executives about turning her bus tour into a series. She'd originally assumed the show would be a onetime thing. "My life was failing. I had no money, no job, and my girlfriend and I had just broken up," she explained. So she turned comedy into her therapist, and used the bus as her exposure therapy.

Her very first show was a terrifying experience. "I basically screamed at everyone for an hour and a half and felt like throwing up every time we got to a new location."

But she forced herself to be honest. Stories of botched dates, relationship shenanigans, and ridiculous encounters poured out. "I was sharing my deepest secrets and shameful moments. It was both frightening and freeing," said Paone.[3]

The next day, while Paone was dealing with what she calls her "vulnerability hangover," people began to talk about the show, and especially about Paone's raw humor and openness. Since then, Paone has done over twenty live bus shows. Every single one sells out.

When Paone speaks, people not only listen—they beg to hear more. Paone accidentally stumbled upon the ultimate shortcut to connection. **She is a storyteller.**

Stories are a communal currency of humanity.
—Tahir Shah

THE SCIENCE OF STORIES

After a lifetime of failed business ideas, toymaker Ty Warner emptied his savings and mortgaged his home, convinced he had an idea worth betting it all on.

It was a radical twist on the sweet, fluffy stuffed animal he'd seen a million times.

He decided that his stuffed animals would come with a name, a birthday, and a story. There was Pinchers the Lobster, born June 19, 1993. He came with a story, too, and it went like this:

> This lobster loves to pinch
> Eating his food inch by inch
> Balancing carefully with his tail
> Moving forward slow as a snail!

And there was Chocolate the Moose and Squealer the Pig and Splash the Whale. Finally Ty Warner created something that flew off the shelves. Kids didn't want just one Beanie Baby—they wanted every single one. At its peak, Beanie Babies pulled in over $700 million in one year.[4]

Warner understood that we feel connected to someone (or something) when we hear their story.

- Stories give us a chance to say "me too," activating the similarity attraction effect.
- Stories create conversation sparks—they give us pleasure when we listen.
- Stories help bond storytellers to story listeners.

Researchers Greg Stephens, Lauren Silbert, and Uri Hasson wanted to know what happens in our brains as we listen to stories. They put participants in fMRI machines and recorded the brain activity of two people—one person sharing a story and one person listening to the story. What they saw was striking—the two brains began to "sync" up. As the speaker told a story, the listener's brain patterns began to match.[5]

Spanish researchers even found that reading words like "perfume" or "coffee" lights up our primary olfactory cortex, where we process smell. If you hear a story about a creamy crème brûlée, your brain pictures the crème brûlée, imagines the taste, and conjures up the sweet smell and smooth feeling on your tongue. Even though you do not have the crème brûlée in front of you, your brain responds as if you do. Imagining a sensory experience activates the same part of your brain as the real experience would. And when someone tells you a story, your brain acts as if you were present in the story. Researchers call this neural coupling. I call it connection hacking.

This cognitive mechanism makes stories the perfect shortcut to connection. Stories help us literally get on the same wavelength as the people we are with. They not only listen to what we are saying but also *experience* what we are saying. **Even simple stories rev up brain activity and sync us up with the people around us.**

> *The shortest distance between a human being and truth is a story.*
>
> —Anthony de Mello

STORY HACKER

Confession: You know those people who call you during dinner and ask for money? I used to be one. I was that person you hung up on. Yes, I used to be a telemarketer. Well, not quite a telemarketer, but close. To make extra money in college, I worked at the Emory Telefund. Every night for three years, I called Emory alumni and asked them to donate to their alma mater.

This was the worst and best job I ever had. It forced me to get out of my comfort zone, bond with people quickly, and become numb to the word "no." Most importantly, it taught me the ultimate connection hack: telling stories.

The first few weeks on the job were the hardest. On the first night, you sit down at a large bank of computers and plug your headset into an autodial system. As the call connects, you have five to seven seconds to speed-read the contact card that pops up on your screen and quickly memorize any relevant details about the caller. I typically aimed to recall their name, graduation year, and major. If you were lucky, you got four to five rings to memorize the data. And then:

"Hello?"
"Hi, Mr. Smith. I'm calling from the Emory University Telefund. I would like to ask you about making a donation—" *Click.*

A click wasn't as bad as some of the more expletive-filled alternatives. If you managed to keep someone on the line, you had to quickly, and in my case, awkwardly, ask for a small donation to the school. In my first two hundred calls, I was lucky to keep one, maybe two people on the line. Getting donations from those two people, well, let's just say, I wasn't earning my keep.

Finally, one night a manager took pity on my abysmal numbers and constant hang-ups. He came over, unplugged my headset, and said simply, "Do you love Emory?"

"Yes, of course! That's why I'm here trying to raise money for us."

"Okay, great," he said. "Why do you love Emory?"

This was easy: "Well, I love Emory because I think it has some of the best teachers in the country, it has an amazing community, and the campus is beautiful . . ."

"Stop," he interrupted me. "That's how I want you to approach these calls. You love Emory, these alumni love Emory. Just tell them stories about that."

My manager was right. It didn't matter that these alumni had graduated fifty years ago, or that we had different majors, or that we lived in different areas of the country. We had stories to share.

From that point on, I approached my calls with two goals. In the first part of the call, all I wanted to do was share a story about Emory—maybe about homecoming weekend, the new gym, or a fun professor prank on campus. I didn't realize it then, but this first story was **aligning** the alumni and me.

In the second part of the call, my goal was to get them to tell me a story. I wanted to hear about their time at Emory—what had changed, whether they had been back for a visit, or what their favorite moment at the school was. In the end, if they donated, great. If not, that was okay, too. My single goal was to hunt for stories.

Slowly, as my stories got better, my calls got better, too.

"Hello?"

"Hi, Mr. Smith, my name is Vanessa and I am a sophomore at Emory University. I was wondering if you had a few minutes to reminisce about Emory?"

"A sophomore, huh? How is our football team doing these days?"

"Great, sir, still undefeated." (Emory doesn't have a football team, so this is a campus-wide inside joke.) "Actually, this past weekend was homecoming, and we had a giant float made of Georgia peaches. Did you do that for homecoming back in 1978?"

"Oh goodness, let's see. I think we had a parade, but we had water balloons back in those days."

"No way! We would get in huge trouble if we had water balloons on campus today. You know how they are about the flower beds."

"Ha, yes, I remember how angry the gardeners got when we played soccer on the lawn! Well, what can I help you with, young lady?"

"Yes sir, I am calling from Emory Telefund. Last year you gave a very generous donation of one hundred dollars, and I was wondering if you would be willing to make a donation of $150. I can also mark it especially for the history department, since that was your major."

"You can do that? Well, that would be great. And please say hi to Mr. Talbott if he is still there."

Not only did the donations start rolling in, but I began to *love* my job. I learned about hidden nooks in the library, I got tips on how to game the housing lottery system, and I learned so much about my fellow alumni. Every week, I would save stories to tell on my calls and think of new ways to ask for stories. I became a story hunter and a story hacker. And now you can, too.

HACK #10: The Story Stack
Share, tell, and hunt for captivating stories to capture
imagination and attention.

Many of us instinctively understand the power of stories, but have trouble knowing how to use them in everyday life. I want to give you an easy way to swap, share, and hunt for stories. I call this your Story Stack.

STORY STACK

Computer programmers use "stacks" to organize the various components of a software system. For example, my website ScienceofPeople .com is hosted on WP Engine, runs on WordPress software, and uses Cloudflare as a content delivery network. This is the stack of tools that works together to create my website.

The easiest way to harness the power of stories is to have a Story Stack with your favorite anecdotes, narratives, and follow-up questions all in one place, ready to use. Here's how it works:

- **Trigger Topic:** You know how the same subjects tend to come up over and over again in conversations? I call these trigger topics. When chatting over drinks or meeting new people, we constantly hear about the weather, traffic, weekend plans, and latest TV shows. These are commonly talked about, safe, generic areas. These are the first level in your Story Stack. When you hear a trigger topic, you can use it as a launching pad to tell your stories. Take a look at the list below and add any topics that frequently come up in your conversations.
- **Sparking Stories:** We have stories about everything, but we very rarely stop to take stock of them. Sparking stories are those anecdotes that produce laughter, ahas, groans, and great follow-up conversation. Use the prompts below to hunt for at least one story for each trigger topic.
- **Boomerang:** After you are done telling a story, you always want to bring the conversation back around to the other person you are speaking with. They can then answer and send it back to you. I call this throwing a boomerang—at the end of your story, how can you tie the idea back to them? What question can you ask to hunt for their stories? How can you get them talking? Or how can you make them laugh?

Let me give you an example of how this works before you begin on your own Story Stack. Let's say I am at a business lunch and someone brings up the latest comedy special on HBO. Comedy is one of my trigger topics. I wait to see if there will be a lull in the conversation and then bring out a story from my stack. It goes something like this:

COLLEAGUE: I just finished the Aziz Ansari HBO special. So good.

ME: Yeah, I could spend a whole weekend watching comedy specials on Netflix. I used to watch Bill Maher all the time, but after I humiliated myself in front of him, I could never watch him the same way again.

COLLEAGUE: What?! What do you mean?

ME: One time, my husband and I were waiting in a crowded parking lot in West Hollywood after a movie. It was freezing and the attendant was taking forever to bring us our car. All of a sudden, I see this giant black SUV roll up into the lot, and the attendants wave it right to the front. My husband and I immediately start wondering out loud whose car it might be. We joked that the rims weren't cool enough to be a rapper and the license wasn't short enough to be a politician. Right as we began to riff on the leather seats, I turn to see Bill Maher standing there giving us death stares. Yes, it was his car and yes, he heard the whole exchange. It was so awkward!

COLLEAGUE: Oh no! That's so embarrassing! Did he laugh or was he serious?

ME: He didn't even crack a smile, so I felt really bad. Anyway, have you ever seen a celebrity in real life?

COLLEAGUE: Oh yeah! This one time . . .

I used a story to bond with my colleague and hack what could have been a predictably boring conversation. Then I threw a boomerang to get him telling me a story.

Now, it's your turn. Fill out the Story Stack below with as many trigger topics, sparking stories, and boomerangs as you can think of.

Remember: Your stories don't have to be originals. Heard a funny story at work? Add it to your stack. Read a funny anecdote in this book? Add it to your stack.

YOUR STORY STACK		
Trigger Topic	**Sparking Story**	**Boomerang**
Current Events Recent News A Shocking News Story		• What's one news story you will never forget, and where you were when you heard it? • Where were you when you found out?
Hometown Childhood Growing Up		• Do you miss your hometown or are you glad you escaped? • What's a funny memory you have growing up?
Names Forgetting Names Interesting Names Hard to Spell Names		• What's the history of your family name? • What's the most interesting name you have ever heard? • Do you like your name?
Jobs First Job Career Choices Dream Jobs		• What advice would you give a teenager entering into this kind of work? • What surprised you most about the job you are in? • Did something surprising happen to lead you to what you do now?
New Activities Travel Weekend Adventures		• What's on your bucket list? • Where do you take out-of-town guests when they come to visit you? • Tried any new activities recently? Did you love them or hate them?
Holidays Vacations Holiday Traditions		• Where are you going next on vacation? • Best vacation spot in the world? • What's the best or worst vacation you ever had?
Parties Birthdays Gifts		• Best party you've ever been to? • Best gift you ever received? • Best childhood party you ever had?
Summer Seasons Outdoors Camp		• Do you have big plans this summer or a story from last summer? • What does summer remind you of? • Did you go to camp?
Weather Storm Stories Extreme Weather		• Ever get caught in terrible or unexpected weather? • What's the worst sunburn you've ever had? • What's your favorite season?

YOUR STORY STACK		
Trigger Topic	**Sparking Story**	**Boomerang**
Traffic Commuting Driving Road Trips		• Do you listen to audiobooks on tape when you drive? • What's your favorite driving playlist or station? • What's your favorite podcast? • Do you have a long commute?
TV Shows Books Movies Classic Books / Films / Shows Documentaries		• What are you reading or watching right now? • What was the last thing you read or watched? • What's the most interesting documentary, book, or article you've ever seen? • What's your favorite character? • What actor would play you in a movie?
Celebrities Role Models Famous Stories Fascinating People		• Have you ever met a celebrity? • Have you heard any interesting real-life tidbits about celebrities? • If you could meet any celebrity, who would you meet? • Do you have a famous role model?
Events Conferences Music Festivals Parades Fairs		• Have you been to events like this before? • What's the craziest event you've ever been to? • Do you go to conferences? • Do you go to music festivals?

THE ART OF STORYTELLING

Having a great Story Stack isn't much good if you're not a great storyteller. Three simple elements differentiate an okay story from an awesome one:

- **Start with a Hook:** You have to grab attention from the start. A hook is a provocative question, stimulating statement, or open-ended idea to pique interest. I started my Bill Maher story with the hook, "I used to watch Bill Maher all the time, but after I humiliated myself in front of him, I could never watch him the same way again." Invariably, this hook gets people curious.

- **Champion a Struggle:** The best stories have at their center some kind of a struggle. A question, a problem to be solved, or a challenge to be overcome. In the Bill Maher story, the struggle was "Who's in the car?" Or think of it as creating suspense. Can you hint at something? Are you facing off against someone else? Is there a punch line on the way?
- **Utilize Provocative Words:** Remember how the brain's olfactory system lights up when it hears the words "perfume" and "coffee"? The more descriptive your story, the more your listeners' brains will light up. Spice up your story by adding expressive, interesting words.

You can use all three of these elements in under two minutes—and you *should* keep your story short. After three minutes you become a conversation hog.

Once you start using this model, it becomes easy to turn a boring anecdote into a laugh-worthy story. The author Susan Cain used this structure to get over 14 million views on her TED Talk on introversion.[6] She used the hook, struggle, and boomerang format to captivate her audience.

Hook: When I was nine years old, I went off to summer camp for the first time. And my mother packed me a suitcase full of books, which to me seemed like a perfectly natural thing to do. Because in my family, reading was the primary group activity.

Struggle: And this might sound antisocial to you, but for us it was really just a different way of being social. You have the animal warmth of your family sitting right next to you, but you are also free to go roaming around the adventureland inside your own mind. And I had this idea that camp was going to be just like this, but better.

Unique Words: I had a vision of ten girls sitting in a cabin cozily reading books in their matching nightgowns. But camp was more like a keg party without any alcohol. And on the very first day, our counselor gathered us all together and taught us a cheer that she said we'd be doing every day for the rest of the summer to instill camp spirit. And it went like this: "R-O-W-D-I-E, that's the way we spell rowdie. Rowdie, rowdie, let's get rowdie."

Boomerang: Yeah. So I couldn't figure out for the life of me why we were supposed to be so rowdy, or why we had to spell this word incorrectly.

Cain could have told this same story in a boring way by simply saying:

Even though many people see reading as antisocial, for me, it was a family activity. When I went to camp, it was incredibly hard to find my place.

Instead, she added elements to get people hooked to her struggle. And her boomerang was getting the audience to laugh—which is the best kind of boomerang in front of a large group.

Having trouble thinking about how to fit your own stories into this structure? No worries! I've got you covered. I created a fill-in-the-blank game for you to practice. The trigger topic here is "Commuting." Sound boring? No way, we are going to turn it into a mini-story using the formula above. Just fill in the blanks:

1. Hook: You want to know the most _____ I ever saw while driving?
2. Struggle: I was driving down the road and all of a sudden, I look over and see _____.
3. Unique Words: And it was so _____!
4. Boomerang: Have you ever seen someone do something _____ in their car?

Let's try this again with the trigger topic "Fascinating People." This one can be a bit longer. Think of a person you were very excited to meet—this can be anyone you were excited to meet at any time in your life.

- Hook: One time, _____ years ago, I encountered one of the coolest people I have ever met.
- Struggle: It might sound _____, but I had always wanted to meet _____ because _____. Beforehand, I was so _____. Finally, the moment came.

- Unique Words: And it was _____ ! What surprised me most about meeting them was _____. I'll never forget _____.

- Boomerang: Who is the coolest person you have ever met?

Practice this formula with the middle column "Sparking Story" in your Story Stack above. Go through your Story Stack and see if you can think of hooks and struggles for each anecdote.

Another fun way to hear casual stories in action is by watching sitcoms—this is how I learned to tell short, witty stories. Sitcom writers have to condense character-building stories into funny anecdotes. The TV sitcom *How I Met Your Mother* has dozens of examples of this. In the pilot, Ted asks Robin, "What do you do?" (Trigger Topic) and she says:

I'm a reporter for Metro News One . . . well kinda a reporter" (Hook)
I do those dumb little fluff pieces at the end of the news you know like "monkey who can play the ukulele." I am hoping to get some bigger stories soon." (Struggle)

A few minutes later he asks her about her future plans (Trigger Topic).

Ted: "Hey, you want to have dinner with me on Saturday night?"
Robin: "Oh, I can't, I'm going to Orlando for a week on Friday. (Hook)
Some guy is attempting to make the world's biggest pancake. (Struggle)
Guess who's covering it. (Boomerang)

Notice these mini-stories all have a bit of humor in them. Humor often comes from something unexpected or surprising. Don't be shy about testing your jokes on different audiences. Just practice telling your story and see when and where you get laughs and smiles.

Use audience feedback to make adjustments to the stories in your stack. Don't be afraid to play around with nonverbal emphases, pauses, and embellishments as you practice telling your stories.*

One of my favorite classrooms for learning the art of storytelling? The

---

* Want to add some humor to your stories? We included our article "How to Be Funnier" in your Digital Bonuses at www.ScienceofPeople.com/toolbox.

New York Times. Award-winning journalists, editors, and writers help make the *New York Times* a world-renowned news agency. And we can learn from them.

One of my researchers, Robby Smith, and I designed a small experiment to analyze the types of *New York Times* articles that go viral. Over the course of four months from October 2015 to January 2016, Robby logged and coded all of their most-read pieces. He analyzed the topics of each article, the format of the titles, headlines, and the promise of each article.

We were particularly interested in the promise of an article. What does the title suggest the article will offer? In other words, if the reader clicks on it, what will it give them? A new outcome? A lesson? A surprise? An update? Here are the categories we used:

- **Question:** For instance, the article titled "Can You Get Smarter?" from October 2015.
- **How to:** Many headlines suggested tips, self-help, or a way of doing something new. "What You Can Do about Climate Change" was the title of an article from December 2015.
- **History:** Other titles referenced a time, period, or moment in history, such as "The Hard-Working Italian Origins of the Rockefeller Center Christmas Tree" from December 2015.
- **Snark:** This category included any headline that had a clever, funny, or punny title. We all laughed when we came across "This Column Is Gluten-Free."
- **New:** For example, "Everything You Need to Know about the New SAT" came out in October 2015.
- **Story:** Well-crafted headlines can imply you're on the brink of reading a great story about a person or place. "My Dark California Dream" or "Lady Gaga and the Life of Passion" are two examples.

Thirty-five percent of the articles on the viral list promised a story—195 out of 559 total articles—making it by far the most effective category.[7]

Promise Over 4 Months

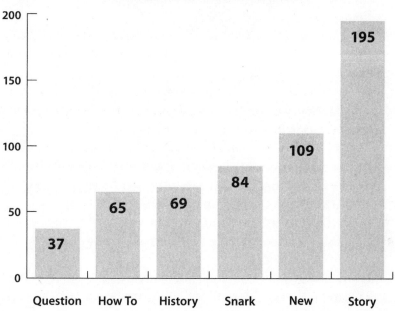

Take a look at the most e-mailed article list on the *New York Times* website for yourself. You'll see how the same storytelling formula comes up over and over again. First, the writers hook you with the slightest hint of a story in their title. Then, they quickly introduce a struggle or challenge that needs to be solved, and finally, they paint a picture with attention-grabbing words.

Whether you want your pitch to go viral, your e-mail to be read, or people to like your status updates, hook people with the power of stories.

REALITY BITES

You can use your Story Stack and the three-step storytelling technique in person, in e-mails, and even in your profiles.

Every week, we send out a free Science of People insights e-mail to over 100,000 subscribers. It's filled with cool people science, human behavior hacks, and communication tips. I once sent out a link to one of our articles called, "Why Couples Fight." Instead of just plopping the link in the e-mail, I decided to include a short story about my husband and me. It went like this:

Subject: The Top 5 Issues Couples Fight About

Darling, will you please pick up your sock?

Babe, please pick up your dirty socks!

PLEASE pick up your smelly, germy, practically decayed socks!!

If you were a fly on the wall of my house, you might hear this sequence occasionally. Do you have the same argument with your partner over and over again? You're not alone!

Get this crazy fact: **According to Dr. John Gottman, 69 percent of relationship conflicts are never solved!**

Whoa, whoa, whoa, it'll all be okeydokey, let Mama Vanessa fix it! Sixty-nine percent of us fight about the same things over and over again—that's the bad news. But here's the good news:

If we know what we fight about and how it happens, we can turn down the heat on our arguments.

Find out what your top issues are and how to solve them. [Link]

This e-mail had a far higher open rate and click-through rate than average. Why? Yes, I told a story, but I was also being real. I told an honest story about my real husband and something we really fight about. In fact, my husband even texted me that he thought he really did forget to pick up his socks that morning.

Comedian Nicol Paone is popular for her bitingly real stories. They're funny, they're heart-wrenching, and most importantly, they connect us to her.

"I think in some ways people relate to my stories. Sure, they laugh, but they also can imagine being in that same spot themselves. Maybe they made a similar mistake," says Paone. "There is connection through failure. When you hear someone else's failure you are less judgmental of your own," she added.

The best stories are the ones that share both failures and successes. Don't be afraid to share something a little embarrassing, a little vulnerable, a little scary. These are the stories that build the best connection.

CHALLENGES

1. Think of three stories that you enjoy telling.
2. Find the hook, struggle, and expressive words to best share them, and then practice them on a friend.

3. Create a note in your phone or on your computer to remember great stories when you hear them.

CHAPTER REVIEW

Stories are your shortcut to connection. Stories spark our attention and align the listener's brain patterns with those of the storyteller. Using your Story Stack is the best way to get someone in line with your way of thinking.

- Stories light up and sync up our brains.
- Find stories for common trigger topics that come up in conversation, then use boomerangs to ask people to share their own stories.
- Not all stories are created equal. Every story should have a hook, a struggle, and vivid words.

My biggest takeaway in this chapter is: _____

CHAPTER 11

EMPOWER

How to lead people

You would think Mark Gordon's illustrious career as a film producer is enough for a lifetime. He's won Oscars and Emmys. He's worked with Hollywood's top celebrities, from Tom Hanks to Matt Damon to Sandra Bullock. But he's also a hero—albeit unsung—in the world of education.

Gordon first took on increasing responsibilities in the private schools his daughters attended. Then he became chairman of Teach For America Los Angeles. Then, in 2010, Gordon had an idea—and it wasn't a small one. He wanted to create a school that shaped kids into global citizens. This was a tremendous undertaking—especially coming from someone who knew little about schools. Would the leadership skills he'd developed on movie sets translate into this new setting?

When I sat down with Mark Gordon, he summed up his leadership approach in three steps: "I always start with something I am passionate about, outline one goal, and then find a really smart, capable person to work with."

The passion was there. And a daunting goal was set: Open a charter school by September 2010. This would give him nine months to find a location, form an education charter, hire teachers, enroll students, and create a curriculum.

The third part of the equation was Kriste Dragon. Gordon met Dragon while she was executive director of Teach For America. As a Juris Doctor, former math teacher, and mom of three, Dragon had the right experience and perspective.

"I called her and told her: I want to start a school and I'll pay for the whole thing. How do we do it and how do we do it fast?" recalled Gordon. Instead of being overwhelmed, Dragon was hooked immediately. "My mom was an immigrant and my dad grew up in the projects outside of Birmingham, Alabama, so diversity and inclusion have always been something that mattered to me," said Dragon.

The duo hammered out a mission together: "We hoped to create a tuition-free school that was incredibly racially, economically, and intellectually diverse. We also wanted to foster sophisticated thinkers who have a deep sense of service," said Dragon.

Within a few weeks, Citizens of the World Charter School was born. But they had just a few months to get the school ready for kids. Eager to shield her from the work of drawing donations or forming committees, Gordon encouraged Dragon to use her talents. "I told her to build a team, find her ideal location, and tell me exactly what she needed," said Gordon.

Dragon internalized Gordon's philosophy in her own hiring process. "Get the right people, connect them to something bigger than themselves, and let them do their thing," said Dragon. She found the right principal, assembled an outstanding teaching team, and located the perfect spot for their flagship location in East Los Angeles.

When Citizens of the World Charter School opened up applications for their fall class, they received hundreds of applicants and had a full class starting in September 2010.

"The reason we were able to do so much, so quickly was due to Mark's leadership style. He is very clear on the goal, he knows my skills, and he lets me run with them. I couldn't ask for a better partner—he gives me the resources I need to solve problems and the freedom to solve them my way," explained Dragon.[1*]

In 2012, Gordon and Dragon opened their second school in the Silver Lake neighborhood in California. Just a year later, they launched their third school in Mar Vista, and expanded to Brooklyn, New York, where two schools (in Crown Heights and Williamsburg) opened. Citizens of the World now has seven schools, serving over 1,850 students across three cities.

Slowly, Citizens of the World schools are empowering the next generation of leaders. And Gordon is a testament to the fact that if you are a leader

---

* Watch the Citizens of the World Charter School video in your Digital Bonuses at www .ScienceofPeople.com/toolbox.

in one area, you are a leader in every area. His approach to people works whether he is influencing the film industry or the education system.

Gordon and Dragon are changing the world by empowering people. Now you can, too.

> *I've come to believe that knowing where to go is important, but explaining why and how to get there is even more important.*
>
> —Patti Sanchez

THE SCIENCE OF OWNERSHIP

Have you ever tried to build something from Ikea? If you're like me, here's what happens: First, you see a great-looking item in a perfectly designed room on the floor of Ikea. You fall in love! You snap a pic of the tag—because you'll never remember the bizarre-sounding name—and burn 1,000 calories pushing a giant flatbed cart around stacks of identical-looking aisles. Once you have procured all twenty-seven pieces of wood for your item, you proceed to the checkout. You stop for a cinnamon roll.

Once you get home, you unload and unpack all twenty-seven pieces of wood onto your living room floor. The amount of discarded cardboard is staggering. You make small piles of nails, screws, himejababs, and plastic nubs. (I don't know what a himejabab is, but it is what I call the tiny weird things Ikea gives you to build furniture.)

You are delighted to see only four pages of instructions—and there are pictures! Forty-five minutes into your assembly, you realize your starting piece is upside down. You throw it across the room. You get a glass of water and yell at your spouse. Five and a half hours later, your item is finished—wobbly, but finished.

Over the next few months, you watch as it slowly begins to disintegrate and then collapse when used or nudged. A friend suggests buying a new (preassembled) item from the store down the street. You are horrified—you invested eight hours of your life for this item, it will crumble into dust before you get rid of it.

This delightful little experience is universal. We place a disproportionately high value on self-made products. And it is appropriately called the Ikea effect. Researchers Michael Norton, Daniel Mochon, and Dan

Ariely wanted to investigate this interesting phenomenon around ownership.

They asked participants (builders) to make a small origami frog or crane. Then the researchers offered to buy their handmade creations from them, and asked how much of their own money the participants might pay for such an item.

The researchers then showed the origami to new non-builder participants and asked how much *they* would pay for it—they wanted to know how far above market price builders would pay for their own creations.

Finally, the researchers had expert origami makers create perfect cranes and frogs, and asked a final group of non-builder participants how much they would pay.

As you might have guessed, "While the non-builders saw the amateurish creations as nearly worthless crumpled paper [worth less than 5 cents], our builders imbued their origami with more value [23 cents]," said the researchers.

The researchers also tested this using actual Ikea furniture and Lego creations—with the same results.[2] We love things that we have made because we see them as an extension of ourselves. This means we place a higher value on them.

We can leverage this effect to empower those around us. Mark Gordon didn't call Kriste Dragon and say, "Hey, I want to start a school and I want to do it my way." From the beginning, he wanted Dragon to create a school with him. He gave her the financing and the support she needed, and then stepped back. **When we give up control, we gift power.**

I call this hack: Own It!

HACK #11: Own It!
Empower people by giving them buy-in, control, and ownership.

Leading people is about communicating a mission and then letting them take part in it. If you want to motivate a colleague, empower a team, or inspire a friend, all you have to do is figure out how to give them ownership.

People appreciate directness and honesty. The best bullshit is truth because it's totally disarming.

—Mark Gordon

EMOTIONAL OWNERSHIP

Have you heard of the famous study about copy machines? It goes like this: In 1977, psychologist Ellen Langer at Harvard University wanted to hack the copy machine line.

Langer had her research assistants try to cut to the front of the copy machine line using three different lines:

Request #1: "Excuse me, I have five pages. May I use the copy machine?" (Request Only)

Request #2: "Excuse me, I have five pages. May I use the copy machine because I'm in a rush?" (Request + Logical Reason)

Request #3: "Excuse me, I have five pages. May I use the Xerox machine because I have to make copies?" (Request + Silly Reason)

Request #2 is the only request that makes any sense. Request #1 is nonsensical because the line is clearly to use the copy machine. Request #3 is also ridiculous—everyone in the line has to make copies.

The first request worked okay—60 percent of people let the researcher cut in line. The second two requests worked incredibly well. The logical reason persuaded 94 percent of people to move aside, and the silly reason got 93 percent of people to say yes![3]

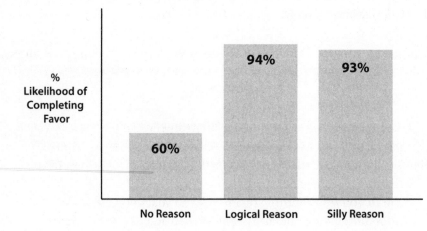

% Likelihood of Completing Favor

60% — No Reason
94% — Logical Reason
93% — Silly Reason

Why are reasons—even illogical ones—so powerful? Humans are purpose-driven creatures. We want to believe there are reasons behind everything we do. **Before leaders can inspire action, they have to get emotional buy-in.**

When we explain the motivations behind a goal, it allows listeners to feel partial ownership of that goal. Have you ever donated to a charity? Were you initially arrested by an emotional plea? Charities typically open a pitch by sharing their mission with you. Take my favorite nonprofit Kiva as an example. This is the first paragraph of the "About us" page on their website:

> We are a nonprofit organization with a mission to connect people through lending to alleviate poverty. Leveraging the internet and a worldwide network of microfinance institutions, Kiva lets individuals lend as little as $25 to help create opportunity around the world.

Kiva wants you to know there is a purpose behind their actions, and they hope that their purpose will become your purpose.

If it sounds like getting emotional buy-in might be hard, I have an easy trick for you:

Always use the word "because" when asking for something.

"Because" implies purpose. Whether you are pitching yourself, trying to get a date, or convincing a friend to choose your favorite restaurant for dinner, you always want to have your why at the ready.

We know from the copy machine example that even ridiculous reasons can successfully persuade people, but I want you to find powerful whys, like Mark Gordon's passion for changing the future of education or Kiva's goal of alleviating poverty. Here is how you can give your "because" more impact.

- **Tie to Them:** The best "because" benefits the listener. What's the payoff? What's the end result? What's the advantage? Think of L'Oréal's slogan, "Because I'm Worth It," which appeals directly to the customer's needs.
- **Tie to You:** If something means a lot to you, or would make you incredibly happy, harness that authentic passion to create a

powerful "because." Gordon believes fervently in equality and diversity. He also has two young daughters whom he wants the best for. Even if those aren't your own goals, hearing him speak is powerfully moving. Or think of the United States Marine Corps slogan, "The Few. The Proud. The Marines," which shows what the marines stand for and their elite mission.

- **Tie to Us:** You can also tie your "because" to a mutual benefit, or the way something could help an entire community. When pitching Citizens of the World Charter Schools, Gordon underscores how raising future world leaders will make the world better for everyone. Of course, the schools help students and their families most directly, but they also benefit the world they will enter after graduation. Similarly, Apple's "Think Different" slogan is an appeal to both the user and the world to challenge the status quo.

Always share a because, and when you can, tie it to as many emotional appeals as possible. You might even be able to check all three boxes. For example, in my online course The Power of Happiness I give three whys for people to buy—you will be happier, I will be able to fund more research on happiness, and we will all live in a more fulfilled and aware community.

Here's how everyday requests could be improved by this hack:

Typical Request: We would love to have you as a customer.
Hacker Ask: We would love to have you as a customer because you will love our product and it will make you stronger/better/more awesome.

Typical Request: Let's get Indian food for dinner.
Hacker Ask: Let's get Indian food for dinner, because it's delicious—and you mentioned you wanted to try something new!

Typical Request: Can I have your number?
Hacker Ask: Can I have your number? Because I think we could have a great time together!

Typical Request: Are there any aisle seats available on this flight?

Hacker Ask: Are there any aisle seats available on this flight, because I tend to get up a lot and don't want to disturb the people around me?

Typical Ask: Would you mind helping with my résumé?
Hacker Ask: Would you mind helping with my résumé? Because I am hoping to finally move out of my parents' house, and your help would mean the world to me!

Knowing your why starts with being **mission driven**. Simon Sinek calls it the "start with why" approach in his book of the same name. Kriste Dragon hires only teachers who believe in the Citizens of the World Schools mission. Mark Gordon works only on projects where he can tell a powerful story. Even when they're action movies, Gordon said, "They are *about* something. They are big spectacles and they are certainly big popcorn movies. But they aspire to at least make the audience think in a very broad way."[4]

If you want to get buy-in from people in any area of your life, you have to know your why: the mission that is driving the action.

Scenario	Why?	Mission
Applying for a new job	Why do you want to help this company? It's not just about getting a paycheck.	What can you do to help this company achieve their mission and yours?
Interviewing a new hire	Why is your company looking for exceptional employees? It's not just about filling a position.	What can you do to help this employee to be a part of the company's mission? Why do you want them as part of the team?
Asking friends to donate to the charity you are working with	Why does this charity matter so much to you? It's not just about raising money.	What is this charity doing to make an impact? Why will your friend's donation count?
Bonding on a first date	Why do you think you can make someone happy? It's not just about not being single.	What do you bring to a relationship? Why are you hoping to find the perfect partner?
Giving your elevator pitch	Why have you chosen your career path? It's not just about what you do.	Why do you do what you do? What's your career purpose?

The why is your launching pad for inspiration. You cannot empower people without knowing what drives you—because it will also be what drives your people.

Bottom Line: Give people emotional ownership over ideas, goals, and projects.

SKILL OWNERSHIP

When Mark Gordon was creating the Showtime series *Ray Donovan*, he partnered with Emmy Award–winning writer Ann Biderman as the showrunner. "Ann Biderman and I worked very closely to develop the script together. She was incredibly collaborative. It was one of the most joyous experiences that I've had developing a piece of material," said Gordon in an interview with *Fast Company*.[5]

Gordon knows how important it is to know not only your own skill set, but also the skills of the people you are working with. "I only work with people whose talent I have tremendous respect for. That way, when you are working with them they have as much of a chance of being right as you and you produce something really good," explained Gordon.

After working with Biderman on casting and the pilot, Gordon knew it was his time to step back and let Biderman run the show. "Once you're on a clear path, my involvement is less, because she doesn't need it. I look at cuts and share my thoughts, but we're sailing smoothly," said Gordon. In other words, **let the right person use their skills and then step back.**

I call this process "skill ownership." Every time someone uses their talents to accomplish part of a goal, they feel more ownership over that goal—and this makes them want to achieve it even more.

Say you're in your best friend's bridal party. The bride and groom— let's call them Rachel and Brian—have asked you to spearhead pre-wedding activities and logistics for the bridesmaids and groomsmen. The wedding planner hands you a long list of items that need to get done, from grabbing ice for the rehearsal dinner to putting the flowers in water before the wedding.

The first step is to give everyone emotional ownership. You assemble everyone in the hotel suite and introduce yourself. "It's so nice to finally meet all of you! The wedding planner just gave me a list of some things we could all help out with **because** Rachel and Brian are a little over-whelmed. I know **our goal** is to make this wedding as smooth as possible for the bride and groom and get everything done so we can party up at the wedding."

This ties in the goal (getting the list done) with both helping the couple and ensuring a good time for everyone on the wedding night. People nod and go around introducing themselves—great! You have everyone on board.

Next, you want to turn that emotional buy-in into action. Here's what most people do, which doesn't work:

- Can someone finish the table name cards? . . . Anyone, anyone?
- Who can go pick up the ice before the rehearsal dinner? . . . Please? Someone?
- Who wants to assemble these frames and hang them? . . . Come on, guys! We all have to pitch in!

Splitting up tasks this way is not the best way to encourage action. People might grudgingly say yes, but it will be like pulling teeth.

Instead of randomly delegating or hoping people will self-select, you want to divide the list by skills. **This highlights people's abilities so they feel capable, as opposed to burdened.** To do this, use what I call Skill Solicitation. Skill Solicitation is when you ask people to self-identify based on capability:

- Is anyone good at _____?
- Do you know anything about _____?
- I need someone who is strong with _____.

For the wedding, it might go like this:

- Does anyone have nice handwriting? Great! Susie, would you mind finishing up the table name cards?
- Does anyone have a car here? Wonderful! Steve, would you mind picking up the ice before the rehearsal dinner tomorrow?
- I need someone who is really handy—anyone good at fixing things? Thank you so much, Greg. Will you assemble and hang these picture frames?

This is not only a faster way to delegate, but it also lets tasks be skill oriented as opposed to duty oriented. Use this tactic on corporate teams, sports teams, with kids, with friends, and with family. Direct invitations can be as effective as open questions. For example, Mark Gordon knew Kriste Dragon had the right skill set, so he called her and asked her to use those specific skills to achieve his mission. Some other examples:

- Uncle Jim, you are so good at mixing cocktails—can you man the bar tonight?
- Rene, I know you are very good at nailing those cold calls—can you tackle this list tomorrow?
- Julie, you always pick the best restaurants—do you want to plan the birthday dinner?

Do you notice something else about these examples? They also secretly use Hack #4: The Highlighter. Skill Solicitation is a great way to emphasize someone's strengths and use them toward a common goal.

Bottom Line: Focus on someone's skills to turn their emotional buy-in into action.

CUSTOMIZED OWNERSHIP

I have a postcard on my desk that says:

Hey, I found your nose. It was in my business again.

Micromanaging kills leadership. The best leaders know when to give up control. They also know that the more power they can give people over *how* something gets done, the better they will be able to get it done. No one does this better than Mark Gordon.

"For me the hardest part was learning that there's something between being 100% engaged in something and not being engaged at all. . . . I learned to be where I'm needed when I'm needed," said Gordon.

Leadership is not about doing or overseeing everything in a project. It is about getting involved in the right things and letting the right people handle the rest. "Real learning experience for me, to be able to know when to come in, and when to leave people alone," explained Gordon.[6]

"Shonda Rhimes doesn't need me every day helping her make *Grey's Anatomy*. You can't feel the need to just go over there and mess around with stuff either because you can, or because you feel guilty, or because it's expected of you," said Gordon.

This approach has been astoundingly fruitful for both Gordon and Rhimes. *Grey's Anatomy*, one of the most popular shows on television, has received 174 nominations and has won 63 awards including Golden Globes and Emmys. Rhimes herself has won a Producers Guild award, a GLAAD Media Award, two Writers Guild awards and five NAACP awards. She has also gone on to be the showrunner for *Private Practice* and *Scandal* and executive producer for *How to Get Away with Murder*. **When you give up control, you let other people take ownership, and everyone wins.**

Now, I am not saying you should give up total control. Rather, I want you to think about how you can allow people to add their own flair. Researchers found that consumers are willing to pay a premium for products that they have customized.[7]

Kiva does an amazing job incorporating this ownership into their business. As discussed previously, Kiva is an organization that allows people to give interest-free microloans to entrepreneurs around the world. But they don't just ask you to give money so they can dole it out as they see fit. Instead, they let you search a database of entrepreneurs so *you* can decide exactly where your loan goes and how it will be used.

I donate to Kiva every year on my birthday, and I *love* the process of picking my entrepreneurs. Kiva uses the three steps of Own It! in their donation model:

- First, when I go to their website, I see a list of people I can "lend" to. Every person starts off with their why—to get emotional ownership. I see a loan to a bookstore in Guatemala will help them purchase a computer for logging sales. Or that Fatima in Lebanon will use her loan to buy more merchandise for her retail shop.
- Then I get to use my skills and values. Female entrepreneurship is incredibly important to me, and entrepreneurship happens to be a talent of mine, so I tend to give to women-owned businesses. I enjoy reading the different revenue models and picking women I think have sturdy business plans.
- Last, I decide exactly how much of my loan goes to each entrepreneur. Talk about customization!

The more you can allow people to customize a process or implement their own strategy, the better their participation will be. Christine Day, CEO of Lululemon Athletica, didn't realize this until she was neck-deep in the business of running a company. "I was a very bright, smart executive, but I think I majored in being right." She realized that "being right" wasn't the best way to motivate a team.

Day began to create spaces for employees to brainstorm and come up with their own solutions instead of being told what to do by upper management. "When I was trying to get other people to have ownership or engagement, it wasn't about the telling, **it was about letting other people come in to the idea and being purpose led**," said Day.[8]

Day wanted to create jobs where people were utilizing their skills and taking ownership of the company's performance. And she believes this is the crux of her leadership ability: "That was so powerful for me to shift from having the best idea or problem solving into actually being the best leader of people."

Under Day's leadership, Lululemon went from having 71 stores to 174, and took their revenue from $297 million to almost $1 billion.[9] Being a good leader is not about micromanaging—it is about empowering your team by letting them customize their work.

How could the typical (boring!) requests we already improved be customized at the end?

Typical Request: We would love to have you as a customer.
Hacker Ask: We would love to have you as a customer because you will love our product and it will make you stronger/better/more awesome.
Customized: We can build a custom package for you. Here's how . . .

Typical Request: Let's get Indian for dinner.
Hacker Ask: Let's get Indian for dinner, because it's delicious—and you mentioned you wanted to try something new!
Customized: You can pick the appetizers!

Typical Request: Can I have your number?
Hacker Ask: Can I have your number? Because I think we could have a great time together!
Customized: Do you want to enter your number into my phone?

Typical Request: Are there any aisle seats available on this flight?

Hacker Ask: Are there any aisle seats available on this flight, because I tend to get up a lot, and don't want to disturb the people around me?

Customized: I'm also happy to take your suggestion on the best seat options for this aircraft.

Typical Request: Would you mind helping with my résumé?

Hacker Ask: Would you mind helping with my résumé? Because I am hoping to finally move out of my parents' house, and your help would mean the world to me!

Customized: If you send me a template that you like, I can reformat it based on your experience in the industry.

You can hack any ask to get buy-in. All you need to do is to help them own the result with you. **Bottom Line:** To get people motivated, give them ownership.

FAST FACT BOX

Over 80 percent of respondents believe that leaders are made, not born. I agree—anyone can be a leader with the right tools.

Vanessa Van Edwards
@vvanedwards   👤 Follow

[POLL] I believe good leaders are born not made.

20% True

80% False

152 votes · Final results

BONUS: PASSION OWNERSHIP

When Gordon began working on *Saving Private Ryan*, he did it because he loved the idea—not because he thought it would make a lot of money.

"*Saving Private Ryan* was a movie that was purely from my heart and that I worked on for a long time with Bob Rodat, the writer. And we were fortunate enough to have Steven [Spielberg] and Tom [Hanks] jump on board. But that was not necessarily expected to be a big commercial movie, so when you can make something of it that is truly meaningful *and* it's a commercial success, that's the best thing of all," said Gordon.

Gordon always hopes his movies will be big blockbuster successes, but they don't have to be. "Movies like *The Details*, which we just finished and premiered in Sundance . . . and some of the other smaller pictures that we've done are all about love of film, and things that I just fall in love with. And those films have to be in a category where we say, *It's not about the money on any level*. It's all about feeling good about making something that we're in love with. Very few people have the opportunity to do that, and I'm very grateful for that," said Gordon.

Gordon's success comes from the fact that he works only on projects he cares about. When he sits down to write a script, he begins with a subject he is fascinated by and explores it.

"The thing for me is: Am I emotionally engaged in the idea? Is there something special about it? Does it capture my imagination? So everything that I do is simply something that turns me on," explained Gordon in an interview with the *Hollywood Reporter*.[10]

If something captivates your imagination, your passion, your energy, it is much more likely to captivate the imagination, passion, and energy of others. And isn't that what we are all here to do? I believe *everyone* is a leader in some way.

You can both solve people problems and empower people to solve problems.

CHALLENGES

1. Why do you want to lead people?
2. Think of one thing you should be delegating. Pick someone who would be good at it. Back away.
3. **Bonus:** Add a "because" to your next three requests—even if they are silly. See what people do.

CHAPTER REVIEW

When you want to lead someone, inspire a team or motivate people:

- Share your mission—and tie it to mutual interests as much as possible.
- Figure out how to use each person's unique skill set.
- Step back and let others take control of the process.

My biggest takeaway in this chapter is: _____

CHAPTER 12

REVEAL

How to build lasting relationships

Frank Warren is a keeper of secrets.

Every week, strangers send him postcards divulging confessions they've been bottling up. In total, Warren has received over a million secrets, and every week he receives one thousand more. The flow is so constant that the walls of his house are lined with stacks of secrets.

Some of the secrets are funny. Like this one, which I'm sure you can relate to:

Some of them are sweet and make you smile.

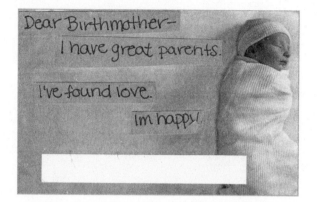

Some are incredibly sad and thought provoking.

Some are troublesome confessions.

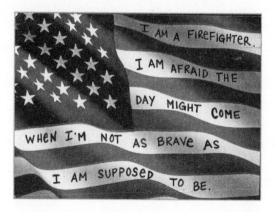

And some make you laugh and cringe.

Warren gets secrets about infidelity, depression, parenting, office politics, repressed fantasies, and friendships.

Warren never expected to be the landing pad for all of these truths. It all started in 2004. "I printed up three thousand postcards with my home address. On each postcard, I asked people to anonymously share a secret," said Warren. He handed them out on the streets of Washington, DC. He posted them on bulletin boards in coffee shops, he hid them in books in the public library, and he left them in bathroom stalls.

When I asked Warren about his expectations, he was not optimistic. "I had no idea if anyone would actually send me any back. I was going to be really happy if I got 365 back over the course of a year," Warren told me. He didn't have to wait for long. Within a few weeks, he had one hundred postcards. Fascinated by what people would share to a stranger, he turned them into an art exhibit. Eventually he began posting them on his blog, which he calls *PostSecret*. Over the course of a few years, the blog went viral.

When I first stumbled upon *PostSecret,* I spent hours scrolling through people's secrets. I completely understood the attraction of a blog about secrets—we all like to read other people's confessions. But why would anyone submit them?

Then I sent Warren my own secret postcard. And it all made sense. Secrets are about releasing a vulnerability. When we share them—even with strangers—we get relief. We feel less alone.

"Every day, we make a decision about what to reveal and what to conceal about who we are," explained Warren. "Those decisions affect what we talk about, who we talk to—and can weigh us down."

A few years into *PostSecret*, Warren created an in-person event where he asked audience members to share secrets—live. "I was worried that it would be a total fail. That the anonymity of the blog is what gave the secrets power," said Warren. But he didn't need to worry.

At one university event, a professor came up to the microphone and admitted, "I have been stoned for every single lecture this semester." The shocked crowd embraced her. "The audience is on an emotional roller coaster, too. Everyone is incredibly supportive. Sometimes we can't support the secret, but we can support the courage of sharing it," explained Warren.

The live events draw hundreds and sometimes thousands of people to share and hear confessions. "People bond incredibly fast at these events. It's as if secrets are the door to connection people have been looking for," said Warren. When he signs books, he often notices people in line forming friendships and collecting each other's contact information. The secrets act as a catalyst for turning strangers into fast friends.

He has tapped into something I call the vulnerability effect. "Sharing our most vulnerable stories is a courageous act that channels intimacy with others and builds lasting relationships," said Warren.

Revealing, as opposed to concealing, not only brings us relief, it also brings relief to the people who we reveal to. "People often find that when they let their secret go, they hadn't been keeping it to begin with. Their secret had actually been keeping them," said Warren. As humans, we can't help but feel bogged down by what we perceive as our limitations and failings. So we try to hide them. We hold back from connecting with people for fear that they might see our ugly parts and judge us. What we don't realize is that **our secrets don't have to prevent connection— they can encourage it.**

Warren is in a unique position to see the patterns in our most private worries. Want to know what secret Warren gets most frequently? "By far, the most common postcard we get is: I pee in the shower," said Warren. "The second most common secret we get has to do with belonging. Someone trying to find a community, someone shunned from their community—it seems everyone is trying to find someone or a group where they don't have to have any secrets at all," said Warren.[1]

Reading through thousands of submissions from unrelated strangers, Warren kept seeing the same narrative: We want to belong, and to be accepted for who we are. Here's the funny thing: **We are afraid that our secrets will cause people to not accept us. But oftentimes, sharing our secrets is the fastest way to find acceptance.**

Now, before we go on, let me be very clear on something. The goal of this chapter is not to get you to confess your secrets to anyone who will listen. That would be both terrifying and weird. Instead, you don't have to feel weighed down by secrets in your interactions. This hack will teach you to leverage your vulnerability to elevate your relationships.

SECRET SCIENCE

Think back to the last time you had a zit.

Did you venture out into the world praying no one would notice the volcano about to erupt on your chin? When talking to people, were you petrified that the only thing they would notice was the giant red bump on your face? Did you become convinced that everyone was talking about it?

We always feel our vulnerabilities are painfully obvious. That people are scrutinizing us at every turn. That our blemishes define us. I hate to break it to you, but no one really cares—and I mean that in the nicest way possible.

Our mistakes are not noticed nearly as much as we think. This cognitive bias is called the spotlight effect. In one study, researchers Thomas Gilovich and Victoria Medvec at Cornell University decided to humiliate students for the sake of science.[2]

First, researchers asked students to put on a Barry Manilow T-shirt—chosen for its high level of potential embarrassment. Then they asked each student to estimate the percent of people who would notice their Manilow T-shirt in a crowded classroom. The students made fairly high guesses, thinking most other students would notice (and probably make fun of the Manilow shirt). And then finally, they asked the students to walk into a classroom and join fellow students taking a survey. The results? The T-shirt-wearing participants grossly overpredicted how many students would notice. The estimates were twice as high as the actual number.

The researchers concluded:

Most of us stand out in our own minds. Each of us is the center of our own universe. Because we are so focused on our own behavior, it can be difficult to arrive at an accurate assessment of how much—or how little—our behavior is noticed by others. Indeed, close inspection reveals frequent disparities between the way we view our performance (and think others will view it) and the way it is actually seen by others.[3]

The things we dread—tripping while walking down the street, making a social gaffe at a party, or misreading something in a classroom—are rarely picked up on. And if they are noticed, they are usually forgotten.

This is great news! If you mess up or expose your vulnerability, most people won't even notice. Now I know what you're thinking: "But Vanessa, even though most people don't notice, what about the few people who do?"

I'm so glad you asked!

VULNERABILITY IS ATTRACTIVE

Most people will not notice your flubs and failings. But what about the people who do?

Researchers Elliot Aronson, Ben Willerman, and Joanne Floyd wanted to know what people really think about those who make mistakes. In their study, they asked participants to listen to a recording of a student explaining how well he did on a quiz. The student talked about his background and then modestly described his 90 percent score on the exam.

Here was the catch: One group of participants hears the student knock over a mug of coffee and ruin their clothes at the end of the recording. The other group hears no such spill. The researchers then asked both groups, "How likable was this student?"

Can you guess what happened? The student who spilled his coffee was rated as far more likable and socially attractive than the non-spilling student.[4]

Why? Mistakes humanize us. We all make mistakes, and we like people who are like us. (Remember Hack #5: Thread Theory?) Having above-average people skills is not about being perfect. It's not about never making a social blunder again. Rather, people who have great interpersonal intelligence leverage their vulnerability.

If vulnerabilities were bad, *PostSecret* never would have turned into a phenomenon. Frank Warren wouldn't be the author of five books and the founder of a secret empire.

And let's be real: **Trying to be perfect is not only impossible, it's boring. Trying too hard smells like desperation. And staying in hiding is exhausting.**

Vulnerability is sexy—it shows we are relatable, honest, and real. That is attractive. And the science proves it: "A blunder tends to humanize him and, consequently, increases his attractiveness."[5]

Vulnerability sounds like truth and feels like courage.

—Brené Brown

HOW TO BE VULNERABLE

I'm standing on tiptoes in a dark, stinky hallway. My high-heel-clad feet are killing me, and the wall I am leaning on is pulsing with the pop music blaring in the next room. I'm fifth in line for the tiny, crusty bathroom.

Amazingly, this dank little corridor is actually my temporary escape from sitting at the sticky high-top tables and yelling over the loud music to people I barely know. It's my friend's thirtieth birthday party and she wants to "party like a twenty-one-year-old." In sum, I'm in my personal social hell.

I'm searching my clutch for some Advil when a girl I recognize from our party stands in line behind me. "Ugh," she moans, "Seriously? This line is going to take forever!"

Now, I have a choice. I could nod empathetically and carry on waiting, or I could be honest . . . and a little vulnerable. "Yeah, I'm not sure what's worse—standing in line in these heels or sitting out there at those tables," I say.

She looks at me, looks down at my heels, and then bursts out laughing. "At least you're not also wearing Spanx. My feet are numb and I can't take a deep breath," she says.

Thank goodness! A fellow human. I counter, "But would you really want to take a deep breath in here? It smells like stale beer."

"Very good point. I'm just dreaming of my couch and my bathrobe right now," she says.

"I think I might cry tears of joy when I get to go home, put on my slippers, and turn on Netflix," I confess.

By the time it's my turn in line, we are exchanging info and promising to get brunch next weekend. Later that night, I realize none of this would have happened had I not taken a small risk. I was uncomfortable—physically and socially—and I was not the only one. All I had to do was reach out.

Living in truth and embracing vulnerability doesn't mean walking up to strangers and saying, "Hi, my name is Vanessa and I'm a recovering awkward person." Well . . . that works, too. But there are much subtler (and less scary) ways you can use the power of vulnerability in your life.

FAVOR ME?

There's a famous story about Benjamin Franklin—no, not the one involving lightning. This one is far less dramatic, but just as intriguing.

In the 1700s, Franklin was an influential writer and politician. While working in the Pennsylvania state legislature, Franklin had to win over a particularly difficult politician who was not a fan of his policies. Franklin could follow the typical route and grovel for his favor . . . or he could try something different.

Franklin—a lover of books—knew that this politician owned a copy of a rare book in his large home library. Franklin wrote him a letter asking if he could borrow the book. He said yes. After a few days, Franklin returned the book with a note of thanks. In subsequent meetings, the politician was friendlier and more attentive than ever before. Franklin had stumbled upon an interesting phenomenon: When someone does a kindness for you, they are more likely to like you.[6] This is dubbed the **Franklin effect**.

Over a century later, Jon Jecker and David Landy wanted to confirm that the Franklin effect really works. In their experiment, they told participants they could win some money by completing a series of surveys. The "administrator" of these surveys was actually an actor tasked with treating the participants as rudely as possible while they completed tests. When finished, the participants received a small amount of cash.

Now, here's where it gets interesting. In trial one, the fake administrator follows the student out of the lab and asks for a favor. "Would you mind returning the cash? I'm funding the study with my own money, and we're almost out of funding."

In trial two, a fake "secretary" runs after the students and asks for the same favor.

In trial three, the participants were able to keep their winnings and no one asked for a favor.

A few days later, the researchers asked the participants in all three trials to rate the administrator on likability. Guess what? **The first trial participants rated the administrator as the most likable.**[7]

Let's think about this for a hot second: Imagine you are a student taking some surveys for extra money. The administrator of the survey is rude to you, telling you to hurry up and dismissing you abruptly. Then—after you have spent all this time completing the survey, the administrator has the gall to ask you to give back your winnings. Do you think you would rate him as likable? I don't think so! But research shows that in reality, this would work.

The Franklin effect is counterintuitive—which is what makes it so powerful. And it is our next hack:

HACK #12: The Franklin Effect
Don't be afraid to ask for advice, share a vulnerability, or admit
a weakness—they bond you to people.

When the administrator asked for help and admitted a vulnerability, he became more human, more relatable.[8] How can we use the Franklin Effect hack authentically—without just asking for favors from everyone we meet? Three words: Ask for advice.

ASK FOR ADVICE

Asking for advice is one of the best ways to get along with people and build lasting relationships. Here's why:

- **Asking for advice softly admits a vulnerability.** When you ask for advice, you are admitting a gap in knowledge or a need for help in an authentic, non-scary way.

- **Asking for advice gets people talking.** Remember how much people like to talk about themselves? Rather than being a burden, you spark pleasure (Hack #3: Conversational Sparks) and have the opportunity to highlight someone's strengths (Hack #4: Highlighter). Being asked for our opinion shows that someone values what we have to say.
- **Asking for advice helps you solve someone's matrix.** When someone gives you advice, you learn so much about them. You get insight into their perspective (Hack #7: Speed-Read) and the things that matter most to them (Hack #9: Primary Value).

Asking for advice doesn't have to be a formal process. In fact, it is one of the simplest ways to stimulate fascinating conversation. Listen for anecdotes people tell about themselves, and then follow up by asking for advice in those areas. If an interviewer mentions loving to read, you can ask for recommendations. If a date says she grew up nearby, ask for hidden coffee spots. If someone mentions loving to cook, ask for any secret kitchen tips.

Or kick off a conversation by asking for advice. These conversation sparkers work nicely:

- Have any good restaurants you like?
- I'm thinking about taking a vacation at the end of the year—have you been anywhere great recently?
- I'm looking for a new book to read this summer—have anything you would recommend?
- What do you think I should get my girlfriend for our anniversary?
- I'm playing in a new fantasy football league—how do you think this season will end up?
- I'm thinking about buying a new car—do you like yours?
- My in-laws are coming for dinner—have any recipes you like?
- I have to open my speech next week with a joke—got any good crowd-pleasers?
- What do you think I should do for my birthday coming up?
- Seen any funny YouTube videos recently?
- My college friend is coming to visit—have any ideas for must-see hidden spots to take him?

If you're ever worried about running out of things to say in a conversation or meeting, you can switch to the topic of advice. Try these seamless transitions:

1. So, I would love your advice on something: _____
2. Hey, can I brainstorm some ideas with you about this new project I'm working on?
3. Speaking of which, do you have any thoughts on how to fix/change/solve _____?

You will notice that these transitions make people perk up. Their eyebrows will raise, they'll lean in, and they'll say something like, "Oh really? Happy to help." We love to be helpful and be asked for help—and hopefully, their advice will actually help you.

Remember: Never ask for advice you don't actually need. Vulnerability is about honesty, it's not a trick to be used without integrity.

LOOK FOR ADVICE OPPORTUNITIES

Never miss an advice opportunity. You get them more often than you might realize.

Don't miss casual opportunities for favors. When I go to someone's home, I always accept a glass of water when offered. People frequently tweet me cool links of studies about people—I almost always retweet them and thank them for the recommendation. Every few weeks, I go on LinkedIn and accept the extremely kind recommendations and endorsements people have given me. After speaking events, I regularly ask audience members or meeting planners to write testimonials if they enjoyed themselves.

May I ask you for a favor? If you are enjoying this book, please write a review on Amazon. I would greatly, greatly appreciate it! Cute emojis encouraged. ☺

Don't be afraid to ask for casual advice. You can ask for advice informally on e-mail or social media. I regularly post open questions on my social media to all my followers. Anything from: "Do you like this shirt?" to "Does anyone know any good graphic designers?" to "What's the best way to cook eggplant?"

I also post polls on Twitter asking for advice and votes. Like this one:

Vanessa Van Edwards @vvanedwards · Apr 6
[POLL] Do you have something you did NOT do in your life that you greatly regret NOT doing?

74% Yes
26% No

93 votes • Final results

Don't undervalue unsolicited advice. The Franklin Effect is not just about asking for advice. It's also about taking advice, help, and support when it is offered to you. We tend to be defensive when someone offers unsolicited advice. However, this is actually an opportunity! This is an unsolicited opportunity to harness the power of the Franklin Effect.

BE GRATEFUL

To double the power of the Franklin effect, thank someone when they've given you advice—and show them that you're taking it seriously. You'll make people feel validated, helpful, and included.

My grandma taught me this. Grandma Dee loves to make her own clothes. One day she called me and left me a voice mail asking for my measurements, "From your neck to your toes and your shoulder to your wrist." I had no idea what she was making me, but dutifully called her back with the measurements.

A few weeks later, she showed up with matching muumuus made from her old living room curtains. "Don't worry," she assured me, "I made yours have a slit to the knee since you are younger than me." Oh, and the best part? She had enough material for headbands.

I gave her a hug and thanked her for it. She was pleased—after all, she had spent weeks sewing it. I realized that it would make her way happier if I actually wore it. So I put it on and wore it for the rest of the day. As I am sure you can imagine, my grandma was ecstatic. She insisted on taking pictures and talked about it for weeks with her friends.

Now I try to pull out the muumuu whenever I see her—or at least wear the headband.

Don't be afraid to get creative with your gratitude! I send people

gratitude journals with the first page filled in with the ways I'm thankful for them. I regularly mail people three-leaf-clover seed packets for thanks and good luck. When I ask for testimonials, I put them on my website, take a screenshot, and send it to the person with a thank-you note. When family friends gave my husband and me advice on where to go in Italy for our honeymoon, we followed it, took pictures, and sent them a mini-album with a thank-you card from Italy.

Don't underestimate the basics, either: Always send a thank-you card.

BONUS: ANTI-PERFECT

Perfection is a strange beast. We strive to be perfect so others will like us but don't like people who try too hard to be perfect. The pursuit of perfection not only makes it nearly impossible to connect with people, it also makes us unattractive. Want to connect with people more quickly? Try to embrace these vulnerability cures:

- Admit when you're wrong
- Don't pretend to know a band you've actually never heard of
- Ask for forgiveness
- When you don't know what a word means, ask
- Say sorry
- Be okay saying, "I don't know"

Following these rules will help you build relationships.

While standing in line at that awful nightclub, I opened a conversation with an honest admission and gained a friend. When I started writing this book, I began with a vulnerable confession. And I hope I gained you, as a reader.

I can tie my greatest personal and professional achievements to single moments of vulnerability. For example, at a conference I once admitted to the woman sitting next to me that I had no idea what a speaker was talking about. She heartily agreed and we bonded while reminiscing about speaker horror stories. Later in the conversation, I found out she happened to be the head producer at CNN—a few months later, she created a segment for me to present my research on air and in columns.

In fact, when I share a confession or embarrassing story in my articles, more people read it, comment on it, and share it. It's almost as if my admission of weakness makes people comfortable with their own weaknesses—and then they're more likely to accept help. Luckily, I am always happy to sacrifice my dignity for the sake of my readers.

Special Note: Some people suck. Yes, there will be people who won't welcome your vulnerability. And yes, you might even get people who try to use your weaknesses against you. But you know what? I think that is worth the risk. The way people respond to your honesty instantly shows you whether they are the kind of person you want to have in your life.

If someone unsubscribes from my e-mail because they are offended at my lack of social grace, then they are not going to benefit from my tips.

If that girl in the nightclub had rolled her eyes at my remark, I would have turned right around and kept looking for an Advil.

If a reader picked up this book and couldn't identify with awkward people, then this book wasn't for them.

Bottom Line: We all have weaknesses. The right people will like you for them.

IT'S NOT ABOUT THE SINGING

When I try to sing, I sound like a cat slowly dying of hypothermia. (No animals were harmed in the creation of this metaphor.)

So when I found out karaoke was the theme of my best friend's rehearsal dinner, and I would have to participate as her "Babe of Honor," I started Googling "easiest karaoke songs," practicing in the shower, and generally freaking out.

The big night came. At the karaoke machine, I turned to my husband, frantic. "They don't have my songs!" I whispered.

Ever calm, ever low neurotic, my husband said, "Don't worry! You can do mine with me."

Guess what he picked? "The Real Slim Shady" by Eminem. Have you ever tried to karaoke rap music? Well, let me tell you, it is *hard*. Like, get-tripped-up-on-your-tongue, spit-on-the-audience, and look-at-the-screen-blankly hard.

About two stanzas in, I was lost and feeling pretty humiliated, when an older woman sitting next to the stage leaned over and said something that has stuck with me, "Don't worry about being the best singer, **just commit.** It's not about the singing."

Somehow, this wiped the deer-in-the-headlights expression off my face. I pumped my hands up in the air and led the crowd in an impromptu wave. I threw out a couple of what *I* believed were hard-core hand gestures. Then I tried to breakdance.

The crowd loved it. They laughed at my lame attempts at the worm, cheered when I dropped it like it's hot, and enthusiastically demanded more waves. My "mistakes" were wildly entertaining. Why? I committed to them.

If you will humor me for a moment: I believe this is a metaphor for life. Karaoke is not about the singing, it's about making a song your own. **Life is not about being perfect, it's about living it your way.**

As Frank Warren likes to say, "Free your secrets and become who you are."

CHALLENGES

1. What do you need advice on in your life? Go ask someone.
2. What advice can you get from your Riser?

3. **Bonus:** What is your deepest, darkest secret? Maybe it's time to share it:

CHAPTER REVIEW

Impressing people with fake flawlessness is both impossible and exhausting. Vulnerability is what truly elevates relationships.

- People don't notice your perceived weaknesses as much as you think.
- Even if they do, your vulnerabilities are connection points.
- Ask for advice to harness the power of the Franklin Effect.

My biggest takeaway in this chapter is: _____

CHAPTER 13

PROTECT

How to deal with difficult people

'**ve been screamed at, hung up on, and blown up at more times than I can count," said Xochitl Gonzalez, "but that's part of the job . . . and I love it." Gonzalez organizes some of the most unique, memorable, and incredible weddings around the world, and she will be the first to tell you that she is as much an impromptu family counselor as a wedding planner. In fact, there is no better person than Gonzalez to teach us how to deal with difficult people. Why? The combination of new love, huge budgets, complicated family ties, and unexpected expenditures can make hers one of the toughest interpersonal jobs in the world.

After thousands of weddings, Gonzalez has discovered her own set of people patterns. And her observations are fascinating. A bride with low self-esteem usually has a helicopter mom. An assertive father typically has a daughter who marries a timid husband—"Perhaps because she already has a dominant male figure in her life?" Gonzalez guesses. Very meek grooms typically have either an opinionated fiancée or mother—if it's both, Gonzalez knows it's going to be a tough wedding.

"I'll never forget one bride who became obsessed with the party favors. When the luxury box of chocolates she had finally chosen didn't turn out the way she had hoped, she became extremely upset," explained Gonzalez. The bride screamed at the caterers and became strangely fixated on ribbons.

Gonzalez suspected something more was going on. She knew that in the midst of planning a wedding, the bride would be adopting her fiancé's children, quitting her job, and moving to the suburbs to be a full-time mom. "She had A LOT going on. I knew the favors were just symbolic of something else. So, I called her and said, 'Is this really about the chocolates?'"[1]

Gonzalez was right. The chocolates were only a trigger for the bride's feelings that her life was spinning out of control. Luckily, Gonzalez was able to get to the root cause of the emotion. She encouraged the bride to have a much-needed conversation with her soon-to-be-husband and prevented a difficult situation from exploding into an impossible one.

SOCIAL FEAR

Gonzalez has two rules for dealing with difficult people:

First, **prevent good people from becoming difficult**.

Second, **stop difficult people from being impossible**.

In both cases, the behavior stems from one thing: fear. When a bride freaks out over a dress or a mother-in-law blows up at a caterer, it's usually not about the dress or the food. It's simply fear coming out as something else—fear about not pleasing people, fear about money, or even fear about the marriage. When we are afraid, our worst selves rear their ugly heads.

In social situations, fears can become even more aggravated. When we are around others, we fear:

- Being judged
- Not being liked
- Not meeting anyone we like
- Being rejected
- Being left out
- Being laughed at
- Saying something and having nobody laugh
- Being criticized
- Being perceived as boring
- Being weird
- Being out of control
- Being misunderstood
- Being forgotten
- Being different

Which of these items resonates most for you? **When you interact with people, what are you afraid of?** These are your gremlins.

> **Gremlin:** *n.* An imaginary, mischievous sprite regarded as responsible for an unexplained problem or fault.

Our gremlins give us social anxiety, make us awkward, and muddle up our charisma. They're also largely invisible to us. We very rarely say, "I'm in a bad mood because I'm afraid of being rejected." Or "I yelled at you because I am terrified of being criticized myself."

I like to say that fear is a cross-dresser. It likes to wear different outfits. Sometimes fear can cause us to:

- Be people pleasers
- Be bossy
- Be defensive
- Be gossipy
- Be avoidant
- Be mean
- Be awkward
- Be boring
- Be critical
- Be narcissistic
- Go into denial
- Be needy
- Seek compliments
- Be selfish
- Be dramatic

Looking at this list, which sounds most like your reaction to fear? **How does your fear dress up?**

We each have a gremlin that causes us to be difficult on our worst days. I can tell you my biggest gremlins are being excluded, feeling weird, and being different. My gremlins pop up anytime, anywhere for a host of different reasons. When I'm extremely nervous, I still get hives on my arms and legs. So I have to constantly check for them in awkward social situations and spend most of the time praying I won't have a breakout. I don't like the taste of alcohol, so I'm always nervous about being the party pooper and unfun invitee—and often volunteer as sober driver. I have a really hard time hearing in loud rooms and almost always end up being the last to arrive and first to leave.

Mostly, I'm terrified that who I am will turn people off. My fear dresses up as awkwardness. When I'm in a survive situation, I clam up, make terrible, offensive jokes, and can't stop talking. No really, I don't shut up. Guess what happens next? Yup, exactly what I feared most. People think I'm weird and different. And then exclude me. In a crazy way, our fear makes our gremlins come true.

I have found that our gremlins make us act in quite predictably difficult ways. They fall into these four categories:

Type	Description	Difficulty	Gremlin
Downers Example: The character of sadness in the movie *Inside Out*	Very negative, always complaining, extremely pessimistic.	Impossible to please	Fear of being rejected—so they reject everything and everyone first.
Show-Offs Example: Blair Waldorf from the TV show *Gossip Girl*	Brag, act like they are better than everyone, and tend to be know-it-alls. One-uppers.	Narcissistic	Fear of being forgotten or undervalued—so they feel the constant need to prove themselves.
Passives Example: Toby Flenderson from the TV show *The Office*	Very quiet, never ask questions. Tend to not contribute or be pushovers.	Invisible / Non-Contributors	Fear of being criticized or judged—so they try not to give anyone anything to criticize by shutting down and not participating fully.
Tanks Example: Louis Litt from the TV show *Suits*	Often explosive, bossy, dramatic, and overly emotional.	Dramatic / Over-reactive	Fear being out of control, so they take control. They also fear being forgotten, so they engage in attention seeking behaviors.

All of us tend to fall into one of these categories on our worst days. **Be honest: which sounds most like you in your bad moments?**

Don't worry! You are not alone and it is *not* your fault. There's a neurological explanation for why you feel this way.

THE SCIENCE OF FEAR

Joseph LeDoux, a New York University psychologist and neuroscientist, studies what he calls fear learning: the way our brains learn to detect and respond to external threats.[2]

You might not be surprised to learn that fear is processed in the amygdala (remember, this is also where we process pleasure and produce dopamine). LeDoux found that the amygdala's fear responses can travel by not one but two pathways: the fast "low road" between the thalamus and the amygdala, and the slower "high road," which begins at the thalamus but takes a detour to the neocortex before reaching the amygdala.[3]

Low Road: This is the fast, automatic, primary fear response that
   helps us *react* quickly to a threat. The low road helps us survive.
High Road: This is a slower, more logical secondary fear response
   that helps us *think* through a threat. The high road helps us thrive.

Let's say you're driving down the street and an accident happens right in front of you.

Immediately, your Low Road kicks in—within 12 milliseconds. You hit the brake, your blood starts pumping, you suck in a breath of air, and your eyes go wide so you can take in more of the scene.

About 30 to 40 milliseconds later, your High Road jumps in. It processes what you just saw—should you call 911? Do you need to help the drivers? Should you pull over?

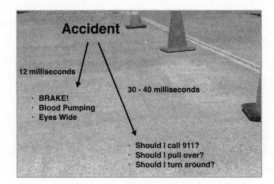

This fear processing system works great—most of the time. The problem is, the Low Road and the High Road have two slightly different goals.

Our Low Road wants us to be safe, protected, and secure. It wants us to survive without bodily harm.

Our High Road wants us to make good decisions that help us thrive. It wants us to have connections, reproduce, and be happy.

Sometimes these goals are aligned, and sometimes they aren't. "The two paths do not always reach the same conclusions," explained LeDoux.[4] For example, if you are afraid of rejection, your Low Road can kick into threat response mode. The moment you enter into a difficult interaction, you get sweaty palms, feel flushed, and have the desire to take flight. This Low Road response makes it impossible to be witty, build connections, or have a relaxed conversation.

Psychologist Dr. Daniel Goleman calls this emotional hijacking.

> **Emotional Hijacking**: When your Low Road is in an emotional fear response, you cannot connect with your High Road, make logical decisions, or act in your best social interest.

He believes emotional hijacking is the reason social situations can be difficult—and why difficult people can be difficult.

Your gremlins are not just distracting; they force you into survival mode. Have you ever tried to have an intelligent conversation when you have dry mouth from nerves? Ever tried to be funny when you felt awkward? It's almost impossible. This is because your apelike Low Road is slowing down your clever High Road.

"Emotional systems tend to monopolize brain resources. It's much easier for an emotion to control a thought than for a thought to control an emotion," explained LeDoux.[5]

Triggers from your past can also condition you to react fearfully to relatively minor events. Let's say your crush laughed in your face when you asked her to dance at your eighth-grade prom. You remember blushing uncontrollably as her friends giggled and pointed at you. You began to sweat and couldn't breathe deeply (Low Road). You had no idea what to do, so you ran out of the room and hid in the bathroom. You decided to wait there until the dance was over (High Road).

As an adult, every time you enter a dark club with loud music and approach a woman to dance, your Low Road kicks in. It recognizes this scenario—and the time it didn't go so well. So you begin to sweat, blush, and hyperventilate before you even talk to the girl. Your Low Road is telling you: "Run!" "Hide in the bathroom!" "Don't talk to her!" Even though your High Road is telling you to approach the girl, and it has been a long time since your eighth-grade dance, your Low Road is **emotionally hijacking you.**

This is why, in the Social Game Plan hack, you narrowed down your survive and thrive places. It's impossible for you to implement people hacks when you're in Low Road, survival mode. I want to get you into situations where your Low Road can stay quiet to allow your High Road to take over and be your awesome self. Difficult people don't do this well.

I don't believe difficult people are bad people. I believe they are being emotionally hijacked the majority of the time. Their fear puts them in constant survival mode. And their gremlins make it impossible for them to compassionately connect or rationally compromise.

"We know that lots of people have fears that they can't come to conscious terms with," said LeDoux.[6] Our emotions are fully capable of overriding reason. The question is: How can we help difficult people overcome their fear and be more socially smart?

THE NUT JOB

Sometimes nutty people drive me bat-poop crazy. When someone's gremlins are too much for me to deal with, I use a simple technique that I call:

HACK #13: The NUT Job
When dealing with difficult people, name the emotion,
understand the feeling, and transform the fear.

The NUT Job both prevents crazy and calms crazy.

This powerful little hack is a simplified version of a hostage release technique taught by Dr. Mark Goulston[7]—yes, dealing with a difficult person can be like negotiating with a kidnapper. Let's put on our big-boy pants.

Step #1: Name
Most gremlins are a product of not being recognized, accepted, or heard. You can quiet these fears by showing someone that you do recognize,

accept, and hear exactly where they are coming from. This is done by the first stage of the NUT Job: naming.

In naming, you are trying to find the answer to:

What is this person afraid of?

The moment you identify the emotion someone is feeling, you open a release valve for their anxiety. Sound easy? It is simple, but for some reason it feels counterintuitive to most of us. **Typically, when someone is emotional and we are not, we try to counterbalance them by staying calm. But this doesn't work**. In fact, it usually only infuriates an upset person even more.

Here's a common example that happens between men and women:

Person	Script	Feelings
Woman	"I'm so upset about the promotion at work! I'm so pissed I didn't get it. It's just so unfair."	Seeking understanding from man

TYPICAL RESPONSE		
Person	**Script**	**Feelings**
Man	"Yeah, but at least your review is coming again in three months. Hopefully you will get it then."	Trying to stay calm
Woman	"Three months! Are you kidding? I have been there for five years—I shouldn't have to wait! This is basically them telling me they don't value me at all."	Getting more and more upset as her fear is not heard
Man	"No way! This is just coincidence. I don't think them hiring her has anything to do with you."	Please, please, please remain calm
Woman	"Are you saying they are forgetting all about me? You're right—they probably hadn't even considered me for the position! If that's the case I might as well quit! You are not helping!"	Officially upset and jumping to crazy conclusions

This conversation quickly escalated. The man was trying to help, but the woman wasn't looking for a solution—she wanted to be heard.

All the man had to do was listen for **emotion words**: words that indicate inner fears. Then he should have worked those exact same emotion words into conversation to validate the woman's concerns and prompt her to say more. That script would go like this:

Person	Script	Feelings
Woman	"I'm so **upset** about the promotion at work! I'm so **pissed** I didn't get it. It's just so **unfair**."	Seeking understanding from man

HACKER RESPONSE		
Person	**Script**	**Feelings**
Man	"I can't believe they did that—it's incredibly **unfair**. I can see why that would be so **upsetting**."	Repeating her emotion words
Woman	"I know I'm just **frustrated**. I've been working there for so long and it seems like they **overlooked** me. I'm **afraid** they will fire me or never give me a raise."	Feeling heard and going deeper
Man	"I get it, so **frustrating**. And it's impossible to do your best work and be happy at your job when you're **afraid** of being fired."	Validating fear
Woman	"Yeah, I just don't **understand**."	Feeling misunderstood by her company, but understood by her man
Man	"Did they give you any explanation at all to help you **understand** it?"	Moving into Step #2: Understand

In this version, notice that the man is simply reflecting the emotion words back at the speaker, trying to get to the root of her fear. This helps him comprehend what's going on and allows her to sort out her emotions. Once she feels heard and validated, then she moves into stage two of the NUT Job: understanding.

My favorite phrases for naming:

- You seem ____.
- Are you feeling ____?
- Give me a sense for what you're feeling.

Special Note: Decoding microexpressions is also incredibly helpful for naming—especially when someone isn't being as vocal about their emotions as you'd like. Naming an emotion you read on their face is just as effective.

Step #2: Understand

Once someone feels heard, their Low Road fear begins to disengage and the High Road starts to kick in. Already, you're dealing with a more logical, rational, and relationship-oriented person.

The goal of the understanding phase is to unpack emotions behind what's being said. During this time, you are trying to:

- Get as much information as possible
- Help them process as much as possible
- Identify their primary value in the situation

You want to find the answer to:

What is this person seeking?

Let's revisit the above example in step one. The points where we get hints of the woman's primary value are underlined. You can use the personality cheat sheet in our Digital Bonuses as a quick reference guide if you need a refresher. See if you can guess what her primary value is:

Person	Script	Feelings
Woman	"Yeah, I just don't **understand**."	Feeling misunderstood by her company, but understood by her man
Man	"Did they give you any explanation at all to help you **understand** it?"	Moving into Step #2: Understand

Person	Script	Feelings
Woman	"Well, they announced it **without any warning** at the meeting today. And they did it in **front of everyone**. I swear it felt like half the room turned and **looked at me** because she got the **title I was hoping for**."	Revisiting the moment of the gremlin attack
Man	"Do you think they will **tell you more about** it next week? Or at least **explain to the team** why **she got the promotion?**"	Seeking to understand the gremlin + fear
Woman	"I mean it's not like I need the promotion right now. I just feel really **out of the loop**. It would be fine if I **knew** that I was on some kind of track for it. I just feel so **in the dark**."	Identifying the underlying fear

Based on her answers, it sounds like her primary value is Information or Status. Say the man asks more questions and narrows it down to Information. This is key information! Wanting a promotion right away is one thing. But merely wanting to know if you're *deserving* of a promotion, and whether there is a timeline in place, is a very different goal. Here's where the next step of the NUT Job comes in: Transform.

My favorite phrases for understanding:

- Tell me what happened that made you feel this way.
- The reason you're so _____ is because?
- What caused this _____?

Step #3: Transform
Once someone is fully in High Road—their fears are disengaged and they've worked through the problem out loud—you can begin to transform the problem into a solution.

Note: Do NOT try to move onto the Transform step until you are fully done naming and understanding. If someone is still speaking in a loud voice, tearful or flushed with emotion—they are not done processing yet.

Once someone gives a big sigh of relief, begins to talk at a normal level, and sounds more like themselves, then you can move on. In the Transform stage, you have two options: speed-read or use their appreciation language. If you can offer answers or facilitate a resolution—even better!

Sometimes, as with many problems, they cannot fully be "fixed." In that case, you are best going into appreciation language mode. You can at least value the person and make them feel less alone.

During this stage, you're answering the question:

What does this person need?

Returning to our previous example, here's how to execute this step:

Person	Script	Feelings
Woman	"I mean it's not like I need the promotion right now. I just feel really **out of the loop**. It would be fine if I **knew** that I was on some kind of track for it. I just feel so **in the dark**."	Identifying the underlying fear
Man	"Do you want to send an e-mail to your boss asking for a meeting to **clarify** early next week?"	Moving into Step #3: Transform
Woman	"Probably. I can ask to sit down with her to **go over** my next quarter goals."	Thinking about how to address her primary value
Man	"Yeah, and we can even **prepare information** for her on what you are working on so hopefully she can give you **more insight** on what's happening on her end."	Helping her get her primary value met
Woman	"That's a good idea."	Feels the problem could be resolved.
Man	"Of course! Hey, I'm so sorry this is rough. I think they are crazy not to appreciate you. What can we do this weekend to make you feel better?"	Success! He got her back to calm and thinking about next steps.

In this situation, the man not only calms down the woman in a difficult situation and difficult mood, but also becomes her support. **When you Name, Understand, and Transform someone out of their difficulty, you become their ally.**

My favorite phrases for transforming:

- How can I help?
- What needs to happen for you to feel better?
- What role can I play in making this better? What role can you play?

The NUT Job system is not about trying to change people—which usually only makes them double down on their bad behavior—but about valuing them and providing deeper understanding of a problem. **You can't argue with a feeling, but you can acknowledge it.**

When you value difficult people, they will be less apathetic, angry, and fearful, and more compassionate, understanding, and open. However, you will meet difficult people that don't respond well to even the most empathetic tactics. Their fear is so ingrained that they become impossible to deal with. I call these people toxic—and not in the poppy Britney Spears spirit, but in the radioactive, poisonous kind of way.

FAST FACT BOX

Unfortunately, most of us have a toxic person in our life. Seventy-three percent of people in our Twitter poll said they did.

BONUS: HOW TO SAY NO

Toxic people constantly throw you into Low Road survival mode. They push boundaries, challenge your worth, and can even turn thrive situations into survive ones by waking up your gremlins. **Toxic people are not worth your energy.**

However, many of us have Low Road fears about saying no. We say yes out of habit, or because it's scary to set up boundaries. Or—let's be real—we feel we don't deserve to stand up for ourselves.

It's time to give yourself permission to say no to the toxic people who drain you. You deserve to interact on your terms, with people you like. **When you say no to the wrong relationships, you make room to say yes to the right ones.** Here's how to say no:

Step #1: Eat Humble Pie
Saying no doesn't mean you should be ungrateful. You can set boundaries and say no without offending anyone.

- "Thank you so much for asking."
- "How wonderful of you to offer."
- "This is a lovely idea."

Step #2: No Hemming and Hawing
Don't beat around the bush. If you hesitate or waver, toxic people will sense weakness and try to change your mind. Be clear and concise.

- "I'm so sorry I won't be able to join."
- "I won't be able to get together."
- "I can't come."

Step #3: No Excuses
This is the most important step! You don't have to defend, debate, or explain your feelings. That's right, you don't need to give a reason. In fact, when you do offer an explanation (even when it's legitimate), it just ends up sounding like an excuse. Offering a why also gives toxic people room to argue with you—and oh, they will. Toxic people do not like when boundaries are placed on them.

Here's what happens when you try to offer toxic people a reason (real or not):

- **Toxic Person:** "You have another party? No worries, just pop over for a little!"
- **Toxic Person:** "You're busy? I'm busy, too—this will only be twenty minutes, you have to get coffee at some point, right? I'll just meet you for a little catch-up."

- **Toxic Person:** "Don't worry about being tired. You'll get energized with all the drinks!"

Special Note: If you have trouble doing this in person, you can always ask for time to think about an invite. Say you have to check your calendar and you'll get back to them in a few days. You can also e-mail or text a response so you can choose your words carefully—sometimes hard to do when face-to-face. You'll get more comfortable with practice.

Optional Step: Step It Up

If you get an invitation you're not crazy about, sometimes you can make a counteroffer. For example, a friend of mine invited me to her birthday at a pool hall. I knew it would not be my scene, nor a good way to catch up with her. I offered to take her to brunch that morning instead, which worked out better for both of us because we got to really talk. You could say:

- "I can't do dinner, but let's grab a coffee instead."
- "A meeting won't work, but let's hop on the phone."
- "Sorry I can't make the party; can I take you out to brunch tomorrow?"

I know it's hard to say no. But this sets you up for growth.

Sometimes farmers have to burn their fields in order to make way for a healthy crop. Fire is a natural part of the ecological cycle. The old crop's residue and weeds must go. They call this process a controlled burn.

Do you need to start your own controlled burn? Clearing out the weeds makes room for new growth.

For Xochitl Gonzalez, learning to say no was one of the most difficult parts of her professional growth. "You want to help everyone. But not everyone can be helped," said Gonzalez. "This job taught me how *not* to be a people pleaser. I don't hold myself to other people's compliments or requirements. I have my own standards for excellence and I hold my ground. If I suspect someone can't handle that, I don't work with them."[8]

You cast the people who you want to play a role in your life. Choose wisely.

CHALLENGES

1. Think about the five most important people in your life. What are their gremlins?
2. Take a hard look at yourself: What are your gremlins? How do they dress up?
3. **Bonus:** Do you have a toxic person you need to slowly release from your life?

CHAPTER REVIEW

Everyone has social fears. When you address someone's fear by seeking to understand it, you can transform a problem into a solution. This approach can make you an ally of the most difficult people.

- Know how your social fears dress up.
- Name the fear, understand the emotion, and transform it.
- Just say no . . . to toxic people.

My biggest takeaway in this chapter is: _____

CHAPTER 14

ENGAGE

How to turn people on

M y hero is coming to dinner." This is what I said to my husband as I frantically prepared dinner, cleaned up the house, and tried to look as presentable as possible. *New York Times* bestselling author of *Predictably Irrational*, behavioral science icon and TED Talk star Dan Ariely would be at my house in thirty minutes . . . and I was freaking out.

A few months earlier, Ariely found my e-mail address and sent me a note saying he enjoyed my YouTube videos. After screaming for joy, briefly passing out, and overcoming a long bout of uncontrollable hiccups, I was able to reply coherently, and even mention some new research I was working on. Thus began our geeky friendship. Now Ariely and his wife were visiting Portland and stopping by for dinner.

The moment Ariely and his lovely wife, Sumi, walked through the door, I was starstruck. But I quickly realized that Ariely wasn't there to impress us. He was there to learn. Over appetizers, dinner, and two bottles of wine, Ariely asked questions. Instead of talking about his groundbreaking work and research, he gently and curiously turned the spotlight on everyone else at the table. My husband's work, his wife's opinions, my goals. By the end of the evening, I was floating. I felt like I was on a relationship high—and it had nothing to do with Ariely's professional accolades or fame. It had to do with his unique approach to people.

Dan Ariely has an intense curiosity. It comes across not only in his work—he has four books and five TED Talks with over 13 million views—but also in his everyday interactions. **His sincere curiosity makes him incredibly engaging.**

Ariely's inquisitive nature is also responsible, at least in part, for his tremendous success—beginning with his decision to follow his current career path. When Ariely was seventeen years old, he accidentally set off an explosion that burned 70 percent of his body.[1] For months, he went through excruciating surgeries and skin grafts. During this process, he faced the ultimate torture: getting bandages removed.

Have you ever had to take off an old Band-Aid? You can either rip it off quickly—a short, intense pain. Or you can pull it off slowly—less intense pain over a longer period of time. "The nurses in my department thought that the right approach was the ripping one, so they would grab hold and they would rip, and they would grab hold and they would rip. And because I had 70 percent of my body burned, it would take about an hour," recalled Ariely.

As soon as Ariely got out of the hospital, he enrolled in Tel Aviv University, where he began to do experiments on pain, tolerance, and relief. "At the end of this process, what I learned was that the nurses were wrong," said Ariely.

It turns out that the best possible way to minimize a patient's pain is not to rip off the bandages quickly, but rather to go slower with less intensity. "My nurses had no idea," explained Ariely.[2] They'd been confident in their opinion to the point of irrationality—despite the evidence staring them in the face.

This simple, powerful discovery was the first of many for Ariely. He has built a career out of making seemingly irrational behavior predictable. He engages people with his distinctive brand of curiosity. And his inquisitiveness has brought him tremendous success.

How can we adopt Ariely's approach? In this final hack, let's find out.

THE SCIENCE OF POPULARITY

What makes someone popular? Researchers at Columbia University were surprised to find that popularity isn't correlated with physical attractiveness, athleticism, intelligence, or humor, but to certain brain patterns. **Specifically, popular people are more attuned to *other* people's popularity.**

In their study, Noam Zerubavel and his team asked participants from two student groups to rank each other by popularity. They then put each participant in a brain scanner and flashed pictures of the group members they had just ranked. They mixed in a few fake pictures. Students had to quickly press a button indicating whether the picture was real or fake.

They found that all of the participants—regardless of their own popularity—had more brain activity in the reward center of the brain when viewing the faces of popular people from their group. Simply put: **Popular people literally make us feel good.** This might be why we are so drawn to watching celebrities on television.

But here's the most interesting part of the study: There was a significant difference in the brain response of the popular students. The most popular participants had the largest neural response when viewing fellow popular students, especially in the "social cognition" part of the brain. In other words, **popular people are more attuned to social signals, social hierarchy, and relationships—and they place higher value on these cues.**

Popular students were also more aware of their own social status and more accurate at guessing how well liked they were by others. The authors suggest that popular people are popular because they enjoy trying to understand what people around them are thinking and feeling. They call this enhanced social attunement.[3]

Now I understand what happened at dinner with Dan Ariely—I was hit full force by his ability to attune to me. The way he *thinks* changed the way I *felt*. First, let's be real, my mental reward center tingled by his world-renowned social status. And then, my social cognition system kicked into thrilling gear by his desire to get to know me.

This is how you turn people on. **You don't impress people by mentioning your accolades, accomplishments, or awards. You impress them by mentally turning on their reward systems.**

Here's the great news: Regardless of how popular you are, anyone can learn how to be more socially attuned.

SOCIAL ATTUNEMENT

Growing up, there were two small letters that sent chills down my spine: PE. Physical Education class was the bane of my awkward, prepubescent existence. The moment I walked into the musky locker room to change, my heart would start to pound. As I surreptitiously tried to change without flashing an inch of skin (sometimes even wearing a second bra as insurance) I would desperately search for any excuse to escape the daily drills and dodgeball games. Paper cut? Haircut? Apocalypse? I tried them all.

Looking back, I realize I liked playing outside. What I really dreaded was the moment my coach said, "Line up, let's pick teams!"

Inevitably, the two jockiest kids were assigned as team captains, and then I spent an agonizing few minutes watching them go through my entire class before picking me or my fellow nonathletically inclined buddy, Smelly Matthew. Then one day, my elementary school social life changed. Our coach decided to allow the new girl to be team captain. She had just transferred from a nearby school and didn't know anyone. In one of the greatest moments in PE history, she picked me *first*!

I was so excited that I ran over to her and then held her hand while she picked the rest of our team. I think we lost in soccer that day, but I was on top of the world. After the game I asked her why she picked me. And then she said one of the greatest things anyone has ever said to me, "I wanted to get to know you."

As humans, we so desperately want to be known. We want to feel like people get us, like we have someone on our side, like a group wants to have us as a member. **Making people feel this way is called attunement— and it is one of the most underutilized social skills.**

When we attune, we are more receptive to and more aware of those around us. Attunement is also about acclimatizing or harmonizing with the people we are with. This is the final hack we will learn:

HACK #14: Attunement
Turn people on by making them feel wanted, liked, and known.

We are often so wrapped up in our own thoughts, schedules, and agendas that we forget to tune into other people's feelings, needs, and values.

Special Note: This is the *only* hack that should be wielded selectively. It is one of the most powerful tools for connection and should therefore be used only with those whom you truly want to build a deep connection with.

Here's how attunement works.

> *The world is full of obvious things which nobody by any chance ever observes.*
>
> —Sherlock Holmes

#1: Reciprocity

Stanford researcher Van Sloan studied the social skills of 2,437 high school students across counties in Northern California.[4] He wanted to know which social skills predicted likability as measured by their peers.

First—and not all that unexpectedly—he found that likable students tended to be more optimistic and upbeat, and had higher self-reported levels of general happiness. But then the results get a bit more interesting: He found that **the most likable students also *liked* the most other people.** Popular students showed their "liking" for others through higher levels of friendliness and smiling. "For females, number of smiles per day was two times more significant to their popularity than physical attractiveness," wrote Van Sloan.[5] The more a student smiled at their classmates, the more their classmates smiled back at them. This made them *feel liked*, which made them like that student even more. **We are more inclined to enjoy being with people who visibly enjoy being with us.**

In social psychology, this is called the reciprocity effect.[6] We like people who like us. We also feel the need to give back the kind of treatment we receive. So if someone smiles at us, we smile back. If someone asks us questions, we feel the need to ask questions back. If someone shares a vulnerability, we feel the need to share a vulnerability back. Every hack you have learned in this book so far was to engage the reciprocity effect.

- **Hack #1: The Social Game Plan:** When you say no to survive situations and embrace thrive situations, you encourage people to also interact in a way that works for them.
- **Hack #2: The Triple Threat:** When you show up with trusting, confident body language, you inspire the people you are with to be more trusting and confident.
- **Hack #3: Conversational Sparks:** When you break social scripts with conversation sparks, you engage your partner's need to respond in kind—with more interesting, exciting tidbits.
- **Hack #4: Highlighter:** When you highlight people's strengths, you not only bring out the best in them, you also encourage them to see the best in you.
- **Hack #5: Thread Theory:** As you search for threads of similarities, you inspire people to hop on the "me too" bandwagon.
- **Hack #6: The Decoder:** As you tap into and respond to people's

true emotions, they are more incentivized to be direct and learn about yours.

- **Hack #7: Speed-Read:** When you respect someone's true personality orientation, you show how you would like to be treated.
- **Hack #8: The Appreciation Matrix:** Finding the energy to appreciate someone on their terms teaches them how to truly care about someone—so they can return it to you in kind.
- **Hack #9: Primary Value:** When you show someone you value them, they are more inclined to respect your primary value.
- **Hack #10: The Story Stack:** The more great, witty, clever stories you share, the more people will want to tell you theirs.
- **Hack #11: Own It!:** The more you empower others, the more they will see you as a leader.
- **Hack #12: The Franklin Effect:** The more vulnerable you are, the more vulnerable people will be with you.
- **Hack #13: The NUT Job:** Your calm and direct communication both calms the people you are with and shows them how to direct communication back to you.
- **Hack #14: Attunement:** The more you show you are interested in someone, the more interested they will be in you.

Here is the key to being popular: Like more people. When you are with someone you enjoy, consciously engage the reciprocity effect:

- Start and end phone calls with "I'm so happy you called!"
- Start and end e-mails with "I'm so glad you e-mailed me!"
- Start and end interactions with "I so enjoyed spending time with you!"
- Invite people to sit with you during lunch, and at parties and conferences.
- When people join your group, table, or meeting, make them feel welcome.
- As people leave your group, table, or meeting, thank them and tell them you appreciate their time.

Duh: I hope it goes without saying that you should do this only with people you actually like and are grateful for. Attunement should always be authentic.

#2: Belonging

TV mogul and entrepreneur Oprah Winfrey has interviewed thousands of people in her years as a TV host. What has she learned from all of these experiences?

> There's one desire we all share: We want to feel valued. Whether you're a mother in Topeka or a businesswoman in Philadelphia, each of us, at our core, longs to be loved, needed, understood, affirmed—to have intimate connections that leave us feeling more alive and human.[7]

The greatest gift we can give the people we encounter is to help them feel accepted for who they are. When my elementary school friend picked me to be on her team, it was one of the first times I felt accepted. When she wanted to get to know me, I finally felt like I was being heard. And when we finally became best friends and sat together every day at lunch, I finally felt I belonged.

Why is belonging so important? It's hard to talk about people without mentioning Abraham Maslow's classic hierarchy of needs. Maslow theorized that all people have five basic needs that must be met in order to thrive.[8] They are:

After our basic food and shelter requirements, our needs become dependent on nourishment from our relationships. If we truly care about people, we can *attune* to them by helping them with their needs for the top three areas:

Love/Belonging:
- Searching for and capitalizing on commonalities that show them you are an ally (Hack #5)
- Getting to know their personality traits and respecting the way they want to interact (Hack #7)
- Discovering and speaking to their appreciation language (Hack #8)

Esteem:
- Asking them meaningful conversation sparkers about who they are and what they are passionate about (Hack #3)
- Having high expectations and finding the best in people (Hack #4)
- Seeking to decode their true emotions and encouraging honest interactions (Hack #6)
- Being vulnerable and encouraging them to be honest about their fears and worries (Hack #12)

Self-Actualization:
- Finding their primary value and helping them realize it (Hack #9)
- Empowering them to customize their ideas and actions and giving them purpose with why (Hack #11)
- Finding the source of their difficult behavior and helping them solve problems, instead of judging them (Hack #13)

As you improve your social skills, you also help the people you care about to meet their needs.

Special Note: Do you feel like you belong? Do you have people who make you feel accepted, heard, and valued? If not, there is a whole community of people just waiting to meet you. Since starting the Science of People, I have made lifelong friends who geek out on people science, love trying out new social experiments, and embrace the upside of awkward at our "Anti-Networking" events. Come join the local readers in your town! We have the link to the Facebook group, forums, and live anti-networking parties that accompany this book in your Digital Bonuses at www.ScienceofPeople.com/toolbox.

#3: Curiosity

Dan Ariely turned a painful, traumatic experience into a learning opportunity. Instead of being paralyzed by the memories of ripping bandages, he got curious about them. His desire to learn more led him to major breakthrough discoveries about pain that have helped thousands of patients, doctors, and nurses around the world. Curiosity cured.

If you're like me, you might have your own painful social experiences. Maybe you were bullied in school. Perhaps even today you feel excluded by peers.

Researchers at UCLA found that physical pain and social rejection activate the same parts of the brain.[9] In other words, when we are rejected, it feels like we are physically hurt.

We asked people on Twitter what would hurt more: a broken arm or being broken up with? Only 24 percent of people said a broken arm, while 76 percent of people said being broken up with would hurt more. So how do we protect against the pain of social rejection? I believe curiosity is a cure-all—and a great engagement technique.

- When you are curious about the people you are with, it is easier to come up with conversation sparkers.
- When you are curious about someone's motivations, it is easier to decode their personality matrix.
- When you are curious about your own interactions, you can find patterns to help you get better next time.

Every single interaction is an opportunity to understand more about yourself and the people you are with. **Being curious about someone is one of the best ways to show you like them.**

My favorite way to get curious is to set up my own mini–social experiments. Now it's your turn to put a personal spin on the human behavior hacks I taught you.

Here are some mini-experiment ideas:

- **What's your go-to conversation sparker?** Try out a few of the conversation sparkers in the next few weeks and pick your favorite one to rely on.

- **Where is your favorite sweet spot on the Social Game Plan?** Try standing in all three of the sweet spots and pick the one that works best for you.
- **What's your favorite story?** Try telling your friends a few stories from your Story Stack this weekend and see which one gets the best response.

Which were your favorite hacks? List your top three hacks below and come up with a mini-experiment for each:

Hack: _____
   Mini-Experiment: _____
Hack: _____
   Mini-Experiment: _____
Hack: _____
   Mini-Experiment: _____

If you want some more ideas, try looking through the summaries and challenges at the end of each chapter. Read the summaries and what you wrote in the "Biggest Takeaway" section. Anything exciting you want to try?

You can also think about mini-experiments you can try with specific people in your life.

- **Your Riser:** What hack would make your Riser feel great? Try one of the hacks with them to connect, bond, or get to know them better.
- **Your Winger:** Would your Winger be brave enough to try an experiment with you? Could you guess each other's appreciation languages or go out for a social adventure to try new sparkers? Think about one mini-experiment you can run with them.
- **Me:** Want to play with me? I would love to do some mini-experiments with you! We are always testing new questions and hacks with mini-experiments in our online lab, and you can jump in, too. We have our latest experiments in your Digital Bonuses at www.ScienceofPeople.com/toolbox.

These mini-experiments not only help you get more curious about yourself and the people around you, but they also enable you to start activating all of the hacks in this book.

Special Note: I hope that as you read this book, you're asking yourself, "Would this work for me? Am I brave enough to try this?" Turn those musings into one big question: **How can I make this work for me?**

Curiosity is the final step in the final chapter of the final hack because curiosity should be the driving force behind every human behavior hack you use.

LEVELING UP

At the very end of one of my phone calls with Dan Ariely, I asked him what advice he would give to people wanting to have more captivating interactions. He told me this:

> From time to time I sit next to people on a plane or at a conference and they want to talk. Even if I am not in the mood, I know that if I want to have a good discussion, it is up to me. I can't blame people for not being interesting or not being good to interact with. I take full responsibility for my interest. Even if I am different from someone, I try to learn from them. Even if I am not interested in something, I try to engage in a new way. I believe we are responsible for having captivating conversations, interactions, and relationships.[10]

You are in charge of how you want to interact. You have the power to be captivating or not. We are the only ones who can level up our relationships—so let's do it!

CHALLENGES

1. Pick your top three favorite hacks in this book and set up a mini-experiment to try this week.
2. Tell one person how much you enjoy spending time with them.
3. Schedule one people skills adventure with your Winger.

CHAPTER REVIEW

Don't impress people; engage them. Turn people on by showing them you are turned on by them. Attunement is about allowing people to be themselves with you. And the more people we truly like, the more people who will truly like us.

- Engage the reciprocity effect by showing people you enjoy being with them.
- Help people feel like they belong.
- Let curiosity drive your interactions.

My biggest takeaway in this chapter is: _____

WHAT'S NEXT?

Congrats—you made it! We have done a lot together:

In Part I: The First Five Minutes, we talked about turning strangers into acquaintances, quickly building trust, and making a lasting first impression.

In Part II: The First Five Hours, I taught you how to speed-read people in order to identify their needs and predict behavior.

In Part III: The First Five Days, we explored how to turn casual relationships into lifelong relationships with stories, vulnerability, and ownership. Your interactions will only get better from here—if you put these hacks into practice.

Albert Einstein once said, "Information is not knowledge. The only source of knowledge is experience." Reading this book is great, but I want you to experience it. Turn back to pages 5–13 and take the PQ Test again. You can use this test as a check-in once a year to make sure you retained the information you learned in this book. And be sure to check out our 7-Day Challenge.

7-DAY CHALLENGE

This end is just the beginning. As you keep leveling up your interactions, I want to help. I have created a 7-day free e-mail follow-up series for you to keep learning after the book. You'll get tips, challenges, and stories to help you put what you learned in this book into action. You will get all of the seven e-mail challenges when you sign up for your Digital Bonuses at www.ScienceofPeople.com/toolbox.

Remember: I'm here for you! **If you'd like to check in about some-thing you read, just e-mail me at** Vanessa@scienceofpeople.com. Tell me your favorite hack, share a story, or just drop a line to say hi! I love hearing from you.

Thank you for letting me take you on this people skills adventure and letting me share my stories with you. People skills changed my life. I hope they are now beginning to change yours.

Cheers,

Vanessa

MORE DIGITAL BONUSES

Along with all of the Digital Bonuses we have mentioned throughout this book, we also included some fun extra resources for you.

- **Invite Checklist:** We have a to-do list from the book that you can use as a checklist before your next event or when you get your next invite.
- **Personality Cheat Sheet:** Have trouble remembering all of the personality traits? Don't worry—we've got you covered with a printable personality cheat sheet.
- **Matrix Practice:** Need some practice on the matrix? Fill out a matrix for your favorite TV characters with our exercises.

Get everything at ScienceofPeople.com/toolbox.

See if we are hosting an Anti-Networking event in your city: ScienceofPeople.com/meetup.

CORPORATE WORKSHOPS

Do you know the personality matrices of each of your colleagues? Do you know if you have a predominant appreciation language in your office? Let's find out!

I love working with corporate teams, doing company retreats, and giving keynotes. My research team builds custom People Analytics reports for your organization based on the content in this book. If you'd like to work with me, please visit ScienceofPeople.com/Speaking.

Want to practice your microexpressions? We made you some that you can cut out of this book to take with you while watching TV or talking with friends. Get more at www.ScienceofPeople.com/toolbox.

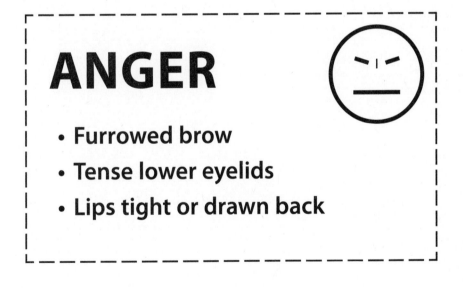

ANGER

- **Furrowed brow**
- **Tense lower eyelids**
- **Lips tight or drawn back**

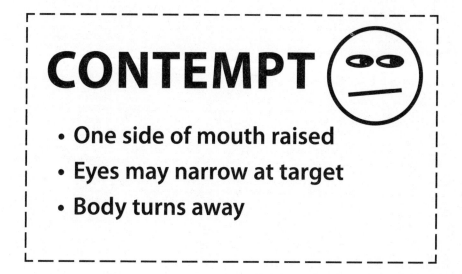

CONTEMPT

- One side of mouth raised
- Eyes may narrow at target
- Body turns away

HAPPINESS

- Lips drawn back and up
- Cheeks are raised
- Crow's feet near eyes

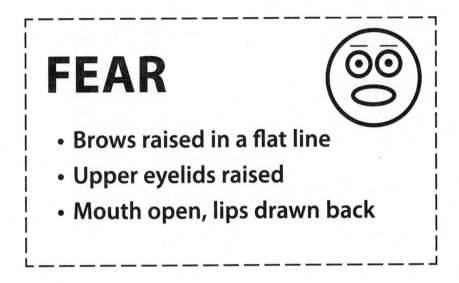

FEAR

- Brows raised in a flat line
- Upper eyelids raised
- Mouth open, lips drawn back

SURPRISE

- Brows raised and curved
- Eyelids open, whites showing
- Jaw drops open

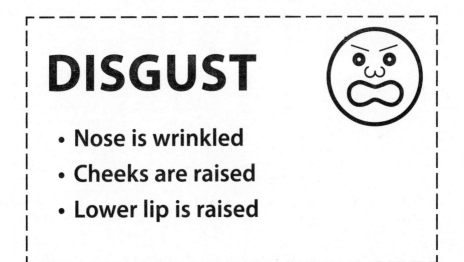

DISGUST

- Nose is wrinkled
- Cheeks are raised
- Lower lip is raised

SADNESS

- Brows drawn in and up
- Corners of lips drawn down
- Jaw comes up

ACKNOWLEDGMENTS

Oh, my amazing husband. He is usually the first person I try experiments on and the last person I explain things to. I have to thank him first and foremost. Thank you for letting me set up secret experiments all over our house. Thank you for letting me have the TV on Monday nights to watch *The Bachelor*—it really is for work. Thank you for letting me have a courageous, out-of-the-box, crazy career and supporting me every step of the way.

Thank you to my incredible agent, David Fugate, who started me on this fantastic whirlwind. And huge thanks to the entire Portfolio team! Especially my tireless editor, Niki Papadopoulos, who has walked me through every step of the process for this book and pushed me to realize its potential. I am truly lucky to have had you and Leah Trouwborst as partners for this book.

I also have to thank my photographer, videographer, and friend Maggie Kirkland, who is the creative genius behind many of the photos used in this book. She also took the cover shot and author shot for this book—you are brilliant and I am so lucky to have you! Another big thank-you to Madeline Roosevelt for cover shoot makeup and hair, Robin Allen for styling, and Christopher Sergio for the design. Thank you to the amazing models and actors throughout this book: Max Dubowy, Orion Bradshaw, Paige Hendrix Buckner, Lacy Kirkland, Scott Edwards, and Danielle Baker.

Thank you also to the team at CreativeLive—Chase Jarvis, Kimberly Murphy, Bryan Lemos, Meg Gayman, Chris Jennings, and Kenna Klosterman for nurturing my courses, making my curriculum come to life, and helping me grow as a teacher. I would like to give a special shout-out to Chris Guillebeau, Jordan Harbinger, Tammy Hernandez, and Helen Raptis for allowing me to share your platform and share my heart with your audiences.

Thank you to all of the wonderful people who let me interview them for this book: Arild Remmereit, Lewis Howes, Jeffer Carrillo Toscano, Dr. Paul Ekman, Richard Nicolosi, Paige Hendrix Buckner, Boyd Varty, Andrew Bohrer, Frank Warren, Nicol Paone, Mark Gordon, Kriste Dragon, Xochitl Gonzalez, and Dan Ariely. Your stories are changing the world. And thanks to Matt Scott, Mark Goulston, Emily McDowell, and Jae West.

Thank you to my masterminders who keep me accountable, read sample chapters, and get together to come up with kick-ass ideas to take over the world—David Moldawer, Stephanie Zito, Dr. Samantha Brody, Devani Freeman, Jamarie Milkovic, Tara Gentile, Amy Yamada, Emily Triggs, Jenny Trygg, Elizabeth Zieg, Gideon Arom, Thursday Bram, Kari Chapin, Katie Lane, Sean Ogle, Tyler Tervooren, Mike Pacchione, Charlie Gilkey, Alex Franzen, David Nihill, Jim Hopkinson, and Zach Suchin for helping me get studies. And thank you to Erin Adams, Dennis Yang, and the entire team at Udemy for giving me the very first online platform to launch my online courses.

Thank you to my amazing Science of People team. First, Danielle Baker for reading every line of this book, being the most amazing support system, and just being a great friend and colleague. You are brilliant and I can't wait to help you grow as much as you have helped me. Thank you Hayley Lucich, Jose Pina, Robby Smith, Emily Lundberg, Ellie Woo, Ben Cook, Lauren Freeman, Nick Pothetes, and Maria Baias for your countless hours, creativity, and strategy with Science of People. I also want to thank our Science of People interns and our Science of People body language trainers around the world for spreading the message to a global audience and taking our work to the next level. I couldn't do this work without you; I am so grateful for all you do for the Science of People!

Thank you to my friends who not only had to put up with me while I wrote this book, but also let me run experiments on them—Margo Aaron, Lacy Kirkland, Brennan Pothetes, Ed Piper, Bari Turetzky, John Boylston, Ana-Lauren Boylston, Stephen Scott, Christine Kelly, A. J. Alley, Kelly Alley, Tony Dal Ponte, Erin Georgeadis, Emily Occhipinti and Alex Occhipinti, Gwen Hickmond, Pam Potts, and Tate Newburgh.

Thank you to my family for getting me through my awkward years and giving me the best education a girl could get at Marlborough School and Emory University—I used every ounce of those writing courses, psychology classes, and science classes in writing this book! Love you Anita First, Vance Van Petten, Stacy Van Petten, Courtney Van Petten, Haley Van Petten, Robert Forrest, and Lindsay Forrest. And thank you to Deborah Edwards, Richard Edwards, and Laura Edwards for welcoming me and giving me Scott Edwards.

And finally I need to thank our Science of People readers. That's you! Thank you for letting me try out new conversation sparkers on you. Thank you for filling out my weird surveys on Twitter and my website. Thank you for letting me smell you in my pheromone experiment. Thank you for letting me film you, interrogate you, and test weird things on you. I could not have written this book without your bravery and willingness!

NOTES

CHAPTER 1: CONTROL

1. David G. McCullough, *Truman* (New York: Simon & Schuster, 1992).

   The Autobiography of Harry S. Truman, ed. Robert H. Ferrell (Boulder, CO: Colorado Associated University Press, 1980).

   Memoirs by Harry S. Truman (New York: Konecky & Konecky, 1955), 68.

   Kenneth T. Walsh, *Celebrity in Chief: A History of the Presidents and the Culture of Stardom* (New York: Routledge, 2015).

2. Andrew Powell-Morse, "A Historical Profile of the NBA Player: 1947–2015." Data Visualizations from *SeatSmart* (blog), March 4, 2015, https://seatsmart.com/blog/history-of-the-nba-player/.

3. Powell-Morse, "A Historical Profile of the NBA Player: 1947–2015."

4. Our Science of People surveys are all digital. Participants opt in to take our surveys via ScienceofPeople.com. This gives us a large sampling of people all around the world, with a variety of backgrounds, races, and religions. In this way, we get an incredibly varied data set.

5. Barbara Wild, Michael Erb, and Mathias Bartels, "Are Emotions Contagious? Evoked Emotions While Viewing Emotionally Expressive Faces: Quality, Quantity, Time Course and Gender Differences," *Psychiatry Research* 102, no. 2 (June 1, 2001): 109–24, doi:10.1016/s0165-1781(01)00225-6.

6. Researchers have found that if we have one happy friend, we are up to 34 percent more likely to be happier because of them. J. H. Fowler and N. A. Christakis, "Dynamic Spread of Happiness in a Large Social Network: Longitudinal Analysis over 20 Years in the Framingham Heart Study," *British Medical Journal* 337 (December 5, 2008): doi:10.1136/bmj.a2338.

7. Veikko Surakka and Jari K. Hietanen, "Facial and Emotional Reactions to Duchenne and Non-Duchenne Smiles," *International Journal of Psychophysiology* 29, no. 1 (June 29, 1998): 23–33, doi:10.1016/s0167-8760(97)00088-3.

8. Barbara Wild, Michael Erb, Michael Eyb, Mathias Bartels, and Wolfgang Grodd, "Why Are Smiles Contagious? An FMRI Study of the Interaction Between Perception of Facial Affect and Facial Movements," *Psychiatry Research: Neuroimaging* 123, no. 1 (May 1, 2003): 17–36, doi:10.1016/s0925-4927(03)00006-4.

9. Paul Schrodt, "Lady Gaga Discovered How to Be Happy When She Started Saying One Word a Lot More Often," *Business Insider*, October 30, 2015, http://www.businessinsider.com/lady-gaga-yale-speech-2015-10.

10. Truman, *Memoirs*, 68.

CHAPTER 2: CAPTURE

1. James R. Oestreich, "Have Baton, Will Travel," *New York Times*, April 24, 2005, http://www.nytimes.com/2005/04/24/arts/music/have-baton-will-travel.html?_r=1.
2. Arild Remmereit, telephone interview by the author, April 12, 2016.
3. Oestreich, "Have Baton, Will Travel."
4. Bill George with Peter Sims, *True North: Discover Your Authentic Leadership* (San Francisco, CA: John Wiley & Sons, Inc., 2007).
5. Nalini Ambady and Robert Rosenthal, "Thin Slices of Expressive Behavior as Predictors of Interpersonal Consequences: A Meta-Analysis," *Psychological Bulletin* 111, no. 2 (March 1992): 256–74, doi:10.1037/0033-2909.111.2.256.
6. Nalini Ambady and Robert Rosenthal, "Half a Minute: Predicting Teacher Evaluations from Thin Slices of Nonverbal Behavior and Physical Attractiveness," *Journal of Personality and Social Psychology* 67, no. 3 (1993): 431–44.
7. Robert Gifford, Cheuk Fan Ng, and Margaret Wilkinson, "Nonverbal Cues in the Employment Interview: Links Between Applicant Qualities and Interviewer Judgments," *Journal of Applied Psychology* 70, no. 4 (November 1985): 729–36, doi:10.1037/0021-9010.70.4.729.
8. Bill McEvily and Akbar Zaheer, "Does Trust Still Matter? Research on the Role of Trust in Inter-Organizational Exchange," *Organization Science* 9, no. 2 (February 1998), doi:10.1287/orsc.9.2.141.
9. Jessica L. Tracy and David Matsumoto, "The Spontaneous Expression of Pride and Shame: Evidence for Biologically Innate Nonverbal Displays," *Proceedings of the National Academy of Sciences* 105, no. 33 (August 19, 2008): 11655-660, doi:10.1073/pnas.0802686105.
10. The Liberators International YouTube page, accessed January 9, 2016, https://www.youtube.com/channel/UCIgioJL7U-TVk2Lf7xg5b4Q.
11. Jae West, e-mail interview by the author, January 9, 2016.
12. Allan Pease and Barbara Pease, *The Definitive Book of Body Language* (New York: Bantam Books, 2006).
13. Michael Argyle and Janet Dean, "Eye-Contact, Distance and Affiliation," *Sociometry* 28, no. 3 (September 1965): 289–304, doi:10.2307/2786027.
14. Brené Brown, *Daring Greatly: How the Courage to Be Vulnerable Transforms the Way We Live, Love, Parent, and Lead* (New York: Gotham Books, 2012).

CHAPTER 3: SPARK

1. Philip Seeman, "Chapter 1: Historical Overview: Introduction to the Dopamine Receptors," in *The Dopamine Receptors*, ed. Kim A. Neve and Rachel Neve (New York: Springer, 1997), 1–22.
2. John Medina, *Brain Rules: 12 Principles for Surviving and Thriving at Work, Home, and School* (Seattle: Pear Press, 2008).
3. Nico Bunzeck and Emrah Düzel, "Absolute Coding of Stimulus Novelty in the Human Substantia Nigra/VTA," *Neuron* 51, no. 3 (August 3, 2006): 369–79, doi:10.1016/j.neuron.2006.06.021.
4. Brian Knutson and Jeffrey C. Cooper, preview "The Lure of the Unknown," *Neuron* 51, no. 3 (August 3, 2006): 280–82, doi:10.1016/j.neuron.2006.07.017.
5. "Novelty Aids Learning," University College London News, August 2, 2006, http://www.ucl.ac.uk/news/news-articles/news-releases-archive/newlearning.
6. Christian Rudder, "Exactly What to Say in a First Message," *OkTrends* (blog), September 14, 2009, http://blog.okcupid.com/index.php/online-dating-advice-exactly-what-to-say-in-a-first-message/.

     Christian Rudder, "6 Data-Driven Dating Facts from OkCupid CEO Sam Yagan," *BigThink*, http://bigthink.com/the-voice-of-big-think/6-data-driven-dating-facts-from-okcupid-ceo-sam-yagan.

7. Michael D. Santos, Craig Leve, and Anthony R. Pratkanis, "Hey Buddy, Can You Spare Seventeen Cents? Mindful Persuasion and the Pique Technique," *Journal of Applied Social Psychology* 24, no. 9 (May 1994): 755–64, doi:10.1111/j.1559-1816.1994.tb00610.x.
8. Dennis P. Carmody and Michael Lewis, "Brain Activation When Hearing One's Own and Others' Names," *Brain Research* 1116, no. 1 (September 7, 2006): 153–58, doi:10.1016/j.brainres.2006.07.121.
9. Gary Small, *The Memory Bible: An Innovative Strategy for Keeping Your Brain Young* (New York: Hyperion, 2002).

CHAPTER 4: HIGHLIGHT
1. Diana I. Tamir and Jason P. Mitchell, "Disclosing Information About the Self Is Intrinsically Rewarding," *Proceedings of the National Academy of Sciences* 109, no. 21 (May 22, 2012): 8038–43, doi:10.1073/pnas.1202129109.
2. Dale Carnegie, *How to Win Friends and Influence People* (New York: Simon & Schuster, 1981).
3. "Alfred P. Sloan Jr. Dead at 90; G.M. Leader and Philanthropist," On This Day, *New York Times* Learning Network, February 18, 1966, http://www.nytimes.com/learning/general/onthisday/bday/0523.html.
    Alfred P. Sloan, *My Years with General Motors* (Garden City, NY: Doubleday, 1964).
    Alfred P. Sloan and Boyden Sparkes, *Adventures of a White-Collar Man* (New York: Doubleday, Doran, 1941).
4. Peter F. Drucker, "What Makes an Effective Executive," *Harvard Business Review*, June 2004, https://hbr.org/2004/06/what-makes-an-effective-executive.
5. Emily McDowell, e-mail interview by the author, April 19, 2016.
6. Geoffrey Miles. *Classical Mythology in English Literature: A Critical Anthology* (London: Routledge, 1999), 326.
7. Christopher J. Bryan, Gregory M. Walton, Todd Rogers, and Carol S. Dweck, "Motivating Voter Turnout by Invoking the Self," *Proceedings of the National Academy of Sciences* 108, no. 31 (2011): 12653–2656.
8. Jen Shang and Rachel Croson, "A Field Experiment in Charitable Contribution: The Impact of Social Information on the Voluntary Provision of Public Goods," *The Economic Journal* 119, no. 540 (October 2009): 1422–439, doi:10.1111/j.1468-0297.2009.02267.x.
9. Alia J. Crum and Ellen J. Langer. "Mind-Set Matters: Exercise and the Placebo Effect," *Psychological Science* 18, no. 2 (2007): 165–71. doi:10.1111/j.1467-9280.2007.01867.x.
10. Robert Rosenthal and Lenore Jacobson, *Pygmalion in the Classroom: Teacher Expectation and Pupils' Intellectual Development* (New York: Holt, Rinehart and Winston, 1968).
11. Elisha Y. Babad, Jacinto Inbar, and Robert Rosenthal, "Pygmalion, Galatea, and the Golem: Investigations of Biased and Unbiased Teachers," *Journal of Educational Psychology* 74, no. 4 (August 1982): 459–74, doi:10.1037/0022-0663.74.4.459.
12. Major Wilburn R. Schrank, "The Labeling Effect of Ability Grouping," *Journal of Educational Research* 62, no. 2 (1968): 51–52, doi:10.1080/00220671.1968.10883758.
13. D. Brian McNatt, "Ancient Pygmalion Joins Contemporary Management: A Meta-Analysis of the Result," *Journal of Applied Psychology* 85, no. 2 (April 2000): 314–22, doi:10.1037/0021-9010.85.2.314.

CHAPTER 5: INTRIGUE
1. Lewis Howes, *The School of Greatness: A Real-World Guide for Living Bigger, Loving Deeper, and Leaving a Legacy* (Emmanus, PA: Rodale, 2015).
2. Lewis Howes, telephone interview by the author, February 19, 2016.

3. Howes, *School of Greatness*.
4. International Encyclopedia of the Social Sciences, Encyclopedia.com, s.v. "Similarity/Attraction Theory," 2008, http://www.encyclopedia.com/social-sciences/applied-and-social-sciences-magazines/similarityattraction-theory.
5. Ellen Berscheid and Elaine H. Walster, *Interpersonal Attraction* (Reading, MA: Addison-Wesley, 1969), 69–91.
6. Tim Emswiller, Kay Deaux, and Jerry E. Willits, "Similarity, Sex, and Requests for Small Favors," *Journal of Applied Social Psychology* 1, no. 3 (September 1971): 284–91, doi:10.1111/j.1559-1816.1971.tb00367.x.

CHAPTER 6: DECODE

1. Paul Ekman and Wallace V. Friesen, "Nonverbal Leakage and Clues to Deception," *Psychiatry* 32, no. 1 (February 1969), doi:10.1037/e525532009-012.
2. Paul Ekman, *Telling Lies: Clues to Deceit in the Marketplace, Politics, and Marriage* (New York: Norton, 1985).
3. Paul Ekman and Wallace V. Friesen, *Unmasking the Face: A Guide to Recognizing Emotions from Facial Clues* (Englewood Cliffs, NJ: Prentice-Hall, 1975).
4. San Francisco State University, "Facial Expressions of Emotion Are Innate, Not Learned," *ScienceDaily*, December 30, 2008, https://www.sciencedaily.com/releases/2008/12/081229080859.htm.
5. Ekman and Friesen, *Unmasking the Face*.
6. There was only one exception: New Guineans could not distinguish between the fear and surprise microexpressions.
7. Ekman, *Unmasking the Face*.
8. Ibid.
9. Janine Willis and Alexander Todorov, "First Impressions: Making Up Your Mind after a 100-Ms Exposure to a Face," *Psychological Science* 17, no. 7 (July 2006): 592–98, doi:10.1111/j.1467-9280.2006.01750.x.
10. Alexander Todorov and Jenny M. Porter, "Misleading First Impressions: Different for Different Facial Images of the Same Person," *Psychological Science* 25, no. 7 (May 27, 2014): 1404–417, doi:10.1177/0956797614532474.
11. Ross Buck, "Nonverbal Behavior and the Theory of Emotion: The Facial Feedback Hypothesis," *Journal of Personality and Social Psychology* 38, no. 5 (May 1980): 811–24, doi:10.1037/0022-3514.38.5.811.

CHAPTER 7: SOLVE

1. John P. Kotter, "What Leaders Really Do," *Harvard Business Review*, December 2001, https://hbr.org/2001/12/what-leaders-really-do.
2. Jerry S. Wiggins, ed., *The Five-Factor Model of Personality: Theoretical Perspectives* (New York: Guilford Press, 1996).

   John M. Digman, "Personality Structure: Emergence of the Five-Factor Model," *Annual Review of Psychology* 41, no. 1 (February 1990): 417–40, doi:10.1146/annurev.ps.41.020190.002221.

   Gerald Matthews, Ian J. Deary, and Martha C. Whiteman, *Personality Traits* (Cambridge, UK: Cambridge University Press, 2003).

   Arthur E. Poropat, "A Meta-Analysis of the Five-Factor Model of Personality and Academic Performance," *Psychological Bulletin* 135, no. 2 (2009): 322–38, doi:10.1037/a0014996.

   Donald Winslow Fiske, Patrick E. Shrout, and Susan T. Fiske, eds., *Personality Research, Methods, and Theory: A Festschrift Honoring Donald W. Fiske* (Hillsdale, NJ: L. Erlbaum Associates, 1995).
3. Brent W. Roberts, Nathan R. Kuncel, Rebecca Shiner, Avshalom Caspi, and Lewis R. Goldberg, "The Power of Personality: The Comparative Validity of Personality Traits,

Socioeconomic Status, and Cognitive Ability for Predicting Important Life Outcomes," *Perspectives on Psychological Science* 2, no. 4 (December 2007): 313–45, doi:10.1111/j.1745-6916.2007.00047.x.

4. Wiggins, *Five-Factor Model.*

5. Sam Gosling, *Snoop: What Your Stuff Says About You* (New York: Basic, 2008).

6. J. C. Biesanz, L. J. Human, A-C. Paquin, M. Chan, K. L. Parisotto, J. Sarracino, and R. L. Gillis, "Do We Know When Our Impressions of Others Are Valid? Evidence for Realistic Accuracy Awareness in First Impressions of Personality," *Social Psychological and Personality Science* 2, no. 5 (January 19, 2011): 452–59, doi:10.1177/1948550610397211.

7. Patti Wood, *Snap: Making the Most of First Impressions, Body Language, and Charisma* (Novato, CA: New World Library, 2012).

8. Christopher Y. Olivola, Friederike Funk, and Alexander Todorov, "Social Attributions from Faces Bias Human Choices," *Trends in Cognitive Sciences* 18, no. 11 (November 2014): 566–70.

9. Lea Winerman, "'Thin Slices' of Life," *Monitor on Psychology*, March 2005, http://www.apa.org/monitor/mar05/slices.aspx.

10. Mitja D. Back, Juliane M. Stopfer, Simine Vazire, Sam Gaddis, Stefan C. Schmukle, Boris Egloff, and Samuel D. Gosling, "Facebook Profiles Reflect Actual Personality, Not Self-Idealization," *Psychological Science* 21, no. 3 (January 2010): 372–74, doi:10.1177/0956797609360756.

CHAPTER 8: APPRECIATE

1. Gary D. Chapman, *The Five Love Languages: How to Express Heartfelt Commitment to Your Mate* (Chicago: Northfield Pub., 1995).

2. Tom Rath and Donald O. Clifton, Ph.D., *How Full Is Your Bucket* (New York: Gallup Press, 2004).

3. Leigh Branham, *The 7 Hidden Reasons Employees Leave: How to Recognize the Subtle Signs and Act Before It's Too Late* (New York: American Management Association, 2005).

4. "SHRM-Globoforce Survey: Companies Need to Fine Tune Employee Recognition and Engagement Efforts," Society for Human Resource Management, April 12, 2012, http://www.shrm.org/about/pressroom/pressreleases/pages/shrmgloboforce2012pressrelease pollengagementrecognition.aspx.

5. Gallup, Inc., "Employee Recognition: Low Cost, High Impact, Attractiveness," Gallup.com, June 28, 2016, http://www.gallup.com/businessjournal193238/employee-recognition-low-cost-high-impact.aspx.

6. Chapman, *5 Love Languages.* https://s3.amazonaws.com/moody-profiles/uploads/profile/attachment/5/5LLPersonalProfile_COUPLES__1_.pdf.

7. John M. Gottman, *The Science of Trust: Emotional Attunement for Couples* (New York: W. W. Norton, 2011).

8. Kim T. Buehlman, John M. Gottman, and Lynn F. Katz, "How a Couple Views Their Past Predicts Their Future: Predicting Divorce from an Oral History Interview," *Journal of Family Psychology* 5, no. 3-4 (1992): 295–318, doi:10.1037/0893-3200.5.3-4.295.

9. Gottman, *Science of Trust,* 155.

CHAPTER 9: VALUE

1. Boyd Varty, *Cathedral of the Wild: An African Journey Home* (New York: Random House, 2014).

2. Boyd Varty, interview by the author, December 26, 2015; telephone interview by the author, January 14, 2016.

3. Varty, *Cathedral of the Wild.*

4. Uriel G. Foa, John Converse Jr., Kjell Y. Törnblom, and Edna B. Foa, eds., *Resource Theory: Explorations and Applications* (San Diego: Academic Press, 1993).

5. Uriel G. Foa and Edna B. Foa, *Resource Theory of Social Exchange* (Morristown, NJ: General Learning Press, 1975).
6. Jerry S. Wiggins and Paul D. Trapnell, "A Dyadic-Interactional Perspective on the Five-Factor Model," in *The Five-Factor Model of Personality,* ed. Jerry S. Wiggins (New York: Guilford Press, 1996), 88–162.
7. A story told in many beginner Karrass Negotiation seminars.
8. Dan P. McAdams, "The Psychology of Life Stories," *Review of General Psychology* 5, no. 2 (2001): 100–22, doi:10.1037/1089-2680.5.2.100.
9. Varty, *Cathedral.*

CHAPTER 10: CONNECT
1. *God's Generals: Vol 7,* DVD, narrated by Roberts Liardon (2005; New Kensington, PA: Whitaker House).
2. Nicol Paone, live performance attended by the author, May 19, 2016.
3. Nicol Paone, telephone interview by the author, November 11, 2015.
4. Zac Bissonnette, *The Great Beanie Baby Bubble: Mass Delusion and the Dark Side of Cute* (New York: Penguin Group, 2015).
5. Greg J. Stephens, Lauren J. Silbert, and Uri Hasson, "Speaker-Listener Neural Coupling Underlies Successful Communication," *Proceedings of the National Academy of Sciences* 107, no. 32 (August 10, 2010): 14425–430, doi:10.1073/pnas.1008662107.
6. Susan Cain, "The Power of Introverts," TED video, 19:04, February 2012, https://www.ted.com/talks/susan_cain_the_power_of_introverts?language=en.
7. Vanessa Van Edwards and Robby Smith, "The Secret Behind How the *New York Times* Creates Viral Articles," Science of People, April 2016, http://www.scienceofpeople.com/NYT.

CHAPTER 11: EMPOWER
1. Kriste Dragon, telephone interview by the author, February 17, 2016.
2. Michael I. Norton, Daniel Mochon, and Dan Ariely, "The 'IKEA Effect': When Labor Leads to Love," *Journal of Consumer Psychology* 22, no. 3 (July 2012): 453–60, doi:10.1016/j.jcps.2011.08.002.
3. Ellen J. Langer, Arthur Blank, and Benzion Chanowitz, "The Mindlessness of Ostensibly Thoughtful Action: The Role of 'Placebic' Information in Interpersonal Interaction," *Journal of Personality and Social Psychology* 36, no. 6 (1978): 635–42, doi:10.1037/0022-3514.36.6.635.
4. Jay A. Fernandez, "SXSW Q&A: 'Source Code' Producer Mark Gordon," *Hollywood Reporter,* March 11, 2011, http://www.hollywoodreporter.com/risky-business/sxsw-qa-source-code-producer-166959.
5. David Zax, "'Ray Donovan' Producer Mark Gordon on How to Leave Good Things Alone," *Co.Create* (blog), *Fast Company,* July 11, 2014, http://www.fastcocreate.com/3032879/most-creative-people/ray-donovan-producer-mark-gordon-on-how-to-leave-good-things-alone.
6. Ibid.
7. Nikolaus Franke and Martin Schreier, "Why Customers Value Self-Designed Products: The Importance of Process Effort and Enjoyment," *Journal of Product Innovation Management* 27, no. 7 (December 2010): 1020–31, doi:10.1111/j.1540-5885.2010.00768.x.
8. "How Lululemon's CEO Learned to Lead," CNNMoney video, :56, accessed March 2016, http://money.cnn.com/video/news/2011/10/28/best_advice_christina_day.cnnmoney/.
9. Brené Brown, *Daring Greatly: How the Courage to Be Vulnerable Transforms the Way We Live, Love, Parent, and Lead* (New York: Gotham Books, 2012), 209.
10. Fernandez, "SXSW Q&A."

CHAPTER 12: REVEAL

1. Frank Warren, telephone interview by the author, November 12, 2015.
2. Thomas Gilovich, Victoria Husted Medvec, and Kenneth Savitsky, "The Spotlight Effect in Social Judgment: An Egocentric Bias in Estimates of the Salience of One's Own Actions and Appearance," *Journal of Personality and Social Psychology* 78, no. 2 (2000): 211–22, doi:10.1037/0022-3514.78.2.211.
3. Ibid.
4. Elliot Aronson, Ben Willerman, and Joanne Floyd, "The Effect of a Pratfall on Increasing Interpersonal Attractiveness," *Psychonomic Science* 4, no. 6 (June 1966): 227–28, doi:10.3758/bf03342263.
5. Ibid.
6. Richard Wiseman, *59 Seconds: Think a Little, Change a Lot* (New York: Alfred A. Knopf, 2009).
7. Jon Jecker and David Landy, "Liking a Person as a Function of Doing Him a Favour," *Human Relations* 22, no. 4 (August 1969): 371–78, doi:10.1177/001872676902200407.
8. Dennis T. Regan, "Effects of a Favor and Liking on Compliance," *Journal of Experimental Social Psychology* 7, no. 6 (1971): 627–39, doi:10.1016/0022-1031(71)90025-4.

CHAPTER 13: PROTECT

1. Xochitl Gonzalez, telephone interview by the author, January 14, 2016.
2. Joseph E. LeDoux and Elizabeth A. Phelps, "Emotional Networks in the Brain," in *Handbook of Emotions*, 3rd ed., eds. Michael Lewis, Jeannette M. Haviland-Jones, and Lisa Feldman Barrett (New York: Guilford Press, 2010), 159–79.
   Jacek Dbiec and Joseph LeDoux, "The Amygdala and the Neural Pathways of Fear," in *Post-Traumatic Stress Disorder*, eds. Priyattam J. Shiromani, Joseph E. LeDoux, and Terence Martin Keane (New York: Humana Press, 2009), 23–38.
3. Etienne Benson, "The Synaptic Self," *Monitor on Psychology*, November 2002, http://www.apa.org/monitor/nov02/synaptic.aspx.
4. Ibid.
5. Ibid.
6. Ibid.
7. Mark Goulston, *Just Listen: Discover the Secret to Gettting Through to Absolutely Anyone* (New York: American Management Association, 2010).
8. Xochitl Gonzalez, telephone interview by the author, January 14, 2016.

CHAPTER 14: ENGAGE

1. Ayelett Shani, "What It Feels like to Know What We're All Thinking," *Haaretz*, April 5, 2012, http://www.haaretz.com/israel-news/what-it-feels-like-to-know-what-we-re-all-thinking-1.422824.
2. Dan Ariely, "Our Buggy Moral Code" TED video, filmed February 2009, transcript and Adobe Flash video, 16:13, TED2009, Long Beach Performing Arts Center, Long Beach, CA, posted March 2009, https://www.ted.com/talks/dan_ariely_on_our_buggy_moral_code/transcript?language=en.
3. Noam Zerubavel, Peter S. Bearman, Jochen Weber, and Kevin N. Ochsner, "Neural Mechanisms Tracking Popularity in Real-World Social Networks," *Proceedings of the National Academy of Sciences* 112, no. 49 (December 2015): 15072–77, doi:10.1073/pnas.1511477112.
4. Mary M. Leahy, "Are You Social?" *Times-Herald* (Vallejo, CA), December 17, 1998, Web. June 23, 2016, http://www.sq.4mg.com/traits_2437.htm#z.
5. Tim Sanders, *The Likeability Factor* (New York: Crown, 2005).
6. R. Matthew Montoya and Robert S. Horton, "The Reciprocity of Liking Effect," in *The Psychology of Love*, ed. Michele Paludi (Santa Barbara, CA: Praeger, 2012), 39–57.
7. Oprah Winfrey, *What I Know for Sure* (New York: Flatiron Books, 2014).

8. Abraham Maslow, "A Theory of Human Motivation," *Psychological Review* 50 (1943), 370–96.

9. Naomi I. Eisenberger, Matthew D. Lieberman, and Kipling D. Williams, "Does Rejection Hurt? An fMRI Study of Social Exclusion," *Science* 302, no. 5643 (2003), 290, doi:10.1126/science.1089134.

10. Dan Ariely, telephone interview by the author, April 1, 2016.

INDEX